# The Digital Television Revolution

*Palgrave Global Media Policy and Business*

Series Editors: **Professor Petros Iosifidis, Professor Jeanette Steemers** and **Professor Gerald Sussman**

Editorial Board: **Sandra Braman, Peter Dahlgren, Terry Flew, Charles Fombad, Manuel Alejandro Guerrero, Alison Harcourt, Robin Mansell, Richard Maxwell, Toby Miller, Zizi Papacharissi, Stylianos Papathanassopoulos, Caroline Pauwels, Robert Picard, Kiran Prasad, Marc Raboy, Chang Yong Son, Miklos Suksod, Kenton T. Wilkinson, Sugmin Youn**

This innovative series examines the wider social, political, economic and technological changes arising from the globalization of the media and communications industries and assesses their impact on matters of business practice, regulation and policy. Considering media convergence, industry concentration and new communications practices, the series makes reference to the paradigmatic shift from a system based on national decision-making and the traditions of public service in broadcast and telecommunications delivery to one that is demarcated by commercialization, privatization and monopolization. Bearing in mind this shift, and based on a multi-disciplinary approach, the series tackles three key questions: To what extent do new media developments require changes in regulatory philosophy and objectives? To what extent do new technologies and changing media consumption require changes in business practices and models? And to what extent does privatization alter the creative freedom and public accountability of media enterprises?

Karen Donders, Caroline Pauwels and Jan Loisen (*editors*)
PRIVATE TELEVISION IN WESTERN EUROPE
Content, Markets, Policies

Michael Starks
THE DIGITAL TELEVISION REVOLUTION
Origins to Outcomes

---

Palgrave Global Media Policy and Business
Series Standing Order ISBN 978–1–137–27329–1 (hardback)
(*outside North America only*)

You can receive future titles in this series as they are published by placing a standing order. Please contact your bookseller or, in case of difficulty, write to us at the address below with your name and address, the title of the series and the ISBN quoted above.

Customer Services Department, Macmillan Distribution Ltd, Houndmills, Basingstoke, Hampshire RG21 6XS, England

# The Digital Television Revolution

## Origins to Outcomes

Michael Starks

*University of Oxford*

First published 2013 by
PALGRAVE MACMILLAN

Palgrave Macmillan in the UK is an imprint of Macmillan Publishers Limited, registered in England, company number 785998, of Houndmills, Basingstoke, Hampshire RG21 6XS.

Palgrave Macmillan in the US is a division of St Martin's Press LLC, 175 Fifth Avenue, New York, NY 10010.

Palgrave Macmillan is the global academic imprint of the above companies and has companies and representatives throughout the world.

Palgrave® and Macmillan® are registered trademarks in the United States, the United Kingdom, Europe and other countries.

ISBN 978–1–137–27334–5

This book is printed on paper suitable for recycling and made from fully managed and sustained forest sources. Logging, pulping and manufacturing processes are expected to conform to the environmental regulations of the country of origin.

A catalogue record for this book is available from the British Library.

A catalog record for this book is available from the Library of Congress.

*To Sue, Mary and Jack*

# Contents

# Illustrations

## Figures

## Tables

# Preface

In October 2012 the United Kingdom (UK) completed the switch-off of its last analogue television transmitters. A couple of months earlier, at the 2012 London Olympics, the BBC, which had only two TV channels back in the five-channel analogue era, showed just what could be done with digital technology. Mainstream Olympic events were carried on BBC One and BBC Three and in high-definition. Digital terrestrial viewers could receive two additional channels of broadcaster-selected events on *Freeview*. Then up to 24 further BBC Olympic channels offered live coverage of individual sports – across the alphabet from Archery, Badminton and Basketball to Tennis, Volleyball and Weightlifting – so that viewers could select their own events. Cable and satellite households could find these extra services on their main TV sets using the Electronic Guide; terrestrial TV households needed to access them on their computers. Away from home, people could watch the Olympics on their mobile phones. The opening and closing ceremonies and the men's 100m final were also broadcast live in 3D. A new television era had arrived.

The shift from analogue to digital television involves more than an enlargement of viewer choice. It has been accompanied by the convergence of the broadcasting, computer and telecommunications industries, now all based on digital technology, which facilitates linkages, including content transfer, between them. This has led to the distribution of television via broadband and mobile telecommunications. It has blurred the interface between television and the Internet, bringing On-Demand TV to the computer and *YouTube* videos to the 'Connected TV set'. Cable and satellite broadcasters have multiplied the choices offered by their video supermarkets. Over-the-air terrestrial television has been able to expand its output dramatically, while at the same time releasing broadcasting spectrum to the hungry world of telecommunications.

Analogue television was mainly viewed simultaneously by mass audiences conforming to timetables set by the broadcasters. Digital television, with digital recording devices and broadband connections, offers On-Demand and self-scheduling options. While large audiences still come together for major events, particularly in the field of sport, viewers are becoming disaggregated, as we each choose what we want from the huge range of options and view it at our own convenience. Digital satellite brings in a wide range of foreign broadcasts while the Internet allows us to view online videos from anywhere in the world. Analogue television was mainly national and regional; digital television is both more individual and more global.

The transition to digital television has taken place rapidly. In 1995 a BBC colleague, Bob Ely, and I presented a paper at the International Broadcasting Convention in Amsterdam entitled 'The Feasibility of Digital Terrestrial Television Broadcasting'. At that stage all terrestrial television, and indeed virtually all television, was analogue and we were reporting on a very early experimental broadcast. Similar R&D work was being undertaken in the United States and in a few Western European countries but the digital equipment was in cabinets the size of refrigerators. It was hard to imagine how it could ever be miniaturised, let alone displace the whole analogue transmission system. Yet by 2012 most countries in Europe and North America had completed the switch-off of their analogue terrestrial TV services and by 2015 the whole of Europe is due to have completed the process. Across the world other countries are following the same course: a few have switched off analogue TV, many more have started digital transmission. The International Telecommunication Union (ITU) provides the framework within which a global transition is taking place.

This book charts and analyses that transition. It is a sequel to my earlier book, *Switching to Digital Television: UK Public Policy and the Market,* which was written during the years 2004–2006 and focussed almost entirely on the UK. As every painter knows, if you revisit a subject at a different time, you see a different picture. So now, in *The Digital Television Revolution,* my aim is to mark the successful completion of digital switchover in around 30 countries by the end of 2012 and zoom out to see the trend spreading across the globe. This book forms part of the Palgrave Global Media Policy and Business Series.

Initially, when the prospect of 'turning off the telly' seemed daunting, the central concern was how to achieve it – and for developing countries in Asia, Latin America and Africa, that remains the case. There are plenty of lessons to be learned and shared internationally. Increasingly now, however, interest is shifting to television after switchover. So, while the early chapters look at the international progress of the transition, the latter part of the book focusses on the world of all-digital communications. How much further will convergence go? What changes does the switch bring to the relationships between those who initiate communications, those who receive and respond to them, and those who govern and regulate this expanding digital domain? Here too I have tried to show the international dimension, while using the UK as a case study to illuminate regulatory and public service broadcasting issues.

The book is designed to be non-technical. It tries to make technical subjects accessible to the non-technical reader and, I hope, shows technical readers the wider political, economic and social framework by which technology change is shaped. My aim is to set out the policy issues and choices associated with digital television switchover in a way that encourages public engagement. When countries first start to formulate their policy, the subject can easily be captured by a small group of technical, economic and legal experts, with the wider civil society either unaware of the issues or persuaded that they are essentially a matter for specialists.

Many of us avoid knowing what goes on at the back of our TV sets, and issues such as transmission standards and spectrum management can sound dauntingly technical, but at the heart of digital television switchover are some vital public policy issues. Together with radio and the Press, television plays a key role in forming opinion and has a significant influence on our political agenda, so major change to the medium affects us all. Do we want more television and, if so, of what nature and from whom? Who will bear the cost? Will our existing TV services be adversely affected? What are the public (as distinct from private consumer) benefits? Digital technology is reshaping our media environment. While it can shape us, we have the ability to shape it – but first we have to understand it.

\* \* \* \* \*

Each chapter starts with a summary of its argument but a brief overview of the structure of the book may be useful at the outset.

After establishing the political importance of the subject, the Introduction explains the basic concept of digital television switchover, covering the different distribution platforms, the reallocation of broadcasting spectrum, the involvement of governments and the role of international spectrum management.

Part I deals with the history, combining narrative with some analysis. Chapter 1 looks at the origins of the digital television transition and at the factors which drove take-up in the market once the new technology had been launched. Chapter 2 describes the diverse experiences of the main pioneering countries, especially the United States, the UK and Spain, and how they stumbled as a result of immature technology and inexperienced commercial and regulatory managements. Chapter 3 charts the UK's recovery from digital TV's financial crisis of 2002, through the success of *Freeview*, to the lengthy analogue switch-off process from 2008 to 2012. Chapter 4 recounts the transition in Europe for which the European Union set a target completion date of 2012. Chapter 5 spans the wider globe and includes an assessment of the position of developing countries.

In Part II, analysis predominates but is supplemented by an element of prescription. The latter has to be circumspect: the digital transition may be global but national differences rule out any one-solution-fits-all approach.

With this caveat, Chapter 6 summarises how to achieve the goal of national digital switchover, insofar as experience to date can be codified. Chapter 7 describes the intertwining of broadcasting, telecommunications and computer technologies. Chapter 8 discusses the implications for regulators, noting the blurred dividing line between broadcasters' websites and the electronic editions of newspapers, and explores the principle of cross-media regulation. Chapter 9 examines the outlook for public service broadcasting during and after the digital transition. Chapter 10 asks whether digital television switchover can deliver a 'democratic dividend'.

Summarising the book's argument, the Conclusion makes the case (acknowledging a counter-argument) that digital television switchover really does constitute a 'revolution' which civil society needs to try and manage.

\*    \*    \*    \*    \*

I should say a few words about my own role in some of the events described here. Before joining Oxford University's Programme in Comparative Media Law and Policy, I was a participant in some of the policy-making and development activity in the UK. Working for the BBC, I directed two major BBC digital television projects involving close collaboration across the industry. I was the Founding Chairman of the UK's industry-wide Digital TV Group. I then worked for the UK government, managing the collaborative UK Digital TV Project which planned the country's digital switchover strategy. I subsequently undertook consultancy work for the New Zealand government and advised the Jamaican Broadcasting Commission. In academic guise I have edited the *International Journal of Digital Television*. My aim in this book is to integrate an academic overview of digital television with some of the insights I gained earlier in helping to make it all happen.

# Acknowledgements

I have several sets of acknowledgements to make. I must begin by recognising how much I owe to those with whom, and for whom, I worked on digital television policy during my professional career – at the BBC, for the UK government and in the industry – over the decade 1994–2004.

Then I must thank those at Oxford University who, from 2005, gave me a base for undertaking academic work in this field: Damian Tambini, and later Nicole Stremlau, at the Programme in Comparative Media Law and Policy; David Levy and the Reuters Institute for the Study of Journalism; David Butler whose 'Media and Politics' seminars at Nuffield College were a regular stimulus; William Dutton and the Oxford Internet Institute; and the Senior Common Room of Lady Margaret Hall. I learned much from my collaborative work with Damian Tambini and María Trinidad García Leiva. I greatly appreciated the opportunities I had as a Research Visitor at the University of Melbourne in 2007 and as a Visiting Fellow at the University of Westminster's China Media Centre in 2008. I also found it stimulating to act as an Editorial Commission Adviser for the research phase of the Open Society Foundations' Mapping Digital Media project.

My third major debt is to my colleagues and contributors at the *International Journal of Digital Television*, which we founded in 2010, especially to Jeffrey Hart, Jock Given, Petros Iosifidis and the publishing staff at Intellect. I acknowledge various IJDT sources in the course of my text but, beyond individual studies, the journal has provided me with a wider vision of broadcasting and communications than I could ever have acquired on my own.

For some of the history recounted in this book I have drawn on my earlier academic publications, in particular on my 2007 book, *Switching to Digital Television: UK Public Policy and the Market*, and I am grateful to the publisher, Intellect Books, for agreeing to this. I have made use of research I undertook at the University of Melbourne in 2007 for a paper on how to plan digital switchover and work I did in 2008 on China's digital switchover, a report of which was published electronically as a Westminster Paper. I have also drawn on an article I wrote jointly with María Trinidad García Leiva in 2009 for *Media, Culture and*

*Society* (published by Sage); a 2011 article about the BBC for the *International Journal of Digital Television* (published by Intellect); and some material I contributed to a Spanish language publication edited by Luis A. Albornoz and María Trinidad García Leiva, *La televisión digital terrestre: Experiencias nacionales y diversidad en Europa, América y Asia* (published by La Crujía Ediciones, Buenos Aires, in 2012).

I would like to thank the following for responding to some specific research inquiries: Ivana Andrijašević, Ram Bhat, Lucia Barmošová, Nan-Shiun Chu, Fred Mattocks, Pham Hai and Eyjólfur Valdimarsson. I am particularly grateful to the following for reading and commenting on draft sections of the book: Martin Bell, Greg Bensberg, Sally Broughton Micova, María Trinidad García Leiva, Jock Given, Raymond Kuhn, David Levy, Andrei Richter, Krisztina Rozgonyi, Russell Southwood, Sue Starks and Roberto Suarez Candel.

I appreciate the inclusion of the book in the Palgrave Global Media and Business Series and the support I have had from Petros Iosifidis and his co-editors. Finally I would like to thank Felicity Plester, Chris Penfold, Cherline Daniel and their colleagues at Palgrave Macmillan, including their former colleague Catherine Mitchell, for all the work involved on the publishing side.

While I am happy to credit others for their role in developing the scholarship on this subject, any mistakes in this book are my responsibility.

# Acronyms and Abbreviations

| | |
|---|---|
| AVMS | Audio-Visual Media Services Directive (European Union) |
| API | Application Programming Interface |
| ATSC | Advanced Television Systems Committee (US) |
| BDB | British Digital Broadcasting consortium |
| BSB | British Satellite Broadcasting (UK) |
| CA | Conditional Access |
| DAB | Digital Audio Broadcasting |
| DBS | Direct Broadcast Satellite |
| DCMS | Department for Culture, Media and Sport (UK) |
| DMB | Digital Multi-media Broadcasting |
| DTH | Direct-to-Home (satellite) |
| DTMB | Digital Terrestrial Multi-media Broadcasting (China) |
| DTT | Digital Terrestrial Television |
| DVB | Digital Video Broadcasting project (Europe) |
| EC | European Commission |
| EPG | Electronic Programme Guide |
| EU | European Union |
| FCC | Federal Communications Commission (US) |
| HDTV | High-Definition Television |
| IBA | Independent Broadcasting Authority (UK) |
| IPTV | Internet Protocol Television |
| ISDB | Integrated Services Digital Broadcasting (Japan) |
| ITC | Independent Television Commission (UK) |
| ITU | International Telecommunication Union |
| MAC | Multiplex Analogue Component |
| MHP | Multi-media Home Platform |
| MHEG | Multi-media and Hypermedia Experts Group |
| MMDS | Multi-channel Multipoint Distribution Service |
| MPEG | Motion Picture Expert Group |
| NTSC | National Television System Committee (US) |
| Ofcom | Office of Communications (UK) |
| PAL | Phase Alternating Line |
| PBS | Public Broadcasting Service (US) |
| PVR | Personal Video Recorder |

| | |
|---|---|
| SECAM | *Séquentiel couleur à mémoire* |
| UGC | User Generated Content |
| UHF | Ultra High Frequency |
| VCR | Video Cassette Recorder |
| VHF | Very High Frequency |

# Introduction

Since it overtook radio in the mid-twentieth century, television (TV) has had a central relationship with democracy as the main source of news for most citizens in the advanced economies of the world. In the ideal democracy it provides accurate and truthful information to citizens, enabling them to exercise their votes and other rights of expression, representation and participation with an understanding of the complexity and context of the decisions made by their government in their name. In recognition of this and of wider cultural benefits, the government provides an independent and well-regulated framework within which television – and, of course, other media – can do this job. Conversely, in an undemocratic society the government controls television, either directly or indirectly, and broadcasters promulgate the messages the government wishes to give the citizens, from whom the full truth is often concealed.

During the twentieth century the number of television stations and channels increased. From a democratic point of view, this was generally judged to be a healthy development – if only because, the more TV stations there were, the more difficult it became for any one political group or commercial magnate to dominate the airwaves and exercise an undue influence on agenda-setting and public opinion. However, even in a pluralist system, television broadcasting was essentially a one-way (one-to-many) communication process.

At the start of the twenty-first century the medium of television began to undergo a radical transformation as analogue technology was supplanted by digital – and as the technologies of broadcasting, telecommunications and the computer converged to begin creating a new all-digital multi-media communications pattern.

One-way TV remains strong and can still command huge audiences. For big occasions, like the Football World Cup, the Olympics, or the

UK's 2011 Royal Wedding and 2012 Queen's Jubilee, it has the ability to bring not just a nation but large numbers of countries across the globe together to witness and share 'live' events. But, more generally, digitisation has disaggregated audiences through a proliferation of new channels, a range of new reception and recording devices and the development of interactivity.

Control of analogue television essentially belonged with the broadcasters – state, public service and commercial – with most of us constituting a mass audience passively watching a relatively restricted range of channels at times of the schedulers' choosing. Control of digital television is much more widely diffused. We can choose what to watch, as members of smaller audiences with shared interests as well as coming together for major events and productions. We choose when and where to watch, to suit our own convenience. We can comment on, and feed into, programme content. We can originate and distribute our own video material with relative ease and at relatively low cost. We can access news and other programme services from around the globe, if we wish. The analogue era of 'They Choose' is being replaced by the digital age of 'We Choose'.

This is a much more radical change than a simple expansion in the number of TV channels. It has implications for the governance, regulation and funding of broadcast television and related broadband communications, and impacts on our democratic processes.

Incumbent analogue broadcasters instinctively endeavour to manage the introduction of new technology in their own institutional interest. So too do governments in countries without a tradition of independent public service broadcasting, where state television and radio services have a dominant role. Regimes which have traditionally controlled television in a confined analogue system do not readily opt for greater pluralism when presented with the opportunity to create many more channels. It is obviously possible, in an authoritarian regime, to replace, say, two state-controlled channels by ten state-controlled channels. A wider civil society debate is needed, therefore, in the early stages of policy design if the potential opportunities for greater choice and freedom of expression are to be taken.

An understanding across civil society is not easy to achieve even in non-authoritarian countries. Governments may issue consultation papers before taking decisions on technical standards, spectrum allocation and the criteria for multiplex selection, for example. While these will be read by, and draw responses from, interested organisations with lobbying skills, there may be great political reluctance to stimulate a wide-ranging and well-informed debate among a broader public for fear of stirring up consumer resistance. Citizens need to understand the subject, however, if they wish to influence the course and potential outcomes of the digital television transition.

## Digital television and digital platforms

In simple terms digital television involves coding and then compressing the television signal. In analogue systems the pattern of transmitted television images and sounds remains *analogous* to the variations in the original camera pictures and microphone sounds. In digital transmission this analogy is lost. Instead the variations are coded using a series of ones and zeros and, once coded, they can be compressed without loss of quality.

Digital coding provides a robust format which retains quality between the transmitter and the receiver. Digital compression brings the additional benefit of increased transmission capacity. This extra capacity can be used for a technically richer signal, providing superior technical quality (high-definition), and/or for additional programme services (more channels). Digital television signals are compatible with computer and telecommunications digital technologies, facilitating interactive services.

Traditionally television was transmitted from the broadcaster to the viewer by conventional 'through the air' transmission from a mast on a hill to a domestic roof-top or set-top aerial. This is what we know as terrestrial transmission and reception. In recent decades it has been joined by, and in some countries largely supplanted by:

- satellite transmission, where the signal is 'up-linked' by broadcasters to a satellite from which it then comes down direct to a domestic satellite dish
- cable television, supplied by a cable running under the ground and coming up into the house (with cable television providers using both terrestrial and satellite transmissions as their source at the cable 'head-end').

Digital coding and compression technology can be applied to all of these forms of distribution, giving the three main digital television transmission 'platforms' of digital satellite, digital cable and digital terrestrial television (DTT).

Digital technology has added a fourth television distribution platform: broadband, normally via a telecommunications wire. Common as a means of delivering the Internet, broadband is increasingly able to handle the much more demanding requirements of television and online video distribution. Wireless broadband, used in advanced systems of mobile telephony, can also handle video distribution but is not a primary means of television distribution.

At the reception end, once a digital signal from the broadcaster has arrived, it needs to be decompressed and decoded before it can be displayed on a TV set. For satellite, cable and broadband, this is normally done by routing it through a set-top box. For digital terrestrial television a set-top box linked to a conventional analogue TV set is often initially the most widespread arrangement, but flat-screen digital TV sets, where the digital terrestrial electronics are integrated into the set, often with widescreen format, are rapidly becoming the norm. At the same time hard-disc digital recorders are displacing the old analogue video-cassette recorder.

Digitisation of the satellite platform has taken place almost entirely on a commercial basis. Digital technology offers satellite operators the advantages of greater capacity, lower running costs per channel, interactive services and the ability to automate pay-per-view booking and billing. For the cable industry the same advantages apply but analogue cable is deeply entrenched in some countries, often with a fragmented industry structure lacking the capability to invest in a major transformation. For that reason the digitisation of the cable platform has proceeded at a different pace in different countries, again largely on a commercial basis.

The conversion of the analogue terrestrial platform to digital, however, is more of a political affair. For most countries the switch-off of analogue terrestrial transmission is the goal at the heart of the digital switchover process, because freeing the spectrum used by broadcasters for wireless 'over the air' transmission is extremely attractive to the rapidly growing mobile telephone and wireless broadband side of the telecommunications industry. The digital television switchover process is generally regarded as having been completed at the point at which analogue terrestrial television transmissions are shut down, even if some analogue services continue on satellite or cable.

## Wired and wireless services

One doorway into the subject of digital television switchover is the concept of the 'Negroponte Switch'. The idea, aired by digital guru Nicholas Negroponte at a meeting back in the 1980s, was that electronic information which was then distributed by wire through the ground (telephony) would in future be sent through the air – while signals that went through the air (television) would in future go through the ground. Wired services would become wireless and wireless services would become wired. Negroponte called it 'Trading Places', but George Gilder who was at the same meeting called it the 'Negroponte Switch' and the label stuck (Negroponte, 1995: 24).

Communications by telephone have indeed made a major shift from the land line to the mobile (or cell). In many countries, in the developing as well as the developed world, the number of mobile telephones now exceeds the number of households. With the invention of 3G (third generation) smart-phones, the technology moved into mobile broadband, combining telephony with access to the Internet. Smart-phone take-up has grown sharply and continues to do so, with fourth generation technology (4G) now entering the market.

The more demand grows, and the more sophisticated the smart-phone becomes, the hungrier the telecommunications industry becomes for additional wireless spectrum. The spectrum allocated to mobile telephony is in a higher band than that used by television terrestrial broadcasters but the frequencies at the upper end of the broadcasters' band are highly suitable for mobile and wireless broadband. From a telecoms point of view, they provide an attractive balance between service capacity and propagation (the distance over which they can travel).

Television meanwhile has moved from relying predominantly on terrestrial transmission to become a multi-platform business. The main driver here has again been demand. Satellite and cable have a far greater capacity than terrestrial television, multiplying the number of channels possible and facilitating a supermarket of choice. They have also opened up the market in subscription television, bringing a new source of revenue into the industry.

The balance between TV platforms varies significantly by country and continues to change over time, but cable now accounts for about 60% of reception on the primary TV set in the United States and Germany and around 90% in the Netherlands. Cable's role is particularly strong in North America and northern Europe and, taking into account the part played by satellite as well, a shrinking dependence on terrestrial transmission is a much wider trend: by 2010 terrestrial reception (for the main TV set) in the UK had fallen below 50% (Ofcom, 2010: 120).

The growing appetite for spectrum on the part of the telecommunications industry and the diminishing role of terrestrial reception by television viewers are at the heart of the process of digital switchover.

## Terrestrial spectrum opportunities

The spectrum used for television broadcasting consists of a specific band of individual frequency channels. In analogue television each frequency carried one TV channel. However, broadcasting five analogue services in the UK required 46 frequency channels in order to cover the whole country in a pattern of some 1100 transmitters. This was because, in order to avoid interference, analogue services could not be broadcast on adjacent or near-adjacent frequencies, nor could adjacent main transmitters use the same group of frequencies. The UK's analogue television broadcasting spectrum in the UHF (Ultra High Frequency) band ran from frequency channel 21 up to frequency channel 68 (with 36 and 38 excluded). It was a generous amount of spectrum for five programme services (Figure I.1).

Using digital terrestrial technology, one frequency channel could initially accommodate at least four (and now many more) standard definition TV services, constituting a digital multiplex. Since digital services are more rugged than analogue, they can be transmitted at lower power and using adjacent frequency channels is much less of a problem. Digital terrestrial television can therefore transmit a much greater number of TV services in significantly less spectrum.

For the telecommunications industry, the invention of digital terrestrial television arrived at the right time. Switching to digital television has allowed the telecommunications industry access to spectrum withdrawn from the broadcasters, not only without broadcasting suffering, but with positive broadcasting benefits. In the UK, digital technology enabled terrestrial television to offer more than six times as many services using two-thirds of its former spectrum allocation, while releasing the other third for, among other purposes, the development of 4G wireless broadband services.

Governments benefit from this process, when the released spectrum is auctioned. The revenue involved can be sufficiently large to give

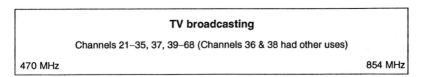

| TV broadcasting |
| --- |
| Channels 21–35, 37, 39–68 (Channels 36 & 38 had other uses) |
| 470 MHz                                                854 MHz |

*Figure I.1*   The UK's use of UHF spectrum for analogue television broadcasting

governments a clear incentive to drive the change. After completing its switchover in June 2009, the United States auctioned 108 MHz of spectrum to wireless broadband providers and raised $19.6 billion (DigiTAG, 2010).

## Digital television switchover

Of course, to achieve such spectrum release, analogue terrestrial television viewers have to be persuaded to migrate to digital television, which poses a challenge to broadcasters, receiver manufacturers, regulators and governments.

At first sight the idea of compelling every TV household to switch to a new method of reception, requiring new equipment by a particular deadline, looks politically thankless, not to say downright risky. Almost all other consumer technology shifts take place at the consumer's pace, even if in the end the old equipment becomes obsolete and impractical to repair or replace. Think of the typewriter giving way to the word processor, the vinyl disc to the CD, or the spread of the digital camera. No one uses quill pens these days but no government ever set a 'quill pen abolition' date! However, to secure the spectrum benefits of digitisation, analogue terrestrial switch-off needs a coordinated compulsory timetable.

The conventional technique for achieving this is to begin by launching digital terrestrial television alongside analogue terrestrial. This is dependent on the availability of some spare frequencies within the analogue spectrum to use for one or more digital terrestrial multiplexes. While this is usually possible, it may not be feasible to achieve full national coverage for digital terrestrial television at this stage. The digital multiplex capacity is then used to carry digital versions of the existing analogue services. This digital duplication of the analogue services is termed 'simulcasting' or 'dual illumination'. Ideally, the digital capacity would also permit the creation of other new digital terrestrial services, to make digital terrestrial television more attractive to viewers than analogue.

A period of time (the digital transition) is then allowed, during which analogue terrestrial viewers are encouraged to purchase digital terrestrial receivers (set-top boxes or a new digital TV set) or, alternatively, should they wish, to switch to another distribution platform. After sufficient time has been allowed for them to migrate, the analogue transmitters can be switched off. At that stage a substantial amount of spectrum is normally released, becoming available for more TV channels and/or to assist a system upgrade to high-definition television (HDTV), as well as for potential use by telecommunications operators. This is usually termed the 'digital dividend'.

The ease with which the switchover process can be accomplished depends to a large extent on the platform mix a country has at the outset. A country whose TV households are largely served by some combination of cable and satellite will have relatively few analogue terrestrial households to convert. Switchover then represents a low political risk for governments – and indeed governments may have an incentive to speed it up, using some form of subsidy, in order to reap revenue from auctioning the released spectrum. In a country where terrestrial reception predominates, the political risk of compelling households to switch is greater. The process is therefore likely to take longer there and the government may wish to see plenty of voluntary take-up of digital television in the market before it names a compulsory analogue switch-off timetable.

## International perspective

While determining the timetable is essentially a matter for national governments, spectrum usage is planned internationally as well as nationally. Within the framework of the United Nations Organisation, the International Telecommunication Union (ITU) has a high-level oversight of the way spectrum is used across the whole range of broadcasting, telephony, mobile communications, navigation and astronomy throughout the world. Its aims are to prevent harmful interference and improve the effectiveness of spectrum use. By agreement, it allocates particular bands of spectrum for particular purposes. This is done within three ITU regions – (a) Europe, the Middle East and Africa (plus Mongolia) (b) the Americas and (c) the Far East and Australasia. Each band of spectrum is given primary and secondary uses, with primary-use services fully protected and secondary-use services protected from one another but not from primary-use services.

In 2015, under an agreement reached in Geneva in 2006, analogue terrestrial broadcasting will formally come to an end in Region 1 – Europe, the Middle East and Africa. This means that analogue transmissions will lose their protection from interference, as the global process of digital television switchover marches on. In practice the impact of this change will be of limited significance in the Middle East, where satellite has a dominant role, and in Africa, where television is less developed and cross-border interference less of an issue. However, in the crowded spectrum of Europe, this deadline is a real one.

The UK was an early starter, launching digital terrestrial television in 1998 but it adopted a cautiously long transition, completing the

*Table I.1* Countries completing digital TV switchover by end of 2012

| Country | Date of analogue terrestrial switch-off |
|---|---|
| Luxembourg | 2006 |
| Netherlands | 2006 |
| Finland | 2007 |
| Sweden | 2007 |
| Germany | 2008 |
| Switzerland | 2008 |
| Denmark | 2009 |
| Norway | 2009 |
| United States | 2009 |
| Croatia | 2010 |
| Estonia | 2010 |
| Latvia | 2010 |
| Spain | 2010 |
| Austria | 2011 |
| Belgium | 2011 |
| Canada | 2011 |
| Czech Republic | 2011 |
| France (including overseas territories) | 2011 |
| Israel | 2011 |
| Malta | 2011 |
| Slovenia | 2011 |
| Ireland | 2012 |
| Italy | 2012 |
| Japan | 2012 |
| Lithuania | 2012 |
| Portugal | 2012 |
| Slovakia | 2012 |
| South Korea | 2012 |
| Taiwan | 2012 |
| United Kingdom | 2012 |

(Author research: sources include ITU, EU, DigiTAG, DVB and http://en.dtvstatus.net. In some cases low power analogue relays may have continued beyond the main switchover completion date shown)

switch to all-digital by the end of 2012. Other countries switched off their analogue terrestrial television much earlier, with Luxembourg, the Netherlands, Finland, Sweden, Germany, Switzerland, Denmark, Norway and the United States ahead of the many others who followed in 2010, 2011, 2012 and since. (Table I.1).

The switchover process has now started on every continent and is becoming a worldwide transition, though in China and India the initial focus has been on digitising the cable TV industry. Terrestrial spectrum release sits within a broader pattern of digitisation, affecting the whole television chain from content provider to viewer, against the background of the convergence of broadcasting, computer and telecommunications technologies. By 2012 around half of the world's 1.2 billion TV households were thought to be equipped to receive digital TV. The speed of penetration has been remarkable: 20 years earlier the technology was only just being invented. Analogue TV is not yet close to global extinction, but the digital television revolution now has global momentum.

# Part I
# Birth and Development

# 1
# The Impetus for Digital Television

## Summary of the chapter's argument

While digital television was invented by Research and Development (R&D) experts, it was adopted for a combination of industrial policy and broadcaster interest reasons in the United States and Europe. An underlying aim was to prevent Japan from achieving a global technical standard for analogue HDTV. Governments perceived the possibility of securing benefits from spectrum release if ever analogue terrestrial television could be closed down but no one initially knew whether this would be possible. It could only become feasible if digital TV reception, on any or all platforms, reached 'take-off' point, but, neither for spectrum release motives nor as part of a wider 'Information Society' policy, were governments prepared to subsidise the costs of the start-up stage. TV set manufacturers were also cautious. Swift take-up was, however, achieved by private sector operators, mainly in the digital satellite sphere, shouldering the risk of subsidising set-top boxes in order to build a pay-TV business. This stage of digital TV development could deliver take-up in the market but a compulsory switch-off of analogue terrestrial could not be based on a foundation of voluntary consumer subscription.

## Origins

Digital television was certainly not invented by broadcast engineers in order to surrender broadcasting frequencies to telecommunications companies. The technical invention, described in depth by Martin Bell (Bell, 2007), was the product of various building blocks – digital coding (already in use in the recorded music industry), digital compression (overseen by the Motion Picture Expert Group, MPEG) and then systems of digital transmission related to the satellite, cable and terrestrial platforms. Broadcast engineers work continuously on ways of improving picture and sound quality, minimising interference and enhancing television and radio capabilities and features. If an innovation promises to have sufficient consumer appeal to support a market, as in the case of colour television and stereo radio (but not quadraphonic radio), the broadcasting and receiver industries adopt it. However, the context for the invention of digital terrestrial television was set by a wider set of commercial and political pressures.

The story can best begin with Japan's desire in the 1980s to develop a new generation of analogue television technology in the form of HDTV. Working with the Japanese receiver industry, whose giant companies were so powerful internationally, the national public service broadcaster NHK developed a studio production system called Hi-Vision, based on 1125 lines of picture (compared with the 525 in use in the United States and the 625 in the UK) and coupled it with a transmission system called MUSE for satellite transmission and reception (Bell, 2007). Far ahead of any rival R&D work elsewhere, Japanese analogue HDTV was ready for submission to the body which approves international technical standards in this field, the CCIR (*Comité consultatif international pour la radio*), at a meeting in Dubrovnik in 1986. The Japanese proposal was that their system should become a world standard.

Technical standards in broadcasting are in effect internationally agreed blueprints for making equipment which is standardised in order to provide interoperability with other related production, transmission and reception equipment (Wood, 2011). They play a vital commercial role in facilitating the creation of markets which are large enough to support major investment in innovation and, generally, they are a friend to consumers: they help ensure that, if you buy a Sony television, for example, it will receive the transmissions of all the terrestrial broadcasters and if you couple it to a Panasonic video-recorder the equipment will all work smoothly.

However, technical standards also play a role in protecting markets: by adopting a set of standards for a particular territory which are different from those accepted elsewhere, domestic manufacturers can try to limit foreign competition. Moreover, foreign manufacturers entering the market, or foreign countries adopting the same standards, then pay royalties to the companies which designed the standards. In analogue television, North America had a system called NTSC (National Television System Committee) while Europe mostly used PAL (Phase Alternating Line) and France used its own SECAM (*Séquentiel couleur à mémoire*).

So the Japanese proposal to make their HDTV system a world standard was a bold jump. The United States was initially supportive of the Japanese proposal: after all, the Americans made TV shows and movies which they wished to sell all over the world, so the concept of a global market, in which, for example, video-recorders in every country would work with American tapes, had a certain appeal (Brinkley, 1997). The Europeans, however, objected strongly, from motives of cultural protectionism in France's case and, more broadly, of industrial protectionism in the interests of European consumer electronics companies like Philips and Thomson. Europe therefore set about creating an analogue HDTV satellite system of its own.

### The United States: ATSC digital television

Back in America, which only had one remaining major electronics manufacturer at the time (Galperin, 2004), a different debate was taking place. The American analogue terrestrial broadcasters were trying to defend their occupation of such a large block of spectrum against pressures from the land mobile industry, championed by Motorola, who wanted to have some of the broadcast spectrum released for use by two-way radios operated by the police, ambulance services and commercial delivery companies (Brinkley, 1997; Galperin, 2004). To the broadcasters' industry body, the NAB (National Association of Broadcasters), HDTV sounded a great idea. Terrestrial HDTV would require the use of the entire under-utilised spectrum at issue with the land mobile lobbyists. So the Americans invited the Japanese to give a demonstration of their Hi-Vision MUSE system in Washington. The result was dramatic in two respects. First, the improvement in picture quality was stunning and HDTV was recognised as the next big development for American television. Second, both American commercial interests and American politicians were outraged at the idea that this business should simply be handed to the Japanese. As Hernan Galperin put it, the Japanese attempt to gain worldwide adoption of the NHK system 'set off an international arms race to develop HDTV' (Galperin, 2004: 35).

In 1987 the Federal Communications Commission (FCC) set up an Advisory Committee on Advanced Television Service (ACATS), chaired by former FCC Chairman Richard E. Wiley, with membership overlapping substantially with the broadcasting technical standards coordinating body, the Advanced Television Systems Committee (ATSC). Its task was to advise the FCC on the technical and policy issues surrounding HDTV. Wiley's committee reviewed the current state of R&D work and announced that it would hold a contest on an open international basis. NHK would be able to submit their entry. As one industry chronicler excitedly noted:

> Nothing like this had ever happened before. Wiley's rules had set off a grand, international competition, sanctioned by the United States government! Anyone in the world could enter. The contestants would be tested and graded. Finally Wiley and his committee would choose a winner, who would hold licensing rights for the next generation of television. Everyone who built and sold HDTVs in America would pay this winner royalties, which would be worth millions, billions!
>
> (Brinkley, 1997: 44)

A key contender was General Instrument who, in 1990, dropped a bombshell on the industry by announcing that it had designed an *all-digital* HDTV system for terrestrial television. Within a few months, three rival all-digital systems were also put forward. Japan's bid for world standard status for its analogue system was doomed.

The FCC Advisory Committee rallied behind the all-digital concept and the proponents of the rival digital HDTV systems formed what they called the Grand Alliance. They set out to design the best combination. As the different components emerged from their tests, the ATSC documented the specifications for what was to become known as the ATSC Digital Television Standard for terrestrial television. The picture format would be widescreen. Following pressure from the computer industry, the question of whether the picture should be based on the traditional broadcasting interlaced scanning system or on the computer industry's progressive scanning technique was left open. Broadcasters would be free to choose and TV sets would need to be able to handle both. Technical specifications were set for standard definition digital television as well as for HDTV. In 1995, when testing procedures were complete, the Advisory Committee recommended adoption of the ATSC standard and the FCC formally adopted it the following year.

In parallel the FCC had done some preliminary thinking on how HDTV, once standardised, could come into operation in practice. Its starting position, formulated in 1991, was that the incumbent terrestrial broadcasters should each be allocated an extra frequency channel on which to launch digital services. There was no policy move to introduce new broadcasting competitors but, while the terrestrial broadcasters had viewed HDTV as a way of clinging on to their spectrum, the FCC now had other ideas: after a transition period, the analogue frequencies would be withdrawn. Thus the seeds of the regulatory strategy of launching digital terrestrial television with the aim of reclaiming spectrum after a transition period were planted early on – though the next FCC Chairman, Reed Hundt, believed that he had inherited a 'crazy policy':

> I never met anyone who truly believed that the broadcasters would give back the analog channels. In the foreseeable future, Americans were not about to throw away their 200 million analog televisions, so broadcasters would not stop sending signals to them.
>
> (Hundt, 2000: 65)

## Europe: DVB digital television

Meanwhile in Europe the major consumer electronics manufacturers and the major national broadcasters had set off down a separate road. They were as keen to be different from the United States as they were from Japan and committed to developing distinctive European standards to protect their European market. The birth of analogue satellite broadcasting in the 1980s had given them the opportunity to revisit the established PAL and SECAM standards and to design a new analogue system around which Europe could unite. They focussed on satellite transmission. The use of medium-powered communications satellites was well-established but, following the World Administrative Radio Conference of 1977, nations were allocated frequencies for the new satellite technology of high-powered direct broadcasting to the home (DBS). Urged on by the European Commission and the European Broadcasting Union, the engineering experts set about designing a new analogue transmission standard on which Europe's DBS services should be based (Bell, 2007).

The MAC (Multiplexed Analogue Component) transmission system was initially designed by engineering experts at the UK's Independent Broadcasting Authority (IBA) and backed, despite some BBC engineering misgivings, by a UK government committee chaired by Sir Anthony Part. Following collaborative work in Europe a group of MAC standards was elaborated and in 1986 a European Community directive mandated the use of the MAC technology for TV services from high-powered satellites.

The European response to Japan's bid to turn its Hi-Vision and MUSE system into a world standard for HDTV was to design a variant of MAC termed HD-MAC. Europe, however, was not convinced at that time that HDTV was ripe for commercial introduction. The technology was too new for receivers to be feasible other than at very high cost. Moreover, to Europeans the attraction of DBS seemed to lie, rather, in its ability to provide many more channels at standard definition. Two factors help explain the contrast with the American perspective.

First, growth in the European television industry had been much more restricted than in the United States. The leading role had been allocated to publicly funded, state-established national broadcasters expected to deliver a service to the whole country and frequencies had been allocated to maximise national coverage. As in the UK, some commercial television had then been introduced as well but European analogue terrestrial viewers typically had far fewer channels to choose from than viewers in the United States. So Europe had an element of pent-up demand for the vista of multi-channel television which satellite, and indeed cable, broadcasting could deliver.

Second, the European analogue television picture quality, based on PAL or SECAM, was better, having been designed later, than the American NTSC system – whose variability European engineers were prone to denigrate as 'Never The Same Colour' (Bell, 2007: 11). American viewers therefore had a stronger interest in the improved technical quality offered by HDTV.

While Europe's HD-MAC system never really became operational, the use of MAC for standard definition satellite broadcasting did become established. For the UK it proved a commercial disaster and its failure more broadly led directly to Europe's conversion to digital television.

The UK had been allocated spectrum for five channels of direct-to-home analogue satellite broadcasting. Two were awarded by the government to the BBC in 1982 for new BBC satellite channels to be launched on a British-made satellite, with no government funding. The scheme collapsed: the receiver industry would not manufacture receivers without prior broadcaster investment, the BBC would not take commercial risks with licence fee investment and the government would not underwrite the venture. An attempt then to construct a broader coalition, including ITV and others, known as 'The Club of 21', also foundered. So the commercial broadcasting regulator, the IBA, advertised a UK satellite franchise and awarded it to a new commercial consortium, called British Satellite Broadcasting (BSB). BSB would use a high-powered satellite capable of being received on a small square aerial – the 'squarial', as it was known – and would comply with the new MAC technical standard required by the IBA and the European directive. Its services would be marketed on a subscription basis. BSB aimed to launch in 1989 and expected to have a monopoly of the brand-new UK satellite TV market (Starks, 2007).

However, in 1988 the press mogul, Rupert Murdoch, announced that Sky Television, then operating a small operation in Europe using PAL technology on a medium-powered communications satellite, would launch a rival direct-to-home service for the UK. It would use a Luxembourg-based Astra satellite outside the IBA's licensing remit. Since the satellite was medium-powered, it fell outside the scope of the European MAC directive (Hart, 2004), so Sky chose to stick with the well-tried PAL standard. Sky was first-to-market in 1989, with four channels. Its services were initially free, relying on advertising, with subscription to follow later. A bidding war began with BSB for Hollywood film rights, and, given its start-up investment and no subscription revenue, Sky went deep into the red.

Meanwhile, BSB, already spending on a much greater scale, discovered that the MAC receiver microchip, technically the key to reception, was still in development – no working version existed, or could exist in time for a 1989 launch. The 'squarials' also had technical teething problems. So BSB did not launch until 1990. Arriving second as a more expensive buy, BSB then subsidised consumer take-up and its losses in 1990 ran to about £8 million a week (Chippindale and Franks, 1991). This was unsustainable. Without telling either its chief executive or the IBA, the BSB Board agreed merger terms with Sky which were tantamount to a Sky take-over. The new company, BSkyB, would be headed by Sky TV's Sam Chisholm and would use the Astra satellite and PAL technology. The BSB satellite with its MAC technology became redundant.

BSB's collapse has been termed 'one of the greatest commercial disasters in British history and certainly the greatest in the history of the British media' (Chippindale and Franks, 1991: xi). The damage was not confined to the UK: European manufacturers had invested heavily in producing MAC receivers. Elsewhere in Europe analogue satellite services began to use PAL. Some MAC services continued in Germany and Scandinavia for a short time but, with the Americans now working on a potential digital system, Europe's bid to create its own new analogue standard reached a dead-end.

The way forward emerged from a secret meeting of seven friends in a German castle in 1991. They came from the German public broadcasting organisations ARD and ZDF, from key receiver manufacturers Grundig, Nokia, Philips and Thomson and from the silicon chip maker Intermetall (Bell, 2007). They wanted to ignore the European Commission's directive on MAC and start afresh down the digital road – and they thought that technical standards should be framed less by technical regulators and politicians and more by the commercial realities of the market. Thus began a process which led to the creation of the European Digital Video Broadcasting (DVB) Project in 1993. Under wise leadership, the DVB established the principle that design work undertaken by a technical module of experts would be governed by requirements set by a commercial module of potential investors. The organisation expanded as an alliance based on a memorandum of understanding and swiftly began to produce results.

For Germany and France, who had not botched their satellite policy in the way the UK had, the priority was the development of a digital satellite standard (DVB-S). This was achieved in 1993. The following year the DVB digital cable standard (DVB-C) was finalised. The third member of the family was to be the digital terrestrial standard, work on which was more complex. It involved a transmission technology called COFDM (Coded Orthogonal Frequency Division Multiplexing), derived from work done on digital radio in another European project, which was different from the VSB (Vestigial Sideband) system adopted in the United States (Hart, 2004). The DVB-T standard for digital terrestrial television was finally approved in early 1996. The Europeans, of course, believed their digital terrestrial technology to be technically superior to the Americans' but failed to convince the United States to change from its ATSC standard.

### Broadcaster push in the UK

In the UK BSkyB was emerging as a powerful competitor to the BBC, ITV and Channel 4 (the UK's last analogue channel, Five, was to start with restricted coverage in 1997). Now that it had a monopoly in satellite pay-TV and was the principal supplier of premium services to the UK's cable operators, it was building a successful business, notably at the tabloid end of the market, with an appeal based mainly on sport and movies but a commitment to serious news too. In 1992 it laid the foundations for a prosperous future by buying the rights to live coverage of Premier League football. By the mid-1990s BSkyB had the financial strength and business acumen to do a lot more competitive damage to the UK's major terrestrial broadcasters, who viewed it with a mixture of fear and awe.

Digital satellite technology was mature and tested in the market now: Direct TV's digital satellite pay-TV service in the United States was thriving and using its huge capacity to provide a Near-Video-On-Demand service, based on staggered starts to movies. The BBC, ITV and Channel 4 saw with alarm that BSkyB could probably launch a digital satellite service for the UK at an early date. In analogue, satellite Sky had already shown the advantage of being first-to-market and had humiliated the British broadcasting establishment. Were they to leave BSkyB unchallenged to establish a *de facto* monopoly in multi-channel digital television now?

Digital terrestrial gave the UK's terrestrial broadcasters an opportunity for a return match in which they might play on their own more familiar ground (Starks, 2007) and they followed the R&D work and the DVB's standardisation progress closely. In 1994 the UK government announced that sufficient frequencies could be found to allow 12 digital terrestrial services to be launched and the terrestrial broadcasters swiftly expressed their interest, mounting trials and demonstrations.

In 1995 Virginia Bottomley, Secretary of State at the Department of National Heritage, published government proposals for launching digital terrestrial broadcasting in the UK – television and radio – and invited comments. The government's aims for television were to

- ensure that viewers could choose from a wide variety of terrestrial television channels
- give existing national broadcasters the opportunity to develop digital services and safeguard public service broadcasting into the digital age
- give terrestrial broadcasters the opportunity to compete with those on satellite and cable
- help a fair and effective market to develop
- help UK manufacturers and producers to compete at home and overseas
- make best use of the available spectrum (DNH, 1995a).

It now appeared that 18 or more digital terrestrial standard definition television channels would be possible (there was no ambition to move to HDTV at this stage). They would be based on six multiplexes whose coverage ranged from over 90% down to around 60%, with the need to protect analogue television's near-universal coverage proving a major constraint. Broadcasters would only be licensed to provide programme services if they had a contract with a multiplex provider. Thus the broadcasters were not, at this point, pictured as being the multiplex providers themselves. However, guaranteed places would be offered for BBC One, BBC Two, Channel 3 (ITV), Channel 4, S4C (the Welsh language service in Wales) and Channel Five to be simulcast 'to maintain public service broadcasting and ultimately to allow analogue signals to be switched off' (DNH, 1995a: 12).

Thus the terrestrial broadcasters were attracted to digital terrestrial television so that they, and perhaps some new entrants, could compete with BSkyB in multi-channel digital television. The UK government welcomed the prospect of competition too. However, significantly, the idea of analogue switch-off was also built into the government's design from the start:

> In the long term the Government wishes to do all it can to release spectrum by switching off existing analogue transmission signals, should digital broadcasting be successful enough to allow it.
>
> (DNH, 1995a: 4)

## Diffusion in the market

Just as not all inventions make it from the R&D workbench into the market, not all marketed innovations prove a runaway success. For a product which penetrates the market fully, take-up normally follows the pattern of an S-shaped curve, starting with a small number of early adopters who are prepared to pay the initially high prices of new equipment. Growing demand then builds a steep take-up curve as the majority of consumers become adopters and the graph of sales tails off during the late adopter phase as the market becomes saturated.

However, some innovations never quite catch on, while others develop with what the industry calls a 'slow burn'. Digital radio, for example, invented back in the late 1980s, launched initially in the UK by the BBC in 1995 and then on a national basis with commercial radio's involvement from 1999, spluttered at the outset. The UK was in the vanguard internationally but by 2004 only 800,000 digital radio sets had been sold (Stoller, 2010: 287).

The contrast between the slow and patchy take-up of digital radio in its first few years and the swift 'take-off' of digital television in its infant years is striking. The greater appeal to governments of spectrum efficiency in television was not the explanation. While the spectrum motive was present in digital television policy from the start, it did not act as a significant driver of take-up until much later. At the outset analogue switch-off was simply not politically feasible. No one had worked out how to do it and the idea of compelling voting consumers to discard their analogue TVs and buy a digital replacement to improve spectrum efficiency looked electorally suicidal. As we have seen, Reed Hundt, who chaired the FCC from 1993 to 1997, was pretty sceptical about the prospect, while in the UK Virginia Bottomley postponed any consideration of a timetable for analogue switch-off until 50% digital take-up had been achieved in the market or, if sooner, until five years of digital terrestrial TV had elapsed (DNH, 1995b).

Governments and regulators could, and did, set legislative and regulatory frameworks which were favourable, for example by awarding free digital terrestrial spectrum for an initial period, but their long-term policy aspirations could not provide the driving force behind early take-up.

So how did digital television 'take off' in its first few years, between 1998 and 2002, to reach the point where switchover did become politically feasible and governments fully engaged?

Henry Laurence has called attention to the possible relevance of general technology diffusion theory to the case of digital television (Laurence, 2011), citing in particular the works of Brian Winston and Everett Rogers.

Winston, writing in 1998, described how inventions which come to the market-place are subject to both 'brakes' and 'accelerators'. New technologies come into an environment dominated by institutional structures based on old technology – and the old has a tendency to suppress the radical potential of the new (the BBC's early attitude to television in the heyday of BBC wireless provides a classic example). This braking force needs some 'supervening social necessity' to overcome it, and Winston cites spare capacity in the electronics industry after the Second World War as the crucial enabling factor which transformed television into a mass market in the United States (Winston, 1998: 111).

Can we relate this analysis to digital television? In some countries the analogue terrestrial broadcasters did indeed provide a brake on the radical potential of digital technology. Digital television was a potential threat in that it would support a much bigger television market, with more competitors and a reduced market share for the incumbents. We have seen how American broadcasters' initial interest in HDTV related to their desire to maintain their hold on spectrum. HD required so much spectrum capacity at the outset that allocating incumbents the frequencies they would need for it went a long way towards maintaining their closed market. Broadcasters in the United States proved keener to secure the spectrum for HD than to start using it and, as we shall see later, the FCC's original strategy had to be revised. Similar commercial pressures operated in Australia, where HD simulcasting was introduced at the start and the risk of new standard definition competitors minimised. In the UK, by contrast, the shock to the analogue terrestrial incumbents of BSkyB's arrival as a competitor produced an enthusiasm for implementing standard definition multi-channel digital terrestrial. The peculiar competitive situation in the UK, stemming from the established broadcasters' failure in the satellite domain, undoubtedly provided an 'accelerator'.

Was there a 'supervening social necessity'? Arguably the pressures on spectrum – and the opportunity digital switchover offered governments and regulators to release terrestrial frequencies – became such a factor subsequently but, as noted above, not in the early years. Indeed in the late 1990s there was some debate about whether digital terrestrial television was a viable proposition in the market at all, so limited was its channel capacity by comparison with digital satellite and cable (Starks, 2007).

Everett Rogers has articulated a framework of variables which influence the rate of adoption of new technologies, spanning the perceived attributes of the technology, the nature of the adoption process, communication channels, the extent of promotion and the social system (Rogers, 2003). Within the perceived attributes of the innovation, relative advantage over existing technology, compatibility with existing systems, complexity, the possibility of trialling and the observability of the benefits are relevant factors. Applying this framework to digital television, Laurence concluded that 'digital TV did not score highly on most of these variables relative to analogue TV in the early years' (Laurence, 2011: 361).

However, comparing digital television's progress in establishing itself in the market with digital radio's, we can note:

- digital television's greater appeal in offering more channels (because there were fewer analogue TV services than analogue radio stations)
- digital television's availability through a set-top box connection to an existing analogue TV set (which offered a low-cost option, retaining existing equipment)
- digital television's interactivity features, including especially the Electronic Programme Guide.

## Carrying the investment risk

As well as looking at the features of the technology, the wider context for its adoption and the significance of any special braking or acceleration factors, we can examine who was prepared to carry the start-up investment risks and why. Given the role of industrial policy in the initial development, we might perhaps have expected the consumer electronics industry to have undertaken major investment in the mass production and marketing of new digital TV sets.

## The TV set market

For a variety of reasons the HDTV market in the United States made a very hesitant start. Having secured their spectrum, the broadcasters were not that interested in providing HDTV simulcasts of their analogue channels: it was a recipe for additional cost with very little additional revenue. They lobbied to be able to provide new standard definition services and for a regulatory regime which made HDTV broadcasting optional, not compulsory.

Then the consumer electronics industry was steadily reshaping itself. America's most famous TV set manufacturer, RCA, had already been sold off by General Electric to the French company Thomson during the 1980s and the remaining major American TV maker, Zenith, was acquired in stages by the Korean firm LG Electronics during the 1990s. Competition to the dominance of the Japanese manufacturers now came primarily from elsewhere in Asia, though a few European companies were also significant players. After the collapse of its ambitions for analogue HDTV, Japan developed its own set of technical standards for digital television and launched its own digital services, initially on satellite, but Japanese consumer electronics firms manufactured receivers to American and European standards as well so that they could sell across the globe. The leading companies were increasingly multi-national in their operations, with bases in each major market and production sited where it was most economic. By the late 1990s, therefore, the patriotic American industrial policy which had originally stimulated the creation of the ATSC standard was fading.

Another factor restricting market development was a degree of confusion surrounding the receiver specification (Hart, 2010). The consumer electronics interest in digital television was not restricted to TV set manufacturers: R&D, silicon chip manufacturing, software development and computer companies had all contributed to discussions during the standard-setting process. The computer industry had been keen to require the Advanced Television receivers to adopt the progressive scanning technique used for computer monitors, rather than the interlaced scanning system historically used by television and, as noted above, the ATSC standard allowed for both possibilities. The broadcasters had argued about how many lines constituted high-definition (720 or 1080): again both were allowed. Because many broadcasters focussed on new standard definition services, not all digital TVs were HD-capable, some were labelled HDTV-upgradeable. Then television screen technology was in flux, with the cathode-ray tube still in production but flat-screen TVs beginning to appear as well. As Jeffrey Hart observed,

Broadcasters and manufacturers were left to figure out what types of signals customers would be willing to pay for at premium DTV [digital television] prices.

(Hart, 2010: 19)

The result was small production volumes, high prices and a degree of consumer bafflement in the shops. Satellite and cable digital television, which was based on set-top boxes, took off and flew but American digital terrestrial television bumped along the runway. By 2001 it had penetrated only 80,000 United States homes, by which time digital satellite was in 17,900,000 and digital cable in 15,200,000 (Galperin, 2004: 121). Around the end of 2000 the price of an HDTV digital set was in the range $1000–$14,000, while analogue TVs cost between $100 and $700 (Grimme, 2002: 239). American shops continued to sell around 25 million analogue TVs per year.

In Europe digital satellite in particular grew rapidly. France and Germany, two of the major markets, were in no hurry to embark on digital terrestrial TV, judging the technology as untried and the market as uncertain. The first countries to launch digital terrestrial in Europe were the UK, Sweden, Spain and Finland. The BBC took the opportunity of digital simulcasting to shift its output from the historically conventional TV picture format (4:3 ratio of width to height) to widescreen (16:9) which was better suited to drama, films and sport. The main European TV manufacturers, backed by the European Commission, had been trying to engineer this shift within an analogue framework and it had not fully worked. Digital terrestrial therefore enabled the industry to market a whole new generation of TV sets, with widescreen, digital quality and extra services as the combined selling proposition. However, the initial prices were high, teething problems both in transmission and reception made consumers cautious about investing in them at this stage, and the volume of integrated digital TV sets in the market remained low.

Europe's digital terrestrial launches were therefore essentially based on set-top box reception. Only in the UK, which started first in 1998, did the digital terrestrial set-top box penetration become significant, reaching 1.3 million households in 2001 (Galperin, 2004: 214). However, the cost of even set-top box receivers was too high for an open and unsubsidised consumer market to develop. After the traumatic experience of MAC technology, manufacturers and retailers were risk-averse. So, generally, during the early years of digital television the consumer electronics industry was only willing to produce set-top boxes in large volumes if their sale to the public would be subsidised.

## 'Information Society' infrastructure

Might subsidies be provided by governments, if not yet for spectrum release reasons, then from another motive? Hernan Galperin, in his early study of digital television in the United States and the UK, included in his account of the reasons why governments sought to promote digital television their policy agenda in the 1990s of creating the infrastructure of the 'Information Society' (Galperin, 2004).

With the spread of the Internet beyond the academic and business fields, and a realisation of the potential of digital coding for the convergence of communications technologies, came a sense of riding one of the big waves of history. The nineteenth century had seen the Industrial Revolution, based on iron and coal and railway transport. The late twentieth century was seeing an electronic information revolution, centred on semi-conductors, computer software and digitisation, ushering in a quite different post-industrial society in which e-commerce, e-education and e-government would flourish. Advanced economies needed to lay the foundations for e-prosperity. In the United States Vice President Al Gore popularised the concept of Information Superhighways and President Clinton established an Information Infrastructure Task Force. In Europe the European Union Commissioner Martin Bangemann led the work on *Europe and the Global Information Society* (European Commission, 1994).

The heart of this governmental activity was telecommunications: the realisation that linking networks of computers across the nation, and across the globe, required a step-change in the level of investment in telecommunications infrastructure to cope with the explosion in electronic traffic. However, digital television was swept into the current. Since the penetration of the personal computer was at that time so much lower than the near-universal ownership of TV sets, politicians seized on the idea of the digital television receiver as a surrogate computer, offering an entry point into the new e-economy.

In the UK Virginia Bottomley declared that

> Digital broadcasting will offer many people their first experience of the new information society. It will help develop interactive services like home shopping, home banking, information and education services.
>
> (Bottomley, 1995)

Enthusiasm for this concept grew, despite the limited consumer interest in the decidedly clunky interactive services which first emerged.

Interactive digital TV channels for government services were envisaged in a Cabinet Office report published in 2000:

> The introduction of DTV – and in particular the use of such technology to provide interactive services – represents a major new opportunity for the delivery of government and information services directly to the household....Many public sector organisations will find that DTV is an increasingly significant factor in the realisation of their service delivery strategies.
>
> (CITU, 2000: 2)

Were governments therefore willing to be a source of subsidy for the fledgling digital terrestrial TV industry? Generally, the answer was quite the opposite. In the United States, in response to a report by the American Electronics Association (AEA), the government had signalled long before that it was not in the business of pumping subsidies into the consumer electronics industry (Hart, 2004). In Europe the European Commission had devised an Action Plan, laden with subsidies, to support its analogue HDTV MAC strategy but this was a policy which had failed. Under Martin Bangemann, digital TV was brought within the European Information Society strategy, the main thrust of which was to liberalise the telecommunications industry by privatising state providers and/or encouraging competition to them. Only in Italy, in 2002, with Prime Minister Berlusconi also the owner of the country's major commercial television company as well as in charge of the state broadcaster, did a government decide to subsidise interactive digital television receivers on the basis of their notional role in providing publicly desirable e-services. Otherwise, the early providers of digital television had to look elsewhere for sources of subsidy.

### The Pay-TV industry

During the period 1998–2002 digital television was bankrolled through its infancy in the market primarily by the pay-TV industry. The major financial risks of taking the technology from its developmental stage through to commercial reality were carried by a set of private sector broadcasting 'merchant venturers'. They reckoned to make their money by signing up subscribers on the strength of the wide and attractive range of new channels and services they offered, especially premium sports and movies, and, in order to sign up subscribers, they were willing to subsidise digital receivers. It was a risky business, with heavy upfront costs: some companies would make losses before they made profits, others would just make losses.

Most of the pay-TV operators based their businesses around digital satellite. In the United States itself the drive came from both cable and satellite, with DirecTV an early provider of Near-Video-On-Demand movies. Digital TV penetration in the United States topped 33% by 2001 (Galperin, 2004: 121).

In the UK, however, a new digital terrestrial television subscription service entered the market. With the analogue terrestrial services spread across three of the UK's six digital terrestrial multiplexes, the regulator, now the Independent Television Commission (ITC), had held a competition for the award of the three remaining multiplexes. They could be bid for *en bloc* and whoever secured them would play the lead role of the digital terrestrial platform. The criteria for applicants were:

- their proposed investment in infrastructure
- their proposed investment in promotion, including the take-up of receivers (widely interpreted as code for a receiver subsidy)
- the variety of the programme services they would offer.

A consortium called the Digital Television Network (DTN), headed by the American-based cable company Cabletel, was one of the two main contenders. Its rival was the British Digital Broadcasting consortium (BDB) formed by ITV's two main broadcasters, Carlton and Granada, in alliance with an interesting third partner, BSkyB. BDB was further strengthened by a last-minute promise of support from a pay-TV channel joint venture, UKTV, in which one of the partners was the BBC's commercial arm.

After a period of public consultation, the ITC decided in favour of BDB. However, at that point the European competition authorities advised that BSkyB's membership of the consortium would be anti-competitive, so the ITC required BSkyB to withdraw from the consortium, thus ensuring that, when digital terrestrial television entered the pay-TV market as a newcomer, it would be in head-to-head competition with BSkyB's digital satellite television, not only in the sale of pay-TV services but also in distribution infrastructure and technology and the marketing of proprietary receivers.

In the event BSkyB launched its digital satellite services in October 1998. Digital terrestrial followed a month later, spearheaded by Carlton and Granada's BDB pay-TV operation which was initially branded ONdigital.

BSkyB had formed a consortium with BT, the Midland Bank (HSBC) and Matsushita to subsidise set-top boxes in the expectation of revenue from interactive services and they were able to offer £500 receivers for £200. Then, when digital satellite take-up swiftly rose to 1 million, they offered potential subscribers their boxes for free. ONdigital felt obliged to match this but it was never part of its financial plan.

In the UK, therefore, competition within the pay-TV field, fuelled by subsidy, drove digital TV take-up to over 38% by 2001 (Galperin, 2004: 214), with 1.3 million households subscribing to ONdigital's terrestrial proposition, 5.9 million to BSkyB's runaway success in digital satellite and 2 million to digital cable.

Elsewhere digital take-up in pay-TV was largely confined to satellite and cable. Sweden launched digital terrestrial in 1999. Spain followed in 2000 – like the UK, with a new digital terrestrial entrant to the pay-TV market (whose fate will be described in the next chapter). Finland then began in 2001. All experienced low penetration at the start. In France and in Germany, digital satellite operators made the early running. Australia and South Korea also launched digital terrestrial services in 2001, the former based on simulcasting its existing services in HDTV on sets with little market appeal at that stage, and the latter undertaking an agonising reappraisal of whether it had been right to select the American ATSC standard.

From the point of view of governments with an eye on spectrum, digital terrestrial take-up was of vital interest but the success of digital satellite and cable was also good news, since satellite and cable homes (whether digital or analogue) were not dependent on analogue terrestrial anyway. Shrinking the number of analogue terrestrial homes would facilitate analogue terrestrial switch-off, so in that respect, the rival platforms complemented one another.

Conscious that governments were not carrying investment risk, but that pay-TV companies were, the European Union grappled with the issue of encryption, or Conditional Access (CA). The pay-TV companies who were subsidising receivers were insistent that their set-top boxes should only use their own proprietary CA technology, ensuring essentially that their subscribers could not transfer to a rival provider without acquiring a new set-top box incorporating the rival's CA. This gave them more direct control over the security of the CA system and helped tie in their customers. Public service broadcasters and consumer-focussed politicians wanted all digital TV receivers to include a common interface which would allow the set-top box to handle a multiplicity of CA systems and allow the customer to change providers at minimum cost. Major lobbying exercises characterised a prolonged wrangle on this (Levy, 1999). The outcome was a European Directive which made the common interface mandatory for integrated digital TV sets, but left the pay-TV industry free, under conditions of fair third party access, to use their own proprietary technology in set-top boxes.

As interactivity initiatives proliferated in the market, the DVB sought to standardise the Application Programming Interface (API) used in conjunction with DVB transmission standards. It designed and developed the Multi-media Home Platform (MHP) as an interface between interactive software applications and the receiver hardware. It was, however, regarded as both complex and expensive to implement. The European Union, which had made DVB digital transmission standards obligatory, did not mandate it. While it was recommended, many operators adopted alternatives. There would be no standard European TV receiver: the market took precedence.

The business model which emerged was one in which virtually every digital TV household (apart from those few who bought an integrated digital TV set) needed to have a commercial service provider, with whom it had a contractual relationship and to whom it normally paid a subscription. This was very similar to the telecommunications business model. In the UK at that time you might choose to watch only BBC, ITV, Channel 4 or Channel Five digital channels, but you needed to have a contract with BSkyB or ONdigital or a cable company in order to receive them on a proprietary set-top box.

The early digital TV set-top box industry was thus very different from the open market in receivers from retailers and manufacturers with no vested interest in pay-TV that characterised analogue television. It was, however, providing subsidies and promoting digital take-up.

Full digital switchover could not be achieved on this foundation, though. Subscribing to pay-TV was essentially voluntary. It was bound to leave a rump of households, possibly a very large rump, who had no desire to subscribe and wished to rely on free-to-view channels. To implement analogue terrestrial switch-off, those households would, in the last resort, have to be compelled to switch. At that stage, during the period 1998–2002 when digital television was growing in the market, no one quite knew how – politically – to achieve this.

# 2
# The Digital Terrestrial Pioneers

## Summary of the chapter's argument

The pioneers of digital terrestrial television had a turbulent time during the period 2000–2002. Having created the framework for launching the new platform, governments stood back, leaving implementation largely to the market. The combination of inexperience and immature technology caused problems. In the UK and Spain, where new digital terrestrial broadcasters entered the pay-TV market in head-to-head competition with established satellite and cable operators, the newcomers collapsed into bankruptcy. The digital terrestrial TV platform in both countries was subsequently repositioned to focus on free-to-view households and their progress towards analogue terrestrial switch-off was to take several more years. Other early starters – the United States, Australia, Sweden and Finland – faced difficulties as the take-up of digital terrestrial receivers stalled in the market. Each had to undertake a significant policy re-think before it could recover. The period 2000–2002 was characterised by financial and regulatory crises. In 2003, however, Berlin showed the world how analogue terrestrial switch-off could be speedily accomplished in a market dominated by cable and satellite. Thereafter digital television switchover proceeded smoothly in a number of heavily cabled countries in northern Europe and the Netherlands was the first large country to complete the process nationally in 2006.

## Immature technology and inexperienced management

The digital terrestrial pioneers struggled. Famously in the UK and Spain new digital terrestrial broadcasters collapsed into bankruptcy. Other early starters had difficulties too. The period 2000–2002 was characterised by financial and/or regulatory crises. The national case studies reveal an overlapping set of contributory factors, with inexperience the over-arching explanation.

- Digital terrestrial technology was very new, only just off the workbench and out of the laboratory, so the interaction of new transmissions, new receivers and old aerials was insufficiently tested.
- Regulators had no history as the basis for modelling how a new multi-channel platform spearheaded by pay-TV would play into the established satellite and cable multi-channel market – and they were naive in their expectations of the effect of introducing additional platform competition.
- The commercial managers and boards of new digital terrestrial companies were in some cases over-optimistic in their financial assumptions and risk analysis.
- The managers and boards of incumbent analogue commercial broadcasters, by contrast, were in some cases inclined to hang back, being in no hurry to face increased competition.
- Broadcasters were inexperienced in judging the respective attractions of high-definition quality pictures, additional TV channels and interactive features – and were dealing with technology which was not yet mature, either in performance or in cost.
- Cross-industry coordination was in its infancy, with companies often failing to see the need for greater collaboration with their competitive rivals than had been necessary in analogue television.
- Governments had not yet learned how digital switchover, complete with analogue terrestrial switch-off, could be accomplished and had not fully thought through how public policy needed to complement the dynamics of the market – so they stood back.

## Broadcaster bankruptcies

### The UK
The Conservative government which presided over the design of the regulatory framework for digital terrestrial TV's launch in the UK was in favour of market forces doing the work and avoided committing public expenditure. It gave the BBC a modest licence fee increase for a two year period between 1998 and 2000 to cover its digital launch costs, but intended to offset this by a reduction in the following period, and it privatised the BBC's transmission arm. The initial award of digital terrestrial spectrum to the six new multiplexes was without charge but otherwise

the commercial broadcasters who would be making the bulk of the investment were expected to fund their own costs. The major commercial risk was carried by the new pay-TV broadcaster, ONdigital, which was responsible not only for three multiplexes but also for specifying, commissioning, marketing and subsidising all the digital terrestrial set-top boxes.

The European Union, having had its fingers badly burned by becoming so closely committed to the analogue MAC technology, also stood back, seeing its role primarily as one of ensuring fair competition in the market. At this stage, therefore, there was no public policy strategy, either at national or at European level, charting a course to switchover. It was for the market to drive sufficient consumer take-up to make the policy goal credible.

With around 25 million TV households, an average of more than two sets per household, some 35 million video recorders and a growing interest in pay-TV, the UK was a lively television market. Most households had fewer channels than viewers in the United States, Canada and Germany, for example, and the market looked ready to break out of the constraints of analogue terrestrial into multi-channel TV.

In the vanguard of innovation was Rupert Murdoch's 'upstart' satellite company, Sky, now transformed into BSkyB following the collapse of its analogue rival BSB. While its analogue satellite business had in the end flourished, digital satellite technology provided it with greater capacity, lower running costs per channel, interactive services and the ability to automate pay-per-view booking and billings. BSkyB aimed to switch the whole of its customer base to digital and recruit new subscribers, so that it could switch out of analogue technology entirely, avoiding a lengthy period of simulcasting.

A key strength was its proven proprietary system of conditional access. While the European Union had mandated a common interface in integrated digital TV sets, there was no such requirement for set-top boxes. BSkyB was free to commission its own set-top boxes designed to work with its own proprietary encryption system – to which other broadcasters had to be given fair access. BSkyB negotiated a new satellite with Astra, at a new orbital position – so even its analogue customers would need a new satellite dish (smaller in size) as well as a new set-top box. The enticement was a line-up of some 200 broadcast services, with a strong reliance on sport and movies, a steadily improving Sky News, and (from the same satellite) the BBC's digital services and the UKTV channels. The new automated pay-per-view system and the interactive features relied on a telephone 'return path'. A well-designed Electronic

Programme Guide provided navigation around this 'digital supermarket' of choice – and the receivers, initially subsidised by a consortium of interactivity partners, were offered 'free' to subscribers from 1999.

The early years of digital pay-TV involved high debt and risk: the cost of customer acquisition was high, especially with platform competition, and a 10% or so churn rate could be expected. The business demanded deep pockets and a strong nerve. BSkyB had both, plus experience. It drove up subscriber numbers, passing the 5 million mark around the end of 2000, and in 2001 was able to complete its plan of closing its analogue service.

The UK cable industry was not in such good health. In the United States and in Germany, Holland and Belgium, for example, the cable television infrastructure – initially, analogue – was extensive. The UK's cable industry, however, had historically been weak and fragmented. The 1990s saw major restructuring and consolidation, initially leaving three major players: Cable and Wireless, Telewest and Cabletel. This last bought NTL, the privatised transmission company serving commercial terrestrial broadcasters, and then adopted its name for its whole business. Digital cable services were launched in 1999 but the restructuring continued, with Cable and Wireless selling its cable business to NTL. The two survivors, NTL and Telewest, began to market consumer packages combining digital TV, interactive services and telephony. Reaching around 2 million customers in 2001, they were well behind BSkyB, with a much higher churn rate. Having spent heavily first on industry consolidation and then on the launch of digital, they were also deeply in debt.

However, the weakest platform in the pay-TV field was digital terrestrial. While working with the BBC, ITV, Channel 4 and Channel Five, who provided free-to-view services on the first three multiplexes, ONdigital – the pay-TV company owned by ITV's main broadcasters, Carlton and Granada – drove the strategy. Much to the BBC's concern, all the digital terrestrial set-top boxes had conditional access and essentially viewers needed to become ONdigital subscribers in order to receive the free-to-view channels terrestrially (the alternative was to buy an integrated digital TV set but these were initially expensive and had teething problems). The idea that licence fee payers had to subscribe to a commercial rival in order to receive licence fee funded digital services was, of course, anathema to the BBC – but the BBC was unwilling itself to invest licence fee money in receivers.

Once BSkyB had been expelled from the original Carlton–Granada BDB consortium, it became an outright rival (as the regulators desired).

ONdigital decided to free itself from dependence on BSkyB in order to avoid being left behind when BSkyB launched on satellite. So any idea of sharing the same encryption technology, or the same Application Programming Interface to support interactivity, was abandoned: ONdigital purchased rival products from Canal Plus in France. This ensured that the ONdigital–BSkyB competition was not just between pay-TV programme services but between platforms. The BBC, Channel 4 and Channel Five side-stepped this by reaching agreements with BSkyB to make their services available on satellite as well, but ITV, dominated by Carlton and Granada, refused to do so.

Digital terrestrial technology was still very immature. In a race not to be left behind by digital satellite, the UK's terrestrial broadcasters had hurried the later stages of the R&D work. The calculations of national coverage for each of the multiplexes were untested. In practice, actual coverage turned out to be less than predicted: the levels of transmitter power initially chosen through a hyper-cautious desire not to cause interference with analogue television were simply too low. Issues of local interference arose which had not been anticipated. Aerial issues were also significant. The search for frequencies for digital terrestrial which would not cause analogue interference had led the spectrum planners to select 'out-of-group' frequencies for some areas. Many viewers in such areas would need to replace their existing aerials with new wideband aerials capable of handling the full range of frequencies, but this was not fully explained at first. As a result of this combination of factors, too many households who were sold subscriptions to ONdigital found their reception unsatisfactory. ONdigital's churn rate rose to over 20%.

Those who could receive a good quality signal found the programme services limited in ambition and appeal. The BBC offered a rather incoherent mix of programmes branded BBC Choice, a learning channel called BBC Knowledge and its 24 hour news channel. ITV launched a modestly funded ITV 2, Channel 4 launched a well-regarded subscription movie channel, but Channel Five restricted itself to simulcasting its analogue service. The ONdigital subscription portfolio included BBC Worldwide's UKTV services (but not exclusively, since they were also available by satellite and cable), some lifestyle channels from Carlton and Granada, some Sky sport and movie channels and a pay-per-view offer. The range of choice was narrower than BSkyB's, but ONdigital's prices were comparable. ONdigital offered its customers access to the Internet if they chose to subscribe to an extra ONnet service, with an extra piece of equipment linked to a telephone line, but using a laptop keyboard and reading Internet text across the room was a frustrating experience.

ONdigital did succeed in securing over 1 million subscribers by 2001 but its debts were mounting, especially since it was matching BSkyB's strategy of providing subscribers with their receivers for free. The problems created by BSkyB's eviction from the original Carlton–Granada consortium were serious. Steve Morrison of Granada was to remark later, with hindsight:

> The minute that Sky wasn't allowed to stay in, it became the enemy and it was much bigger... We should have got out... We should all have taken a deep breath when the regulators said, 'OK, go out there and fight a well-established pay provider with less programming, less good equipment and less bandwidth'. At that point what we should have asked was: 'Is it likely to be successful?' We didn't because we had just won the franchise. We were carrying on against unbeatable odds.
>
> (Broadcast magazine, 2003)

In April 2001 ITV decided to rebrand ONdigital as ITV Digital and to re-launch the venture with heavy promotion. It then attempted to compete with BSkyB for football viewers. Unable to prise away the Premier League games, ITV Digital paid £315 million for the rights to the Nationwide League. The audiences for these second rank matches proved tiny and it steadily became obvious that this contract had been a disastrous mistake. ITV Digital's financial position, already precarious, worsened. Carlton and Granada had originally calculated that they would need to invest about £300 million before their pay-TV operation could reach break-even. They now faced the prospect of having to spend at least four times that figure.

As ITV Digital's commercial problems grew, so did its interest in the public policy goal of digital switchover. If ITV Digital's pay-TV proposition was not working in the market, could the prospect of a compulsory national switch to digital television help drive consumer take-up of digital terrestrial equipment and thus rescue the company's fortunes? Political lobbying became a key strand in ITV Digital's survival strategy: the government, it argued, should outline a road-map and a timetable for achieving analogue switch-off and appoint a 'Digital Csar' to champion the task.

However, the idea of making an early announcement of the switchover date was a political step too far. Chris Smith, Secretary of

State for Culture, Media and Sport in the Labour government, consulted consumer representatives and devised two criteria designed to protect viewers who simply wished to continue receiving their traditional channels and did not wish to subscribe to pay-TV. These were (a) the availability of the main terrestrial channels in digital form to 'virtually everyone in the UK' and (b) the affordability of digital reception equipment, a measure of which would be take-up. While 70% take-up would provide a significant milestone, he wanted take-up to reach 95% before switchover could be completed (Smith, 1999). He envisaged his criteria being met to allow switchover to take place between 2006 and 2010, but the criteria took precedence over the dates.

Government enthusiasm for getting on with the task was briefly kindled in 2000 when the UK auctioned the spectrum allocated to third generation (3G) mobile telephone systems for over £22.5 billion. The idea of some public subsidy which could be recouped from the auction proceeds was considered. However, it soon became apparent that the telecommunications companies had massively overpaid for spectrum and the risks of public intervention were judged too high, especially in view of the uncertainty surrounding the commercial future of ITV Digital. Chris Smith's successor as Secretary of State, Tessa Jowell, made it clear that an early government-driven initiative on digital switchover was off the agenda. There would be no political rescue for ITV Digital.

By the end of 2001 ITV Digital's financial position was dire. It could no longer afford to continue single-handedly subsidising digital terrestrial set-top boxes and pressed other broadcasters to do more to support the platform. The BBC, by now funded much more generously by the Labour government, was developing a set of new free-to-view services of much greater appeal – and ITV Digital took soundings about some form of 'digital coalition' to support a free-to-view digital terrestrial receiver initiative. The stumbling block was a conditional access facility which ITV Digital wanted every digital terrestrial receiver to include, and for which the BBC had no requirement. However, BBC Director-General Greg Dyke subsequently revealed that, as early as December 2001, the Managing Director of Carlton, Gerry Murphy, had warned him to be careful since, even if a BBC–ITV Digital agreement did prove possible, 'he doubted whether there was enough money to keep ITV Digital going' (Dyke, 2004: 185).

Share prices for Carlton and Granada, already hit by an advertising recession, suffered as both companies reported major losses. Break-even plans for the digital operation were revised but, against a trend of falling subscription numbers, high 'churn' rate and a continuing bad press, they looked unconvincing. The company attempted, amid dreadful publicity, to reduce the cost of its misjudged £315 million contractual commitment to Nationwide League football by threatening to go bankrupt (in which case Carlton and Granada would not be liable for ITV Digital's debt). At the end of March 2002 ITV Digital went into administration and the digital terrestrial pay-TV services were suspended, though the free-to-view multiplexes continued to broadcast (Starks, 2007). On April 25th the administrators announced that they were preparing for the short-term sale of the business and its assets. The next day Tessa Jowell, the Secretary of State, declared in Parliament:

> Yesterday's announcement represents the collapse of a brave commercial enterprise to launch an entirely new digital platform. The business has made commercial judgements which have turned out to be unsuccessful. There is always a risk in such ventures, especially in relation to markets built on new technology...
>
> The success of DTT (digital terrestrial television) should not be equated with the position of one commercial operator. The fact that ITV Digital has not succeeded will not deflect us and the broadcasting industry from making a reality of the digital future. Digital TV and the promise it holds is more than ITV Digital.
>
> (House of Commons, 2002)

Though not everyone was confident about the prospects for digital terrestrial TV's recovery, the BBC had already developed the thinking behind the free-to-view strategy which, under the brand name of *Freeview*, was to rescue the platform.

### Spain

Meanwhile Spanish digital terrestrial television followed a course which, in many respects, mirrored the crisis in the UK.

Spain, one of Europe's larger television markets, started digital development with around 14 million TV households and a complex structure of three layers – national, regional (there are 17 Autonomous Communities) and local broadcasting. Terrestrial reception accounted for over three-quarters of the population and, during the 1990s, terrestrial television had been transformed from domination by the public broadcaster RTVE to a mixed economy at national level with two public channels and three private ones (Antena 3, Telecinco and Canal Plus).

The satellite market was particularly strong, with two major players, Sogecable (owners of Canal Plus) and Vía Digital (in which the telecommunications company, Telefónica, had a major stake). When digital satellite began in 1997, it was characterised by fierce rivalry between them which the pro-competition Conservative government sought to encourage (Suárez Candel, 2008). The cable sector grew less vigorously, especially after Telefónica pulled out of it to concentrate instead on broadband.

The Conservative government's strategy for digital terrestrial television was to introduce further competition. The incumbent analogue broadcasters were allocated a multiplex for simulcasting their services but were not incentivised by being awarded any extra channels. Instead, two new free-to-view ventures, Net TV and Veo TV, were licensed. Another multiplex was allocated to regional channels. The majority of the available capacity, however, was awarded to a single company, Onda Digital (rechristened Quiero), for national pay-TV services. The aim here was to provide digital terrestrial competition to the satellite and cable platforms. Quiero's main shareholder was Retevisión, a recently privatised terrestrial transmission company which saw digital technology as critical to the future of the platform. It was very keen to start and launched in May 2000.

The other digital terrestrial broadcasters, old and new, held back. The regulatory deadline by which they had to launch was 2002. They were challenging the government's desire to introduce MHP (Multi-media Home Platform) as a standard Application Programming Interface – for the government this appealed because it would support relatively sophisticated interactive features, while for the broadcasters it represented an avoidable production and reception expense. Also the free-to-view broadcasters had little to gain by launching their services until Quiero had built up a customer base of subscribers with digital terrestrial receivers. No organisation existed to coordinate stakeholder decisions effectively.

Like ONdigital in the UK, Quiero felt obliged by the policies of its competitors to provide receivers free of charge to its subscribers. It also invested heavily in football rights, without being able to secure the premium events. In marketing and promotion, it laid great emphasis on its interactive capabilities, which included access to the Internet, but, as in the UK, this had limited appeal. Quiero managed to recruit around 200,000 subscribers by 2002 but by then it had also accumulated losses of nearly 400 million euros (Arrese and Herrero, 2005: 197). It went bankrupt in May 2002.

The simulcast broadcasters had launched on digital terrestrial the preceding month and Net TV and Veo TV followed in June. This led to the bizarre position of six digital terrestrial broadcasting companies pumping out services which could only be received on the proprietary receivers of a seventh company which had gone bankrupt. The digital terrestrial market was thus completely stagnant and the government's aspiration to switch off analogue terrestrial TV seemed a fantasy.

The digital satellite operators were far ahead in terms of take-up, having secured over 2 million subscribers, but the internal competition between the two operators became too intense and in 2003 they merged: Sogecable emerged as the main operator with a satellite monopoly service branded Digital+ (rechristened Canal Plus in 2011). The conservative government's strategy of using the arrival of new technology to increase competition in television was now a wreck. It was inherited in that state by the socialist government which came to power in 2004.

After a period of frustrating inaction for the industry, the new government announced a redesigned regulatory framework and technical plan, learning from Spain's previous mistakes and from the early success of *Freeview* in the UK. Stakeholder coordination was addressed in two ways. Under the Ministry of Industry, Tourism and Trade, a Monitoring Commission for the Transition towards Digital Terrestrial Television was set up. Then the public and private broadcasters, together with the transmission provider Abertis, created an association called Impulsa TDT to promote the digital terrestrial platform in collaboration with various public authorities (Fernández Alonso and Díaz González, 2010). The multiplex capacity left vacant by Quiero was reallocated as part of a transition plan designed to achieve analogue terrestrial switch-off in 2010, in accord with broadcaster licences.

The public broadcaster, RTVE, was allocated two multiplexes and expected to provide a range of free-to-view services, ultimately covering 98% of the country. The three incumbent analogue terrestrial commercial broadcasters – Antena 3, Telecinco and Canal Plus (owned by Sogecable) – were each awarded frequencies for two extra channels each. Canal Plus (terrestrial) converted itself from a pay-TV service into the free-to-view Cuatro channel. Net TV and Veo TV were given an additional channel each. A new broadcaster, La Sexta, was chosen and given an analogue licence, as well as a digital simulcasting one, to help establish itself. Additional digital capacity was allocated for regional and local television. On this basis a wholly free-to-view digital terrestrial platform was re-launched in 2005.

Essentially the new strategy worked, though reservations have been expressed about the quality of the output and the lack of appeal of the interactive service applications available on expensive MHP-enabled receivers (Suárez Candel, 2011). An open market in digital terrestrial receivers flourished and take-up was steady. The free-to-view character of the platform was altered by a decision in 2009 to allow a limited number of pay-TV channels – permitting the entry of a new subscription service, Gol TV, with rights for First Division football. A further 2009 change was an easing of the ownership restrictions on mergers between commercial licensees.

Meanwhile plans for a regionally phased analogue terrestrial switch-off were laid in 2007 tied to the target date of 2010. A transition coordination body was established and pilot projects undertaken. The task was a complex one, given the mountainous terrain with some 1500 masts, the national–regional–local structure both of the services and the political authorities, and the predominance of terrestrial reception (Suárez Candel, 2011).

Spain successfully completed analogue terrestrial switch-off according to plan in April 2010. However, in a climate of economic recession and the problems affecting the Euro common currency, its digital terrestrial television industry underwent further restructuring. Antena 3 acquired La Sexta in 2012, creating a concentration of commercial ownership. Both at national and regional level, public service digital terrestrial television faced financial cutbacks, entailing regional channel closures (Fernández Alonso and Díaz González, 2013). Spain also found that it had to reorganise its spectrum to accommodate a wider European plan for 4G mobile telecommunications.

## Stalled starts

### The United States

The United States market presented one of the greatest challenges for digital switchover. It had around 100 million TV households and some 1700 terrestrial broadcasters, consisting of commercial stations affiliated to the major networks (NBC, CBS, ABC and Fox), independent commercial stations and public broadcasting stations. Around 60% of American homes had cable and around 20% (and growing) subscribed to direct broadcast satellite. Terrestrial television therefore accounted for less than 20% of reception and was diminishing. However, the transmission and frequency allocation pattern, based primarily on local commercial stations, was highly complex, in contrast to the national transmission systems which had been designed in many European countries.

The FCC's initial approach, as we saw earlier, was to loan all the existing terrestrial broadcasters an additional digital terrestrial frequency (sufficient for an HD channel), require them to invest in HDTV production and transmission, oblige them to simulcast their analogue service in digital HDTV for perhaps 15 years, then shut down all analogue transmission and take back the extra frequency. The 'carrot' for terrestrial broadcasters lay in free new spectrum and the absence of any new competition.

However, this plan involved major broadcaster expenditure without bringing in any corresponding level of additional revenue – simulcast advertising carried on the HD channel would initially be to tiny audiences since HDTV sets were likely to be very expensive. Many broadcasters wanted to be able to introduce extra standard definition (SD) channels with new content in order to attract extra revenue and lobbied hard for this. Accordingly, the 1996 Telecommunications Act, which provided the basis for the loan of new spectrum, left HDTV as optional: the FCC simply required the broadcasters to

> provide a free digital video programming service the resolution of which is comparable to or better than that of today's service and aired during the same time periods that their analog channel is broadcasting.
>
> (FCC, 1997)

Moreover, the requirement to simulcast the analogue service did not have to start immediately nor be 100% until the analogue switch-off date was imminent (and later the simulcast requirement was dropped entirely).

In return for commercial flexibility, the broadcasters were required to achieve digital switchover on an accelerated timetable. The political focus had shifted via the wider agenda of the Information Society, to the more specific benefit of auctioning released spectrum to reduce the federal budget deficit. TV stations affiliated to the major networks were required to invest first: those in the ten largest local markets had to build their digital facilities by May 1999 and others in the top 30 markets by November 1999. All commercial broadcasters would have to complete construction by May 2002 and public TV stations by May 2003. Digital frequency allocations would be concentrated in a defined section of the current broadcasting band, allowing spectrum to be cleared systematically. The FCC's target was to terminate analogue broadcasting by 31 December 2006.

However, the broadcasters lobbied for a softer switchover date and found ready allies in Congress by highlighting the adverse public reaction politicians could expect from a premature switch-off. The Balanced Budget Act of 1997 therefore introduced an escape clause whereby analogue broadcasts could continue in specific areas after 2006 if either a major network affiliate was not broadcasting a digital signal in its local market, or receiver converters were not generally available, or, more significantly, if fewer than 85% of households in its area were equipped to receive digital television, whether terrestrially, by satellite or by cable. The politicians thus tried to make sure that mass blank screens could be avoided but remained keen to secure the auction benefits. The Clinton administration now included the potential income in its revenue estimates.

The practicalities of implementing the United States switchover policy were hampered by 'considerable confusion on the part of manufacturers, broadcasters and consumers' (Hart, 2010: 19). The formulation of the ATSC standards had involved political compromises, as the FCC endeavoured to reconcile the requirements of both the broadcasting and the computer industries. It had resolved a number of conflicts by leaving several technical options open. Deciding in which format to broadcast or exactly which kind of receivers to manufacture in what volumes caused some commercial hesitation, while consumers had to 'cope with complexity in stores where labelling of DTV sets and equipment includes such unfamiliar terms as HDTV-ready, HDTV-capable, HDTV-compatible, and HDTV-upgradeable' (Hart, 2010: 20).

The policy became one of wishful thinking, with little happening in the market. In 2001 the National Association of Broadcasters warned the FCC that about a third of its members would fail to meet the May 2002 deadline for beginning digital transmissions. Many faced planning or financial hurdles relating to transmission masts. The FCC had the power in theory to compel compliance with its plan by revoking broadcaster licences but, in practical terms, the scale of the problem ruled this out. As Hernan Galperin noted,

Neither the commission nor Congress ever introduced provisions that contemplated an en masse failure of broadcasters to meet their construction requirements.

(Galperin, 2004: 125)

It was not just broadcaster activity which was lagging. The consumer take-up of digital TV receiver sales was very slow, as consumers waited for more digital content and lower receiver prices. HDTV sets cost ten times (or more) as much as analogue sets and even digital terrestrial set-top boxes were priced around $1500 (Grimme, 2002: 239). Analogue TV sales continued unabated. Digital terrestrial households in 2001 accounted for less than 1% of all TV households. The digital switchover policy, after so many debates, decisions and modifications, was stalling. The prospect of analogue terrestrial switch-off looked remote. No date for 85% take-up could be confidently forecast and the target of 2006 had lost all credibility.

The FCC's immediate response was to assess case-by-case the arguments by broadcasters unable to launch on time, accommodating deserving cases and penalising undeserving ones. It then undertook a major policy re-think with three main ingredients: sealing off the sales of analogue TV sets, separating cable and satellite households out from the population which needed to switch and providing subsidised low-cost convertors to the residual analogue terrestrial homes.

In 2002 the FCC initially proposed a voluntary commitment from receiver manufacturers to include digital terrestrial tuners in all new TV sets, with a phased implementation starting with the largest sets. The Consumer Electronics Association (CEA), representing receiver manufacturers, rejected the idea, mainly on the grounds that this would unnecessarily increase the price of TV sets for the great majority of households served by cable and satellite who did not require a terrestrial tuner in order to receive TV – but also because it opposed government intervention in the retail market in principle.

Conscious that each new sale of an analogue TV potentially added to the difficulties of completing digital switchover, the FCC then decided to forget voluntary action and to make the policy mandatory. In order to do so it would use powers it had been granted under the All-Channel Receiver Act back in 1962 when TV stations on the UHF band were being introduced alongside the established stations on the VHF band and manufacturers had to be compelled to make receivers capable of receiving both. The CEA took the FCC to court and lost. So in 2003 the mandatory policy went ahead on the following basis (FCC, 2002):

*For screen sizes of 36" and above*
50% by July 2004; 100% by July 2005
*For screen sizes 25" to 35"*
50% by July 2005; 100% by July 2006 (later modified to March 2006)

*For screen sizes 13" to 24" and for VCRs, DVD recorders with tuners*
100% by July 2007 (later modified to March 2007 and extended
to smaller screens).

In 2003 the FCC blessed an agreement between the TV set manufacturers
and the cable companies on a standardised interface between the digital
cable input and a digital TV set, making it possible for digital TV sets
with a tuner for cable and an ATSC digital terrestrial tuner to be sold as
'digital cable-ready' in an open market.

These initiatives yoked the TV set replacement market to the digital
switchover goal, ensuring that new TV sets, whether sold for terrestrial
or for cable viewing, met the ATSC digital standard. But was it really
necessary to upgrade every household to advanced television technology in order to switch off analogue terrestrial transmissions and realise
the spectrum auction revenue?

Cable companies were already obliged, under 'must carry' rules, to
relay the local broadcast services broadcast on analogue terrestrial TV.
Satellite operators were not obliged to carry local broadcast services
but, if they chose to do so (which, in general, they did, since this
was an attractive business proposition), they had to carry all the relevant local services. These rules would certainly extend to the digital
simulcasts of local services at the point of analogue terrestrial switch-
off, even if there were arguments about how the 'must carry' principle
applied to new digital-only services. A complication was that much of
the cable industry was still analogue: digital cable, although growing,
still accounted for less than half of total cable homes in mid-2005. The
broadcasters wanted cable companies to be obliged to carry their digital
signals for HD and digital viewers. However, cable operators wanted to
be able to 'down-convert' the digital signal at the head-end for continuing analogue distribution to continuing analogue TV viewers, promising
that this would ensure that analogue terrestrial switch-off would not
adversely affect any cable household, whether analogue or digital.

Congress and the FCC could now re-scope the policy. The vast majority of American households, with well over 80% served by cable or
satellite, could be regarded as outside it. While some would, of course,
have second or third sets relying on terrestrial signals, these households
were in no danger of being suddenly deprived of television. The focus
therefore sharpened on the residual analogue terrestrial homes: how
many were there and who were they?

The Government Accounting Office estimated in 2005 that about
21 million households (or 19%) relied wholly on terrestrial television.

It noted that these households were disproportionately non-white and Hispanic and disproportionately poor (GAO, 2005). They were less likely than the average American family to have the spending power to go out and buy expensive new digital TV sets by a government-set deadline. The real policy requirement was therefore for cheap converter boxes which could keep analogue TV sets functioning when fed with a digital signal – and the GAO looked at the possible cost of subsidising them.

By 2005 pressure was mounting to jettison the 85% digital penetration threshold and fix a hard date for full digital switchover. The broadcasters were in no hurry but a High Tech DTV Coalition wanted the business opportunity to use the released spectrum for wireless broadband and other possibilities. Electronics industry companies estimated the potential spectrum auction proceeds at between $10 billion and $30 billion (the outcome was $19.6 billion). In the wake of Hurricane Katrina, and of a report in the aftermath of 9/11, the emergency services had established the need for additional spectrum for operational communications. So both commercial and public interests lay behind the passage in 2006 of the Deficit Reduction Act which set analogue switch-off for completion by the end of 17 February 2009.

A $1.5 billion subsidy fund was created: analogue terrestrial households could have up to two $40 coupons with which to buy converter boxes. The subsidy was financed from the anticipated proceeds of the spectrum auction. However, weak management of the voucher scheme and inadequate public communication gave rise to last-minute anxiety over implementation. While some 40 million vouchers had been issued by the end of 2008, only 16 million had been used: the scheme was running out of funds yet survey evidence showed that over 7 million households were still not ready (Hart, 2010: 24–25). The incoming Obama administration postponed the date by four months to June 12th, topped up the funding and ensured that the FCC's call centre and walk-in centres were well-prepared. The June 2009 switch-off had some rough edges but essentially it worked.

Following an auction raising $19.6 million, released spectrum in the 700 MHz section of the UHF band was licensed to wireless broadband providers (DigiTAG, 2010) and, within a year, the FCC approached the broadcasters with a new scheme for surrendering further spectrum to feed broadband operators' continuing hunger.

### Australia

Australia, while a large country, has a relatively small population and therefore only around 7 million TV households (though over two TV sets per household on average). It was quick to start digital terrestrial television, launching on 1 January 2001. At the time terrestrial reception was dominant, with cable limited in scope and satellite pay-TV still in its infancy. The analogue terrestrial broadcasters at national level were three commercial channels, between them dominating the market, and two public services, ABC and SBS. Terrestrial television was entirely free-to-view and, having seen the UK's early problems, Australia decided that digital terrestrial television should be so as well.

Australia opted for Europe's DVB technology but emulated the United States in basing its initial strategy on HDTV (García Leiva and Starks, 2009). The main analogue terrestrial broadcasters were allocated sufficient spectrum to simulcast their analogue services in full, with a quota of 20 hours in digital high-definition. The broadcasters were expected to create a new market for digital HD receivers with technical quality, not new content, as the selling point. The proposition was a technology upgrade, just as the shift to colour TV had been. The public broadcasters were each allocated an additional channel, for minority-appeal content, while the commercial broadcasters were initially restricted to simulcasting their existing services in standard and high-definition. At this stage there would be no new entrants. The government's intention was to switch off analogue terrestrial transmissions in major cities by the end of 2008 and elsewhere by 2011.

This strategy – in many respects the antithesis of the standard definition multi-channel approach adopted in the UK and elsewhere in Europe – reflected more than early faith in the future of terrestrial HDTV and new possibilities of data-casting. The commercial broadcasters, who were a political force in the land, were 'more concerned about laying claim to spectrum and resisting new entrants than offering more channels' (Given and Norris, 2010: 54). Their instinct not to rush into a new pluralist and competitive digital market was shared by satellite and cable subscription television providers who wanted to build up their own pay-TV customer base before viewers were given the option of digital terrestrial multi-channel television. The Packer group which at that stage controlled the terrestrial Nine Network also had a 25% stake in the main pay-TV company, Foxtel.

The result, perhaps not surprisingly, was very sluggish take-up by consumers of expensive HD digital receivers: by mid-2006 digital terrestrial TV had been adopted by only about 20% of Australian households. Moreover, complex Australian television regulations, reflecting the regional structure of the terrestrial television industry and protective of the commercial terrestrial broadcasters' access to sporting rights, prevented national satellite carriage of the commercial terrestrial channels. Whereas most other countries, in assessing their readiness for switchover, could add the take-up of digital satellite and cable TV to their digital terrestrial figures, on the grounds that these platforms carried digital versions of the main analogue terrestrial services due to close, Australia could not do this (García Leiva and Starks, 2009). It soon became apparent that the 2008 target would have to be delayed.

As elsewhere, a policy re-think took place. The government was unwilling to continue funding the public service simulcasts on an open-ended timetable so a new strategy was devised, recognising the need for new TV services and drawing explicitly on the UK's successful launch of *Freeview*. The analogue switch-off completion target was pushed back to 2013 (Australia's version of *Freeview* and the related switchover policy are described further in Chapter 5).

### Sweden and Finland

Sweden and Finland were also early pioneers of digital terrestrial television, with Sweden launching in 1999 and Finland in 2001. They were success stories in that they were among the first nations to complete analogue terrestrial switch-off, in both cases in 2007. Neither, however, had a straight problem-free run from start to finish and each, for slightly different reasons, experienced an initial stalling of the market.

Sweden has a small market of around 4 million TV households, two-thirds of which subscribed to cable or satellite when digital policy was formulated. Analogue terrestrial viewers received only three national channels (two public service and one commercial). The decision to launch digital terrestrial was in part a cultural and economic defence of home-based Swedish TV in the face of the popularity of foreign-based satellite channels.

The state-owned transmission provider, Teracom, constructed the digital terrestrial network. Two multiplexes were licensed, then a third added. In addition to the analogue simulcasts, an ambitious mixture of new pay-TV and free-to-view channels was planned. Initially all the services were encrypted and customers had to pay for a decryption card even to view the digital simulcasts. Senda, a new technical organisation affiliated to Teracom, provided the conditional access and an Electronic Programme Guide. Another Teracom affiliate, Boxer, was responsible for subscription management, including the sale and rent of set-top boxes and for marketing and promotion.

The structure was cumbersome, technical problems afflicted transmissions, the receiver rental scheme had not been fully designed, and several of the services failed to launch. Diagnosing the reasons for a premature and botched start, Allan Brown noted:

> The launch was also adversely affected by the recalcitrant attitude of the four commercial broadcasters that breached their licence conditions by delaying commencement of their DTTV [digital terrestrial television] transmissions. Their complaint of an insufficient audience tended to be self-fulfilling, as viewers were disinclined to subscribe to DTTV [digital terrestrial television] without the full complement of channels.
>
> (Brown, 2005a: 217)

The market failed to take-off. A re-launch took place in 2000 with a fourth multiplex; Senda and Boxer merged; the public services ceased to be encrypted; and, although a major commercial broadcaster pulled out, a fifth multiplex was added. A hybrid free-pay market for multi-channel digital terrestrial TV developed, with take-up reaching over a quarter of analogue terrestrial homes by the end of 2004.

Many of the new services which had been added were non-Swedish channels already available on satellite and cable, diluting the original cultural strategy. However, the successful re-launch made analogue terrestrial switch-off feasible. In 2004 the government established a Switchover Commission to work with the broadcasters and Teracom to plan the regional phasing for analogue terrestrial switch-off in 2008, with an accompanying public information campaign. Stakeholder coordination was strong and charitable organisations were mobilised to assist the elderly and the disabled. The operation was well-planned and efficient (Suárez Candel, 2011). It was completed early, before the end of 2007.

Finland too is a small TV market with only 2.4 million households, but the country has a strong consumer electronics and communications industry and prides itself on being at the cutting edge here. When it started digital terrestrial television in 2001, it had around 1.4 million terrestrial homes, 1 million on cable and a minor role for satellite. The digital terrestrial launch was based on three multiplexes offering simulcasts, limited new free-to-view content from both public and commercial broadcasters and (it was hoped) pay-TV channels especially for movies. In support of its 'Information Society' goals, and keeping in the technological vanguard, Finland mandated MHP interactive technology and interactive services were envisaged as an attractive feature in the consumer proposition. Analogue switch-off was scheduled for 2006.

However, MHP-equipped set-top boxes were hard to find and expensive. The shortage of set-top boxes with conditional access held the pay-TV companies back from launching the promised movie channels: when they failed to meet the regulatory requirement to commence by the end of 2001, their licences were withdrawn. Interactive service development was incomplete. Consumer interest was not aroused and take-up was low.

> A year after its launch the performance of digital terrestrial television in Finland fell well short of expectations.... There were nine digital television channels on air... but four of these... were broadcast on analogue terrestrial. There were no digital pay-TV services on offer, superteletext was not available, and the EPG was in a rudimentary stage of development. Digital terrestrial television in Finland had a disappointing start.
>
> (Brown, 2005b: 237)

Here too a re-think was necessary. MHP was sidelined. New funding was injected – charges to commercial broadcasters for analogue licences were halved and there was no charge for digital terrestrial spectrum. The Finnish national broadcaster, YLE, was given licence fee increases of 1% p.a. above inflation. The digital service offering was strengthened by the introduction of a selection of pay-TV channels provided by Canal Plus. Combined with the completion of near-universal coverage, these changes encouraged the majority of terrestrial households to switch to digital voluntarily (Starks, 2007). In 2004 analogue switch-off was scheduled for August 2007.

The Ministry of Transport and Communications led a coordinated public communications campaign and established a coordinating project group. The process was well-managed and analogue terrestrial switch-off achieved on time, with the full conversion of cable to digital following early in 2008.

## Cable and satellite predominance

The countries where analogue terrestrial switch-off proved most straightforward were those with very little dependence on terrestrial reception. We have already seen in the case of the United States and Sweden that having a high proportion of cable and satellite homes meant that the households which could potentially be deprived of a TV signal at switch-off were in a minority from the very start (less than 20%

in the United States and around 30% in Sweden). Persuading a minority of homes to adopt digital terrestrial, or move to cable or satellite, was less daunting, and less politically risky, than having to convert the great majority (as in Spain). In a number of northern European countries the dominance of cable and satellite was much greater than even in the United States and it was here that the first analogue switch-offs were achieved.

### Berlin and Germany

The first analogue switch-off in the world took place in Berlin. Media regulation in Germany is devolved to the regions, or *Länder,* and so the initiative was taken by the Berlin city government and the broadcasters. The motive, here and elsewhere in Germany, was to ease pressure on the country's overcrowded terrestrial spectrum. Analogue terrestrial frequencies were intensively used, to the point where it was not possible to simulcast digital and analogue terrestrial television. The only way forward was to switch off analogue at the same time as digital terrestrial was introduced. However, since analogue terrestrial reception played such a small part compared with satellite and cable, this was quite feasible. In a population of around 4 million, Berlin had only around 150,000 who relied on analogue terrestrial transmission for their main TV and another 90,000 or so who used it for second or third TV sets.

In February 2002 the Berlin administration and the broadcasters mapped out a plan for the introduction of digital terrestrial television, with both new services and simulcasts of the existing ones, and for the withdrawal thereafter of the analogue services in two stages. The commercial broadcasters would have about 30% of their transmission costs subsidised for five years. Receiver design would be simple – it certainly would not include MHP – and agreement was reached with the manufacturers to produce the required volumes below a target retail price. Households on social security would be given a voucher enabling them to be given a low price set-top box free. Public communication was undertaken mainly on the analogue TV channels and a call centre established. Digital terrestrial transmissions began in October.

By the end of the year receiver supplies had dried up, partly because the manufacturers had not fully believed that the switchover plan was serious. However, the shortage was temporary, the analogue services of the commercial broadcasters were withdrawn in spring 2003 and the analogue public services closed in the summer. From digital terrestrial launch to analogue terrestrial switch-off had taken less than a year. The European Commission subsequently found the subsidy scheme to have been illegal, in that it favoured the terrestrial platform, but Berlin's digital switchover was an impressive example internationally.

The rest of Germany followed, using a very similar approach. Germany had some 36 million households but, because of the predominance of cable and satellite, only 2.6 million relied on terrestrial reception. The switchover process was designed to happen on a regional basis, in 'islands' formed by large conurbations, under the regulatory authority of the *Länder*. By the end of 2005 analogue terrestrial switch-off had been achieved in nine regions, accounting for around 50% of the population. Digital terrestrial roll-out and analogue terrestrial switch-off were completed in 2008.

Because terrestrial reception had only a minor role, Germany saw no need to make its digital terrestrial coverage universal. The public broadcasters provided a digital terrestrial option to 90% of households but some rural areas (outside the coverage areas and not served by cable) could only receive television by satellite. While most satellite operations switched from analogue to digital satellite, the majority of Germany's extensive cable network for the time being remained analogue (Kleinsteuber, 2011).

### The Netherlands

In the wake of Berlin's example, a number of other heavily cabled European countries undertook digital switchover in order to recoup terrestrial spectrum. Strictly speaking, the first nation to complete was Luxembourg in 2006 but the first major country was the Netherlands.

In the Dutch market of 6.7 million households only 100,000 depended on terrestrial reception for their main TV set and the vast majority, 92%, were cable customers. Applications were invited for the licence to launch a digital terrestrial service, but only one bidder came forward – a joint venture called *Digitenne* whose members included the terrestrial transmission operator Nozema, the telecommunications company KPN and the terrestrial broadcasters. The digital terrestrial provider therefore had a monopoly but of a very small market, much of it targeted at second TVs.

*Digitenne* launched in 2003. While viewers who wanted only the public service channels had simply to purchase a low-cost set-top box, the full service included a number of commercial services requiring a small subscription which positioned the business as a cheaper option than cable. KPN later acquired Nozema and took control of *Digitenne*, combining the television proposition with telephony services.

Given the predominance of cable and the low importance of terrestrial reception, switching off analogue terrestrial television in the Netherlands proved relatively simple and was completed without any major problems in December 2006.

# 3
# The UK's Digital Transition

## Summary of the chapter's argument

The UK's digital transition proved a lengthy one, with analogue switch-off towards the end of 2012 following 14 years after the launch of digital terrestrial in late 1998. The dominant role of terrestrial reception at the outset, the crisis culminating in the bankruptcy of ITV Digital, and the cautious stance of the UK government account for this. From the end of 2002 onwards the process was smooth, characterised by high voluntary digital take-up and by a complementary relationship between a free-to-view digital terrestrial television and the pay- TV operations of the satellite and cable platforms. While the government designed the policy framework, implementation of switchover was led by the broadcasters and the industry, through Digital UK. However, BBC leadership and licence fee funding were central to the whole transition. The role of the regulator, Ofcom, was critical in facilitating the retro-fitting of HDTV to a set of terrestrial multiplexes designed for standard definition services. A government initiative was vital in starting local television. Ofcom continues to manage spectrum release and reorganisation. The pattern of digital television shows a dramatic increase in viewer choice, a major increase in subscription TV, less dramatic change in viewing habits, the greater convenience of easy recording and On-Demand services and a modest increase in total viewing. The full implications of digital switchover, however, go beyond this to include television's synergies with the Internet.

## After the debacle

We left off the story of the UK's switch to digital television in 2002, when ITV Digital collapsed leaving the digital terrestrial platform temporarily in turmoil. A decade later, in October 2012, the UK finally completed the switch-off of its analogue terrestrial TV transmissions. It had started the process like a hare, launching digital satellite and terrestrial services in late 1998. It finished smoothly and successfully, but more like a tortoise by comparison with other nations. Measuring from the launch of digital terrestrial television services to the date when analogue terrestrial TV was fully switched off, its total transition period was 14 years. It is instructive to see this on a comparative basis (Table 3.1).

Why was this? Clearly part of the explanation lay in the initial dominance of terrestrial reception, which back in the late 1990s accounted for around three-quarters of households. In this respect the UK was very different from the United States, Germany and much of northern and central Europe. Another major factor, of course, was the trauma of ITV Digital's bankruptcy, which created both uncertainty and delay. However, Spain was also heavily dependent on terrestrial reception and Spain too had its digital terrestrial pay-TV company failure, yet it completed digital switchover in 2010. The length of the UK's transition had another contributory cause – the political stance of the government.

The UK's Labour government, elected in 1997 and re-elected in 2001, approached the idea of a compulsory analogue terrestrial TV switch-off with some caution. In contrast to the United States government, it was not driven by an urgent desire to secure revenue from auctioning spectrum; nor, in the period immediately following the collapse of ITV Digital, was it facing huge pressure to clear the spectrum for telecommunications purposes. Popular resistance to Mrs Thatcher's attempt to introduce a poll tax in 1990 was still very alive in the political memory and the government had no wish to run too far ahead of popular opinion in pursuing digital switchover. In March 2001 the Consumers' Association had published a research report focussed on those who had *not* adopted digital TV, stating that:

Non-adopters do not seem to be in any particular hurry to go digital. Two-thirds (66%) have not even looked into the possibility of getting it .... Just under a third of non-adopters (32%) said they would never get DTV, and 50% of older and retired people never want to switch .... There are low levels of awareness about the benefits of digital television. 56% of non-adopters feel they don't know enough about the current digital television offering and even a quarter of adopters feel this way.

(Consumers' Association, 2001)

Table 3.1   Transition duration for countries completing switchover by end of 2012

| Country | Date of analogue terrestrial switch-off | Duration of transition (from launch of DTT services) |
|---|---|---|
| Luxembourg | 2006 | 1 year |
| Netherlands | 2006 | 3 years |
| Finland | 2007 | 6 years |
| Sweden | 2007 | 8 years |
| Germany | 2008 | 6 years |
| Switzerland | 2008 | 5 years |
| Denmark | 2009 | 3 years |
| Norway | 2009 | 2 years |
| United States | 2009 | 9 years |
| Croatia | 2010 | 3 years |
| Estonia | 2010 | 4 years |
| Latvia | 2010 | 1 year |
| Spain | 2010 | 10 years |
| Austria | 2011 | 5 years |
| Belgium | 2011 | 8 years |
| Canada | 2011 | 8 years |
| Czech Republic | 2011 | 6 years |
| France | 2011 | 6 years |
| Israel | 2011 | 2 years |
| Malta | 2011 | 6 years |
| Slovenia | 2011 | 4 years |
| Ireland | 2012 | 2 years |
| Italy | 2012 | 9 years |
| Japan | 2012 | 8 years |
| Lithuania | 2012 | 6 years |
| Portugal | 2012 | 3 years |
| Slovakia | 2012 | 3 years |
| South Korea | 2012 | 11 years |
| Taiwan | 2012 | 7 years |
| United Kingdom | 2012 | 14 years |

(Author research: sources include ITU, EU, DigiTAG, DVB and http://en.dtvstatus. net. In some cases low power analogue relays may have continued beyond the main switchover completion date shown.)

Digital switchover would not win votes, it could very easily lose them – and there would be no political appetite for confronting any widespread protest movement against the policy. Having won its second election victory in 2001, Labour would try for a third either in 2005 or 2006, so naming a possible timescale of 2006–2010 and qualifying it by a requirement for 95% take-up before switchover could be completed was politically prudent. The government was in favour of developing digital television but deliberately relaxed about the prospect of a lengthy transition to analogue switch-off.

In support of digital television development, Chris Smith, as Secretary of State at the Department for Culture, Media and Sport (DCMS), had agreed a generous licence fee settlement for the BBC. The preceding Conservative government had given the BBC a modest licence fee increase for 1998/1999 and 1999/2000 to cover the launch of digital TV but planned to offset it by a reduction in later years. The BBC argued strongly against this and made a major pitch for a much larger increase in its funding to equip it to play its part in the nation's digital future, leading Chris Smith to set up an independent inquiry into the issue. In February 2000, he announced that the BBC licence fee would increase by 1.5% above inflation for the period 2000/2001–2006/2007. This laid the basis for the raft of new BBC channels which the BBC was able to launch in 2002 – complementing its digital widescreen versions of BBC One and Two with BBC Three, BBC Four, BBC News 24 and two children's channels aimed at different age groups, CBeebies and CBBC. This was central to digital terrestrial TV's recovery.

## The birth of *Freeview*

Finding a new leader for the digital terrestrial convoy after ITV Digital's collapse was left to the regulator, the ITC (Independent Television Commission). The ITC invited applications for the three vacant multiplexes and, in collaboration with the Digital TV Group, carried out tests on the technical parameters of the transmission system to help bidders see how best to overcome the history of reception problems. Essentially there was a trade-off between maximising the number of channels which a multiplex could accommodate (which commercial broadcasters tended to favour) and optimising the robustness of the signal to enlarge the reception area and reduce interference (which the BBC favoured).

The BBC had concluded that the market could not support three-way competition between satellite, cable and terrestrial platforms for pay-TV subscribers. Its digital terrestrial television recipe was fewer channels, better coverage, quality services and no subscription. This, of course, suited its own public services, which were financed by the licence fee, but would require an open market in unsubsidised receivers available for a modest price. In order to implement this strategy the BBC would need multiplex partners and a close working relationship with receiver manufacturers and retailers.

After unsuccessful talks with ITV and Channel 4 (who put in a rival bid), the BBC teamed up with Crown Castle (the company which had taken over BBC transmission when it had been privatised): the BBC bid for one of the vacant multiplexes and Crown Castle for the other two. A third partner in the organisation which became *Freeview* was BSkyB. The BBC and Crown Castle valued BSkyB's marketing and technical experience. For BSkyB a free-to-view digital terrestrial platform meant the removal of any terrestrial pay-TV competitor. As BSkyB was only an ally, not a bidder for a multiplex licence, and since its potential dominance was in pay-TV which, in this case, would not be involved, the alliance passed muster with the competition regulators.

Pace, Nokia, Grundig, Goodmans, Panasonic, Daewoo and Hauppage – followed by Sony and Humax – committed to creating an open receiver market, a mixture of set-top boxes and integrated digital TV sets. Retailers were trained to be straight with their customers – not pretending they were within a reception area if they were not, and not pretending that they did not need a new aerial if it was obvious (from the selection of digital frequencies for their area) that they probably would. The unsubsidised price for a set-top box was £100 and the target market was those who did not want to pay a subscription but did want a much wider channel choice. The *Freeview* consortium duly won its bid and, in place of just the four or five analogue services, offered terrestrial viewers a line-up of around 30 standard definition TV services which included all the new BBC channels, plus ITV 2, ITV News, Sky News and Sky Sports News and a Community Channel, plus digital radio services.

The channel mix evolved and expanded. ITV, Channel 4 and Channel Five later joined *Freeview*. An element of subscription, in the form of a service called *Top-Up TV*, was added in 2004. This required the consumer either to buy a *Freeview* set-top box which included conditional access or to add a conditional access module to an integrated TV set, but it was planned essentially as a low-cost add-on option at this stage. The main character of the UK's digital terrestrial platform was free-to-view. Following its launch in October 2002, supported by extensive BBC promotion, *Freeview* proved a runaway success and claimed two million customers by the end of its first year of operation.

## Planning the transition to analogue switch-off

With the success of *Freeview*, the idea of analogue terrestrial switch-off became credible again. The government had convened a joint government–industry Digital TV Project to draw up and implement an

Action Plan, having regard to the government's criteria and with 2010 a notional target. By 2003 the Berlin media authorities and the German broadcasters and receiver industry had worked out how to accomplish analogue switch-off in the Berlin area, which provided a model other countries could study. A group of UK government economists undertook a Cost–Benefit Analysis which compared analogue terrestrial switch-off with the alternative of digital–analogue coexistence. Because of the potential value of the released spectrum, the economic case for analogue switch-off was clear (DCMS and DTI, 2003).

The popular appeal of *Freeview* played in, politically. Because of frequency planning constraints, *Freeview's* coverage was limited to around 75% (for the multiplexes carrying public services). It could only be made available terrestrially on a comparable basis to analogue (with 98.5% coverage) if analogue transmissions were switched off and the digital services able to broadcast with more transmitters and at higher power. Since every household was paying the increased licence fee underpinning the BBC's new range of digital services (the government had rejected the idea of a licence fee supplement for digital households only), then every household, so far as practical, should be able to receive them. This 'fairness' case for analogue switch-off carried political weight, especially as the public demand from constituents who wanted *Freeview* but could not receive it began to offset the fears of those attached to analogue. In 2003 the government affirmed its commitment to the switchover goal and quietly included it in its manifesto for the 2005 election.

Spectrum planning was done on the basis that the digital transmitter pattern would match the analogue one, so that existing transmitter sites would continue to serve the household roof-top aerials pointing at them. Switchover would involve moving the digital multiplexes onto freed analogue frequencies and boosting them to high power. Although 94% coverage could then be achieved with 80 main transmitters, it was decided to convert over 1000 analogue relays to digital as well, to enable the four main broadcasters to match their 98.5% analogue coverage and to boost the coverage for Channel Five. Digital-only commercial services with no universal coverage obligation opted to extend to 90% coverage.

The 98.5% coverage commitment was technically elaborate and expensive. Ofcom estimated that, of the 1000 or so extra relay transmitters, 398 would serve fewer than 300 houses (Ofcom, 2004a). There was a reluctance to rely on BSkyB's satellite operation, with its proprietary receivers, to complement more limited terrestrial coverage, since this was a commercial service whose long-term future was not publicly guaranteed: the public service-managed satellite service, *Freesat*, did not then exist – it was only started in 2008.

The plan was, at switchover, to release 14 frequency channels, one third of the 42 used in total for analogue terrestrial. In addition there would be opportunities for new regional or local services whose transmissions could be interleaved within the channels reserved for digital terrestrial services (White Spaces).

The stance taken by the government was that switchover was primarily a terrestrial broadcasters' project (albeit one the government needed to facilitate), partially analogous to BSkyB's policy of migrating its customers to digital satellite and closing down analogue satellite transmissions. This political positioning was two-sided: on the one hand, avoiding financial responsibility and, on the other, offering consumer protection.

Had the driving force behind analogue switch-off been perceived as a government quest for spectrum auction proceeds, with the government the most obvious beneficiary, then there could have been demands for the government to subsidise the receivers that consumers would be compelled to buy. The Chancellor of the Exchequer, Gordon Brown, was adamant that there would be no government expenditure for the project. So, since some public expenditure was clearly going to be necessary, the DCMS decided to use the BBC licence fee.

Then, as the government was not the main driver, it was able to cast itself as the consumers' friend. It would look after the interests of those for whom switchover represented a risk or a source of anxiety. It took advice from a Consumer Expert Group and Ofcom's Consumer Panel. It worked with the industry to develop a 'digital tick' which could be displayed on digital TV receivers that would work through switchover. Together with the BBC, it developed a 'Help-Scheme' for the elderly and disabled, which offered practical assistance in installing set-top boxes as well as a financial subsidy for those who qualified on grounds of need. The government decided that this should be funded by the licence fee and £600 million was duly ear-marked for this purpose.

In line with this political approach, operational responsibility for making the switch would be entrusted to a newly formed company of terrestrial broadcasters, working closely both with the receiver manufacturers and retailers and with the satellite and cable platforms. This company, 'Switchco' (which became Digital UK) would coordinate the practical work of switching frequencies at the transmitters with a full and effective communications campaign. It would be funded by the broadcasters, again primarily by the BBC through the licence fee.

The terms of the BBC's new Charter, due to run for ten years from 2006, and the related licence fee settlement for years immediately ahead, would reflect the BBC's digital switchover obligations. The 2005 Green Paper on the BBC's future proposed that:

> The BBC needs to take a leading role in the organisation and funding of digital switchover, using the licence fee to bring the benefits of digital TV to all. The BBC should:
>
> * help to establish and manage the organisation that will coordinate the technical process of switchover – currently known as 'Switchco';
> * play the leading role in the public information campaign that will tell consumers when and how the switch will happen, what choices of equipment they have and how they can install that equipment;
> * help to establish and pay for schemes to help the most vulnerable consumers make the switch and pay for it (DCMS, 2005).

Essentially, with caveats over its financial responsibility for the Switchover Help-Scheme, the BBC was willing to accept these roles. It was keen to achieve full terrestrial coverage for its digital services and to end the double transmission costs of simulcasting and it was confident of its own future, both in broadcasting and online, as a digital public service.

A new (converged) regulatory body, Ofcom, had been created by the 2003 Broadcasting Act. It presided over the renewal of the licences for commercial terrestrial broadcasters, incorporating the switchover deadline and dramatically reducing the payments ITV and Channel Five made for their licences in line with their progress to full switchover (Ofcom, 2004a). It offered them 'digital replacement licences' to take the place of their analogue licences. These involved a commitment to analogue switch-off, the extension of digital terrestrial coverage to match that of analogue, obligations to communicate with viewers and obligations to collaborate with other bodies involved in the switchover process.

A review of their financial terms followed. The base-line for the review was the *status quo* under which the ITV companies and Channel Five paid the Treasury £230 million in 2004. In 2005, if there were no other change, their combined payment was predicted to be about £180 million. Ofcom undertook an analysis of the market conditions predicted during the run-up to analogue switch-off and estimated that, under the switchover scenario implicit in the digital replacement licences, their combined payment for 2005 would be halved (Ofcom, 2005). It would continue to fall until analogue switch-off and at that point, ITV told its shareholders, the ITV annual payment would be down to a mere £4 million (Starks, 2007: 126). It was an offer the commercial broadcasters could not refuse.

Ofcom also drafted a digital replacement licence for the government to grant to Channel 4 as a commercially funded public service. The government attempted to give Channel 4 a £14 million subsidy from the licence fee to assist digital switchover, but the European Commission subsequently judged this to be contrary to EU state aid rules.

## Deciding the timing

By orchestrating the use of licence fee money, and through Ofcom's regulatory role, the government thus managed to construct a switchover project which, while under the overall direction of ministers, was led, operationally and in public communication terms, by the broadcasters. Consistent with this, it then consulted the broadcasters on the timing. It backed away from its earlier insistence on 95% take-up as a precondition (not least because the analogue restriction of digital terrestrial coverage to 75% made this very difficult to achieve) and recognised the need for a set of hard dates. However, it did not propose to dictate them.

The broadcasters and the wider industry had a preference for a phased regional approach – and this was attractive politically too. It meant that the process could be started on a small-scale and experience acquired before any switch-offs in the major conurbations. The broadcasters' proposal was to start in the (English–Scottish) Border region and leave London until near the end. The broadcasters were unable to reach complete agreement on the timing: the commercial broadcasters, in particular, were in no rush and the transmitter operations experts, whose staff would have to climb the masts, wanted enough time to give them a buffer against the risk of disruption by bad weather. However, a partial consensus emerged around an end-date of 2012 and this was duly entered into the digital replacement licences.

The government knew how to implement digital switchover by the end of 2004, when the Digital TV Project completed its work (DCMS and DTI, 2005), and it knew the broadcasters' recommended regional phasing and preferred timing by then. 2005 was election year and Labour won a further term of office that May. In September, with the support of its manifesto commitment, the Secretary of State at the DCMS, Tessa Jowell, announced the government's blessing for a phased region-by-region analogue switch-off, starting in 2008 and completing by the end of 2012.

By 2005 around 60% of UK households had digital television and the 2008–2012 commitment left time for the continuing take-up of digital television on a voluntary basis. *Freeview* flourished as did the pay-TV sector, with BSkyB the dominant provider and the cable industry further consolidated (NTL took over Telewest in 2006 and later merged with Virgin Media). Thus the industry drove take-up steadily higher in the run-up to analogue switch-off, reducing the number of analogue terrestrial homes still remaining and simplifying the switch-off task. Public policy therefore went with the grain of the market. However, by the time the first UK transmitter was switched at Whitehaven in 2008, the Netherlands, Finland and Sweden had completed their national switchovers.

## Implementation

In the analogue switch-off implementation viewers received ample publicity and advice, with an increasingly practical focus, as the deadline for their area approached. The operation was in two stages. Initially, BBC Two's analogue channel was switched off and the BBC multiplex including BBC Two transferred to a new frequency and given a power boost. Then, usually two weeks later, the remaining analogue channels were switched off and the other digital multiplexes moved to their new frequencies and powers. At that point all the public services (and all the former analogue services) were available near-universally on digital terrestrial and the coverage of the digital-only commercial services was extended. So the analogue viewer who had failed to acquire a digital receiver in time could still do so in the two-week period after losing BBC Two, while the vast majority of terrestrial households, already equipped, had simply to retune their receivers (twice).

The practical side of the operation hinged on close cooperation by the broadcasters with one another, with Arqiva the transmission provider, and with the wider industry including receiver manufacturers, retailers and aerial installers. Digital UK was able to build on a history of collaboration within the industry which had started right at the beginning, in 1995, with the formation of the Digital TV Group and continued with the digital terrestrial broadcasters' coordination of transmission operations. *Freeview* had been divisive for only a short time: ITV and Channel 4 became shareholders in 2005. The government-instigated Digital TV Project had been based on collaborative working, so Digital UK swiftly became a constructive partnership.

The years of caution and methodical planning were rewarded by generally smooth operations. The main practical problems related to poor quality aerials and to the complexities of auto-retuning by TV sets presented with a choice of signals. Call centre advice on manual retuning was needed to ensure reception of the right regional output and, on the Welsh borders, of the right language. Also, the distinction between former analogue services and digital public services with 98.5% coverage and digital-only commercial channels with only 90% had to be explained in areas affected by the discrepancy. This was all 'normal business' and learning from the early regions provided a bed of experience for dealing with the larger metropolitan areas in the later years. For the great majority of the population, with digital take-up on the main receiver over 90%, switchover was a non-event (in this case, a public relations dream).

The government, Ofcom, Digital UK and the broadcasting and receiver industries all gave a sigh of relief when London's Crystal Palace transmitter, serving some five million homes, was successfully switched in April 2012, well ahead of the summer Olympics, and digital switchover was completed by analogue switch-off in Northern Ireland in October 2012.

## Challenges of a long transition

However, there were issues specific to the long transition. Technology did not stand still over the 14-year period. The early receivers had included a silicon chip (known in the business as a 2k chip) which did the job the UK required and was available to do it straightaway, although a technically superior (8k) version was in development. It later became sensible, technically and commercially, to make the move to 8k chips. However, this had been foreseen when *Freeview* started in 2002, so the legacy problem was a modest one.

A much more serious challenge arose around 2005–2006 when HDTV matured as a consumer proposition. In the mid and late 1990s, when the UK first planned its digital terrestrial television, the market lay in multi-channel TV in standard definition (SD). HD would have consumed too much spectrum to allow for a full expansion of choice from five to around 30 channels and cathode-ray HDTV sets were very expensive. So the UK digital terrestrial proposition was designed to be SD and the spectrum plan rested on this design. Ofcom's firm intention was to auction the 14 frequencies released by analogue switch-off without being prescriptive about whether they were used for broadcasting or telecommunications, so no additional spectrum was ear-marked for digital terrestrial's expansion into HD.

However, the rapid spread of new flat-screen TV sets, with the larger screen size models sold as 'HD-ready', changed the market. BSkyB launched HD digital satellite services in 2006 and cable followed. The BBC was making many of its programmes in HD, with the United States export market in mind, and, together with ITV, Channel 4 and Channel Five, was keen to launch its own HD services on terrestrial TV as well as on satellite and cable. The TV set manufacturers, whose new digital flat-screen TVs were essentially digital terrestrial receivers (to which other platforms' set-top boxes could be added), were equally keen. But neither the terrestrial broadcasters nor the receiver manufacturers were in a financial position to compete with the telecoms giants in any auction for the frequencies due to be released.

A period of intensive lobbying against Ofcom's policy stance followed but Ofcom stood firm: its chief executive, Ed Richards, declared that

> we have not been persuaded of the argument that the best way to maximise the social and economic benefit of the released spectrum is simply to gift some or all of the released spectrum to broadcasters.
>
> (Ofcom, 2007)

An ingenious resolution then came from within Ofcom (Bell, 2010). Technically, it involved changing the modulation and utilising statistical multiplexing to increase the capacity of the multiplexes and reshuffling SD channels between them, so as to release one full multiplex for HD. This multiplex could use the DVB's new digital terrestrial standard DVB-T2 plus the more modern MPEG-4 compression system, and could then carry at least four HD channels. (This provides a measure of the extent to which the technology had improved: back in the 1990s, it was an achievement to put four SD channels onto one multiplex). In this way digital terrestrial HDTV could be provided without any initial need for new spectrum.

There was great urgency to coordinate the launch of digital terrestrial HD with the switchover process as soon as possible, so that would-be HD viewers could buy an HD receiver before their region switched. The

| Retain for TV broadcasting | Release | Retain for TV broadcasting | Release |
|---|---|---|---|
| Channels 21–30 | Channels 31–5, 37, 39, 40 | Channels 41–62 | Channels 63–68 |
| 470–550 MHz | between 550 & 630 MHz | 630—806 MHz | 806–854 MHz |

*Figure 3.1*   The UK's original plan for spectrum release

fear was that otherwise they would be forced into the expense of buying an SD box to cope with switchover and subsequently having to replace it for HD. Speedy development was achieved, with terrestrial HD set-top boxes arriving in retail outlets in March 2010.

A further complication then arose in relation to the frequencies due to be released. The UK's original plan was to release a group of frequencies in the middle of the broadcasting spectrum and then another group at the top end (in what was termed the 800 MHz band) (Figure 3.1).

At the top end the frequencies due to be released were channels 63–68. The UK's digital switchover proceeded on this basis. Under the ITU Region 1 agreement reached in Geneva in 2006, spectrum in the 800 MHz band could be used for either broadcasting or telecommunications purposes. However, European dialogue led to a desire for a European Union coordinated approach to use the 800 MHz spectrum for mobile broadband, since cross-border consistency would assist the telecommunications industry. The agreed European Union scheme involved clearing channels 61 and 62, plus channel 69 which was used for broadcasting support services, as well.

So in 2010 Ofcom, Digital UK, the terrestrial broadcasters and their transmission provider Arqiva needed to start changing the frequencies designed for use at and after switchover. A revised plan was implemented in time for the regions due to be switched in 2011 and 2012 but, for areas which had already been switched, further frequency changes now became necessary and some TV set retuning would therefore have to continue in 2013. The new plan resulted in the release of channels 31–37 (550–606 MHz) and channels 61–69 (790–862 MHz).

## Spectrum auction

Ofcom's initial consultation on the so-called 'digital dividend' – the release of the spectrum saved by digital switchover – was published in late 2006. With a substantial amount of spectrum available and the prospect of great competition for it, the regulator could not 'know' the best use and decided that the process should be market-led, involving a spectrum auction. The aim was to maximise the value the spectrum could bring to society over time, and Ofcom stated:

> It is emphatically not our objective to manage the spectrum so as to raise money for the Exchequer – nor, given our statutory duties, is this a consideration that Ofcom takes into account.
>
> (Ofcom, 2006: 8)

It was not necessary for all the spectrum to be cleared before any auction took place, provided the clearance date was known and reliable. The earliest date for an auction would be 2008 (Ofcom, 2006: 97). In the event the auction of spectrum in the 800 MHz band, where mobile broadband was envisaged, was substantially delayed. Once the frequencies to be cleared had been coordinated with other European countries, one cause of the delay was a protracted legal dispute between Ofcom and the telecommunications network operators on the design and terms of the auction process.

Another factor was the identification of potential interference 4G services might cause to some 900,000 digital terrestrial households. This problem could be solved by the fitting of a filter, usually to the receiver but in some cases to the roof-top aerial (if a mast-head amplifier or distribution system was in use). In 2012 the government announced that it would create a £180 million scheme to fund vouchers to enable the affected households to take remedial action free of charge.

The UK was starting to fall behind a number of other countries in spectrum auctioning and 4G telecommunications implementation. By 2011 Germany, Sweden, the Netherlands and Spain had sold off the spectrum required to prepare for the introduction of 4G services in Europe, while 4G services had already been launched in the United States and Japan (*The Times*, 2011b). The UK auction of spectrum in the 800 MHz band finally took place in 2013, yielding £2.3 billion.

## Review of the UK's digital switchover process

Looking back on the UK's lengthy digital switchover process, we can see that, after the ITV Digital crisis, it was essentially well-managed. Digital UK and the transmission company, Arqiva, who undertook the operational work at the transmitter sites, delivered a successful project, within the framework set by the government, the regulator and the stakeholders.

Recasting digital terrestrial as essentially a free-to-view platform in 2002 was of critical importance. The original concept of a pay-TV venture which would provide effective competition to the established satellite and cable multi-channel operators ended in failure. This was probably a feature of the particular market conditions prevailing in the UK around the turn of the century, and of the newness of digital terrestrial technology then, rather than any kind of iron law. While Spain's early experience paralleled the UK's, other countries, such as Italy and France, subsequently showed how pay-TV and free-to-view services could coexist on a digital terrestrial platform. However, an attractive free-to-view proposition is fundamental to the process of digital switchover: governments can compel people to buy a relatively cheap adapter for their TVs, but they cannot realistically compel them to subscribe.

The leading role played by the main public broadcaster in the switchover process was also a distinctive feature of the UK's experience, with relatively generous licence fee funding underpinning the process. The BBC's enthusiasm for digital television from the outset, for competitive reasons and because of the opportunities it offered for modernising and extending its public service proposition, was a major factor. However, the BBC role also reflects the UK government's preference for navigating from the back seat, rather than being the front seat driver of switchover.

In some other countries, the leading commercial terrestrial broadcasters were reluctant supporters of the introduction of digital television, since it obviously threatened their market share. In the UK the commercial broadcasters were mainly keen, again because of the competitive situation: remaining frozen in an analogue world was not a sensible response to the growing challenge from satellite and cable multi-channel. However, the commercial broadcasters' willingness to support analogue switch-off was undoubtedly assisted by the regulator's approach of reducing their payments to the Treasury in line with the switch from an analogue to a digital market.

BSkyB's role in digital switchover was an important one, though that might not have been predicted from its initial public stance either on the introduction of digital terrestrial or on the concept of a compulsory switchover policy. By pursuing its own commercial interest effectively, BSkyB played a major role in building digital take-up by consumers and reducing the number of households dependent on terrestrial reception. By collaborating with the BBC and Crown Castle in the creation of *Freeview*, it both protected its own pay-TV interests and assisted the rescue of the terrestrial platform, without which analogue switch-off would have been impossible.

The public too was generally supportive of the switchover process. Consumer resistance, with the potential to make the policy politically controversial, was low. This was certainly due to the high level of voluntary take-up by viewers attracted by both the pay-TV and the *Freeview* services. However, the smoothness with which every household was converted by a fixed date is testimony to the work of Digital UK and to the care taken by the government, the regulator, the broadcasters and other stakeholders to involve consumer groups in the planning.

Each stage of the policy formulation was characterised by the publication of consultation documents; regular meetings of stakeholders were held; and both the Consumer Expert Group and Ofcom's Consumer Panel made important contributions. The UK Help-Scheme for the elderly and disabled went beyond the public provision made in many other countries and, reinforced by the assistance of charities, created an ethos of looking after the vulnerable. In the event the scheme turned out to have been over-funded, which was good news all round. The extended timetable too was a factor in minimising opposition to switchover.

While the switch-off of the last analogue transmitter marked the end of the switchover process, the spectrum plot continued to develop. There was an intention to begin charging the broadcasters for it. Also, once the 800 MHz spectrum at the top end of the broadcasting band had been auctioned, a further question was how to handle the other frequencies released by switchover in the middle of the broadcasting band (550–606 MHz). Would mobile broadband want to take another bite out of the broadcasting spectrum and, if so, would that require a further reshuffle of frequencies, shifting the broadcasters down into one consolidated bloc in the lower part of the band and releasing more spectrum at the upper end? Clearing the 700 MHz band for wireless broadband would match the approach already taken in the United States and by 2012 Ofcom was already consulting about that prospect.

## Assessment of the emerging outcomes

UK digital television is now clearly multi-platform, with TV by broadband arriving as a fourth platform and BT Vision combining access to *Freeview* over the air with On-Demand services via broadband. The growth of pay-TV during the years of transition proved substantial, fuelled by the transfer of major sports such as Premier League football and premium movies to pay channels. Back in 1995, when the UK government published its proposals for the introduction of digital television, around 20% of households subscribed to multi-channel analogue satellite or cable (Goodwin, 2005: 154). The remaining 80% were served purely by analogue terrestrial TV. By the time of analogue switch-off in 2012, satellite and cable households, taken in combination, accounted for the majority of UK households and subscriptions constituted 42% of TV's revenue (Ofcom, 2012a: 115).

Digital terrestrial TV's market penetration was nonetheless a triumph. Its share of households, classified by the distribution system feeding the main TV set, had grown from 1% in 2002 to 43% in 2011, surpassing digital satellite's share of 40% (Ofcom, 2012a: 119). In addition it supported second and third TV sets in many cable and satellite homes.

The crisp separation of free-to-view and pay-TV by platform has become blurred at the edges. *Top-Up TV* on digital terrestrial now offers an interactive download service for a range of programmes and subscription access to Sky Sports 1 and 2 and ESPN. *Freesat* offers a free-to-view service, with an open market in receivers, via satellite.

The next obvious development has been the huge growth in the number of TV channels, with satellite and cable offering around 500 and *Freeview* now providing around 50 (some of them time-sharing) plus a wide range of radio services.

As well as providing HDTV channels, *Freeview* also markets a hard-disc digital recorder sold, without a subscription, as *Freeview +*. Digital terrestrial television is thus able to support a range of general entertainment and other genres with licence fee and advertising funding.

Channel proliferation has not been matched by an expansion of original high-quality production. The bulk of original UK production continues to be provided by the five former analogue terrestrial broadcasters, much of it now commissioned from independent production companies. Their level of investment in original production fell from £3 billion to £2.5 billion between 2005 and 2011 (Ofcom, 2012a: 115).

With increased choice, total viewing increased from 3.6 hours per viewer per day in 2006 to an average of 4 hours per viewer per day by 2011. With more choice too, of course, the audience has spread itself across the wider number of outlets, reducing the share of the five terrestrial channels which were once so dominant. Their share of viewing across all platforms fell from 70% in 2005 to 54% in 2011 (Ofcom, 2012a: 115). However, despite the difficulties of recession and changing patterns of commercial advertising, these five main broadcasters remain buoyant, their appeal strengthened by their additional digital channels.

The top ten channels by share in multi-channel homes in 2010–2011 were:

1. BBC One
2. ITV 1
3. Channel 4
4. BBC Two
5. Five
6. ITV 2
7. ITV 3
8. E4
9. BBC Three
10. Film4
    (Ofcom, 2012a: 169)

Democratic, social and cultural gains can certainly be identified. The birth of the BBC's 24 Hour News Channel, the growth in the quality and reputation of Sky News, the availability of channels such as Al Jazeera (in English), and improved national services for Scotland, Wales and Northern Ireland have all broadened access to news and information. The development of children's channels for different age groups has offered families much more flexible and convenient access to TV than the fixed slots of analogue Children's Hour. And BBC Four now enables the BBC to carry far more classical music and foreign films.

HDTV has arrived and fully established itself. Digital video recording has made time-shifted viewing much simpler. Audio-description of programmes for the partially sighted and subtitles and signing for hard-of-hearing and deaf viewers have improved access to television. The convergence of television and the Internet has facilitated the development of On-Demand Catch-Up television, with the BBC iPlayer service proving particularly popular. Broadcasts are increasingly linked to, and supported by, complementary online services and features.

While the BBC has in general been strengthened by its importance to government in leading and managing the process of digital switchover, the funding of the Help-Scheme for the elderly and disabled from the licence fee created a precedent, encouraging a not entirely convincing, and in the end unsuccessful, lobbying campaign by Channel 4 for a slice of licence fee money. More significantly, in October 2010 the new Conservative–Liberal Democrat coalition government, in freezing the licence fee for six years as part of its public expenditure austerity programme, ear-marked licence fee money for the BBC World Service (a transfer from Foreign Office funding), for the Welsh language service S4C, for broadband infrastructure and for non-BBC local television. The relatively generous licence fee funding the BBC received during the switchover years proved to have been temporary.

ITV, transformed from a federation of regional companies into a consolidated ITV plc, was adversely affected by the inevitable loss of audience share accompanying the huge expansion in TV channels and by the trend of media advertising away from broadcasting and towards major Internet players. Its worries were compounded by the recession which started in 2008 but, despite continuing national economic difficulties, it subsequently bounced back with some flair. Ofcom recognised the necessity of easing the public service obligations placed upon it in respect of children's, religious and educational programmes, and also in non-news programmes for the regions. In 2009, with Ofcom's approval, ITV reduced the number of its regional newsrooms from 17 to 9 to save £40 million (Barnett, 2011: 188).

### Regional and local television

A reduction in the strength of regional broadcasting thus became a feature of the UK's digital switchover process. This was in contrast to the experience of other countries, such as Spain, where extra digital capacity was allocated to both regional and local services. While both the BBC and ITV broadcast regional and, for Scotland, Wales and Northern Ireland, what were termed 'national regional' services as variations within the schedules of their UK networks, stand-alone local television stations had never been firmly established in the analogue era. There had been several experiments – from community cable stations like Swindon Viewpoint back in the 1970s through to a small number of analogue terrestrial Restricted Service Licences in more recent times – but they struggled to find viable business models. As a result, when digital terrestrial was being designed in the 1990s, and the regulators were looking for multiplex operators with the financial resources to drive the take-up of a brand-new technology, the awards were for national services. Spectrum scarcity then remained an issue during the simulcasting years.

However, the completion of analogue switch-off removed this constraint. In addition to releasing two main chunks of spectrum with national coverage, it opened up the possibility of access to capacity within the broadcasting band (interleaved spectrum) which could be used for local services without causing interference to the six national multiplexes.

The Conservative–Liberal coalition government took a close interest in this topic, with the Secretary of State at the DCMS, Jeremy Hunt, a personal enthusiast. He commissioned a review from Nicholas Shott, Head of UK Investment Banking at Lazard, on the financial viability of local TV services. The advice was that, while the Internet might provide the best means of distribution in the long-term, there was 'a coherent argument' that local TV could be developed on a digital terrestrial basis first in about ten or 12 major conurbations. Both national and local advertising, and assistance from the BBC, would be required. Licences should be awarded by 'beauty contest' rather than by auction. On this basis 'commercially viable local TV may be possible in the UK' (Shott, 2010).

Building on this analysis Jeremy Hunt published a Local Media Action Plan (DCMS, 2011a). The aim was to have 10–20 local TV services operating by 2015; the first services were licensed during 2012 and a licensee for a digital terrestrial television multiplex operator for local TV was selected in 2013. In the BBC's 2010 licence fee settlement, it had been specified that the BBC would provide start-up capital of up to £25 million in 2013/2014 for up to 20 local services and up to £5 million p.a. for the following three years as payment for local material for BBC use.

With local TV still in the development stage, further spectrum reorganisation on the horizon, and synergies between television and the Internet (described in Chapter 7) continuing to develop, the full implications of digital television switchover are still emerging.

# 4
# Europe's Coordinated Timetable

## Summary of the chapter's argument

Within the framework of the ITU, Europe has coordinated its digital switchover process. The 2015 deadline, after which analogue television will no longer be protected from interference, agreed by the members of ITU Region 1, is a real one for nearly all European countries, because with so many small countries so close together, and with such highly developed broadcasting markets, cross-border interference has to be prevented. The European Union largely left switchover policy to be formulated at national level by member states, within a framework of platform-neutrality, but recommended 2012 as a common target end-date. In practice 22 of its 27 members achieved this – though in some cases, particularly after the 2008 economic crisis, only with difficulty. Outcomes have varied considerably, in respect of new services, new content providers, the influence of the state and the power of incumbent commercial TV companies. One of the trickiest questions, on which there proved to be no blanket answer, was whether it was feasible to launch new pay-TV services on the digital terrestrial platform in competition with satellite and cable.

The 2015 deadline will be broadly achieved across the continent, with some stragglers and a few rough edges. The first countries to complete are moving to the second generation of DVB and compression technology, while some of the later starters have been able to adopt this at the outset. In Western Europe a coordinated plan is emerging to use released spectrum in the 800 MHz band for mobile broadband.

## International coordination

While the international framework for the transition to digital television is provided by the ITU, its authority rests on agreements, willingly made by governments representing their regulators, providers and users who know that, in this field, collaboration is generally in the interests of all. The ITU has no sanctions of its own to impose. Much of its radio-communications work is undertaken by collective agreement at the level of its three regions.

Region 1 comprises Europe, the Middle East (west of the Persian Gulf), Africa, Russia and Mongolia and it was this diverse group which committed itself, at Geneva in 2006, to setting 2015 as the deadline for analogue terrestrial switch-off. After that date analogue terrestrial transmissions will lose their protection against interference. In practice the implications of this decision, and the likelihood of switchover having been fully completed by that date, vary within the region. In Europe, where spectrum is intensively used and where, especially in smaller countries, cross-border spill-over is common, nations have a very strong incentive to comply with their agreed switchover deadline.

Within Europe a degree of coordination is managed by the inter-governmental European Conference of Postal and Telecommunication Administrations (known as the CEPT from the French version of its name) encompassing 48 countries. The European Union (EU) has been actively involved in switchover plans of its member states. However, conscious of the unhappy history of technology intervention by its predecessor organisation, the European Community, it initially left policy formulation largely to national governments and the market and judged its own interventions carefully.

## European Union role

In the 1980s the European Community had tried to develop its own analogue satellite system, including high-definition, called MAC (Multiplexed Analogue Component), embodied in a European Directive. As described earlier, it proved technically over-ambitious and commercially disastrous. In the 1990s, therefore, European broadcasters and receiver manufacturers reacted against politically driven high-technology strategies and the DVB (Digital Video Broadcasting project) family of technical standards for digital television was designed largely by industry members with a sharp focus on commercial viability.

From the beginning, due to the failure surrounding the MAC initiative and the liberalising trend in telecommunications regulation, the European Commission (EC) shied away from the possibility of managing the transition to digital television on a coordinated European Union basis. It saw its role as primarily one of preventing market distortion.

On these grounds it initially took the view that member states should not be free individually to mandate digital TV sets in the way that the United States did:

> Free movement of goods within the internal market requires that national authorities do not impose administrative constraints for commercialising digital broadcasting equipment and compulsory technical requirements without previously informing the European Commission. Where such requirements would be necessary, they should be introduced Community wide and be based on European standards.
>
> (EC, 2003)

The EU endorsed and mandated the commercially based and collectively developed DVB standards but, beyond that, it declined to be prescriptive in detail. It thus allowed considerable technical diversity, particularly in respect of Electronic Programme Guides, the hardware–software interface for interactive applications and conditional access. It ruled that integrated digital TV sets had to have a common interface into which different conditional access systems could be plugged, but no such requirement applied to set-top boxes, nor was there any obligation on pay-TV companies to ensure that their proprietary conditional access systems would work via the common interface. The net result was that different set-top boxes were developed for different platforms in different national markets.

The EU also favoured a multi-platform approach, viewing competition between platforms as in principle desirable, and therefore required political platform-neutrality and a regulatory level playing field. It was particularly hawk-eyed on the subject of state aid for the digital terrestrial platform, where, of course, rival platforms were quick to complain. While national governments could promote a specific digital television technology if this was justified by 'well-defined general interests', e.g. to achieve a fast and efficient switchover, 'policy interventions should be transparent, justified, proportionate and timely to minimise the risks of market distortion' (EC, 2003: 4). The Commission took legal action where state aid appeared to have breached EU competition policy in respect of Berlin, Italy and the UK (Wheeler, 2012). Austria skilfully designed a subsidy scheme which met with EU approval by following Commission advice on how to stay within the law.

The actual formulation of policy, however, was left to national governments and the result of this 'hands off' approach at European level was a very varied set of experiences in different European countries, especially at the outset. As switchover gathered momentum, the European Commission became more confident about intervening with the aim of coordinating outcomes. In 2005 it named 2012 as a target date for analogue switch-off within the EU but this was a recommendation, not a prescription (EC, 2005a). It also played a role in facilitating transnational cooperation in planning the re-use of released spectrum for mobile broadband, in the end mandating the release of the 800 MHz band (Stirling, 2012).

## Europe's digital switchovers

With only limited coordination, European countries proceeded with digital switchover at different speeds, following distinctive national policies. Only a few general observations are possible.

As will be discussed more fully in Chapter 9, public service broadcasters played a leading part in most European countries. Progress proved most rapid in countries which were heavily cabled, well-served by satellite and had a relatively small percentage of households dependent on analogue terrestrial reception. Generally, north-west Europe forged ahead. The experiences of Sweden, Finland, Germany and the Netherlands have already been related. Denmark and Norway (non-member of the EU) both completed their switchover after relatively brief transition periods in 2009. The countries of south-west Europe, where dependence on terrestrial reception was much higher, in general required more time – with, as described, the additional complication of early commercial disasters in the UK and Spain.

As a generalisation, central and Eastern European countries which were formerly part of the Communist bloc have also needed longer, with less developed television markets, less wealthy consumers and, in some cases, persistent political problems. Petros Iosifidis has observed:

> Eastern Europe has its own character in terms of DTV developments. With roughly half of TV households in Eastern Europe relying on terrestrial television, the region represents a large market for free-to-view multi-channel television. However, analogue switch-off in this part of Europe has been hampered by political issues, governments' lack of a political priority and lack of political consensus that makes it difficult to reach an agreement. There is a lack of sufficient understanding of the issues involved in the digital switchover by regulators and broadcasters, especially with regards to the programming and market issues involved. Public broadcasters in many transition countries

have still not consolidated in terms of the transition from state to public service television.

(Iosifidis, 2011a: 8)

Kenneth Murphy has argued that undertaking switchover on a multi-platform basis, in line with the EU's insistence on platform-neutrality, is harder in small states where the market may simply not be big enough to support three or four competing technologies (Murphy, 2010). Certainly in the European states which suffered severely in the economic crisis that began in 2008 – Greece, Ireland and Portugal – the digital television investment market struggled. Problems appeared after switchover in Slovenia too. However, Croatia and Estonia completed switchover with relatively few difficulties, while Latvia undertook a crash programme in one year. Market size in conjunction with platform balance is a relevant factor but there is certainly no rule that says switchover is necessarily more difficult for small countries.

While late starters in Europe found themselves undertaking switchover in a deteriorating economic climate, they did have some advantages. They were able to adopt the second generation of technology, using the DVB-T2 terrestrial standard with MPEG-4 compression which gave them many more channels per multiplex and facilitated the adoption of HDTV.

They could also learn from the experiences of the pioneers. However, while the inference first drawn from the commercial broadcaster bankruptcies in the UK and Spain was that terrestrial TV should focus on free-to-view services and leave pay-TV to other platforms, that lesson turned out to be too simplistic. The UK and Spanish pay-TV broadcasters had suffered from the immaturity of the terrestrial technology and the high cost of early receivers and these factors changed. Indeed, some pay-TV appeared on digital terrestrial television in the UK and Spain after free-to-view TV had fully established itself and a number of other countries, including Italy and France, successfully introduced pay-TV elements to their digital terrestrial propositions. Nonetheless, as Ireland and Portugal found, pay-TV multiplexes could be designed, put out to tender and accepted by commercial operators who, when the time to invest came, then backed away and failed to take-up their licences. On the basis of Europe's varying experiences, the viability of digital terrestrial pay-TV seemed to be dependent on:

- the size of the terrestrial market and whether it was stable or contracting;
- the strength of competing pay-TV platforms;

- presence of latent consumer spending power;
- existence of a compulsory payment for public service TV and strength of its appeal;
- attitude of sports bodies towards selling exclusive TV rights to pay-TV;
- ingenuity of would-be terrestrial pay-TV operators in developing attractive content, controlling their costs and forming alliances with some players on other platforms (head-to-head competition with established satellite and cable pay-TV operators was unwise, so a more sophisticated market positioning was required).

Unsurprisingly then, a look across the continent as a whole shows great national variety. As the cross-section of European countries discussed below illustrates, case studies reveal national differences much more obviously than they support generalisations.

### France

France, with a large market of around 24 million TV homes, was a late starter in digital terrestrial television by comparison with its European neighbours. France's early digital TV initiatives were pay-TV services on satellite. Canal Plus had long been providing analogue terrestrial pay-TV and, for a short period, an analogue satellite service, when digital satellite technology arrived in the 1990s. It launched its digital Canal Satellite platform in 1996. It was promptly challenged by a rival satellite platform, TPS, which carried services from the other major analogue terrestrial broadcasters, TF1, M6 and the two public television broadcasters France 2 and France 3. Competition for subscribers and for programme rights was intense and left the broadcasters with little appetite for further competition from digital terrestrial TV. In 2007, however, the satellite rivalry ended in a merger, with Canal Satellite in essence the victor.

Meanwhile the French government had started to take the digital terrestrial platform more seriously, primarily because of the dominance of analogue terrestrial reception in France. Satellite had only a modest segment of the market, cable had less and, although broadband TV was strong and growing, the majority of French households remained with the six analogue terrestrial channels (TF1, France 2 and 3, Canal +, La Cinquième and M6). The Jospin government designed a national pattern of digital terrestrial television and in 2000 introduced a law which helped persuade the big commercial broadcasters, TF1, Canal+ and M6, to accept it. They were offered guaranteed access to the proposed multiplexes both for simulcasting their existing channels and for new services, which had the effect of limiting the extent of new competition (Kuhn, 2011: 273).

France's pattern of digital terrestrial television was finally launched in 2005 under the umbrella brand of *Télévision Numérique Terrestre* (TNT), beginning with free-to-view services and then adding pay-TV channels to complement them. Thus the digital terrestrial business model was a hybrid one, in contrast to the free-to-view models which had rescued the terrestrial platforms in the UK and Spain. The proposition to the consumer was a choice of 18 national channels, including new services of news and youth-oriented programmes and the option of 11 pay-TV channels (two of which later closed). Most of the new channels were also available on other platforms.

While all other European digital terrestrial television, including the French free-to-view services, had hitherto used the well-established MPEG-2 coding system, France decided to introduce the newer advanced compression system, MPEG-4, for its digital terrestrial pay-TV. By providing greater compression MPEG-4 facilitated the inclusion of high-definition services. Thus, by starting later, France was able to build HDTV into its digital terrestrial design, rather than 'retrofit' it, as the UK had had to do. Local TV services were also part of the French digital terrestrial pattern, initially simulcasts of 18 analogue services, then building towards a total of around 50 (Kuhn, 2011: 275).

In 2009 President Sarkozy implemented a major reform of public service television, bringing together within the single organisation of *France Télévisions* the former analogue channels France 2 and France 3 with the new France 4 (youth) and France 5 (educational) digital services and with France's overseas service, plus online services. This reform, which partially reversed the fragmentation of public broadcasting caused by the dismantling of the old ORTF (*Office de Radiodiffusion-Télévision Française*) back in 1974, was accompanied by a reduction of public service television's dependence on advertising to supplement its licence fee income. In place of the lost advertising revenue *France Télévisions* would receive the proceeds of a new tax on Internet service providers and mobile phone operators (Kuhn, 2010: 162). This change, of course, assisted the commercial channels at a time of economic difficulty but also underlined the distinctive public service remit of *France Télévisions* – though, if the idea was to make it more like the BBC, it was an aberration to make the Chief Executive a direct Presidential appointee.

Meanwhile, supported by an enthusiastic level of take-up for TNT, a timetable was set for a region-by-region switch-off of analogue terrestrial

TV. *France Télé Numérique*, a public body formed by the government and the broadcasters, was established to manage the process. Coverage requirements were met and TNT Sat was launched to serve areas where terrestrial coverage was not sensibly feasible. The commercial companies – TF1, Canal+ and M6 – whose analogue licences would be terminated early were promised 'bonus channels' once switchover was complete. They also consolidated their industry position by buying some of the smaller digital channels.

Receiver industry regulations were introduced (in contrast to earlier practice within the EU, and more in line with the United States): HDTV sets were required to have an MPEG-4 decoder and all TV sets sold from 2008 onwards had to have a digital tuner (García Leiva and Starks, 2009).

Analogue switch-off was completed on schedule by the end of 2011 – at which point additional spectrum for new digital terrestrial multiplexes became available. TF1, Canal+ and M6 had been expecting their 'bonus channels' but the European Commission judged that they had already done quite well during the transition and that this would be in breach of European law, so the award would need to be through open competition (Broadband TV News, 2011b).

### Italy

The Italian market of around 22 million households is dominated by terrestrial television: cable penetration is low and satellite services, though they dominate the pay market, have limited penetration compared to other countries. Until 1990 analogue television at national level was formally a monopoly, in the hands of the state broadcaster RAI, though within an ill-regulated and chaotic local TV sector Silvio Berlusconi had built up his Mediaset empire of three quasi-national networks (Gardini and Galperin, 2005). When digital terrestrial television appeared as a practical possibility, analogue TV was essentially a duopoly with three RAI channels and three Mediaset commercial channels accounting for 90% of the audience.

Although Italian regulators saw digital television as an opportunity to introduce more competition, Berlusconi became Prime Minister in 2001 (and continued to dominate Italian politics, with a short break between 2006 and 2008, until 2011) and the duopoly obtained an early grip on digital terrestrial TV. Mediaset was first to launch in 2003 with a multiplex of five channels and RAI followed swiftly with two national multiplexes. As Alfredo Del Monte observed

Not many governments are able to resist the political pressure of interests linked to the current structure of the TV sector. Technology is only one of the factors that affects the structure of the TV industry and is not necessarily the most important. Therefore the transition to digital TV very often follows a pattern determined by the pre-existing structure of the terrestrial analogue sector. The transition to digital TV in Italy lends support to the above hypothesis.

(Del Monte, 2006)

By the end of 2004, however, there were two other multiplexes, one run by Telecom Italia and TV International and the other by a company called D-Free. Approximately 25 national channels and 40 local ones, including the simulcast of the existing national terrestrial channels, were available in total, with a mixture of free-to-view and event-based pay-TV services. The business model was originally all free-to-view, based on advertising revenue. However, led by Mediaset, the broadcasters decided to challenge Sky Italia's satellite premium services and began offering pay-TV events (football especially) through pre-pay rechargeable cards.

Take-up was kick-started by the Italian government's decision to offer subsidies to licence fee-paying consumers purchasing set-top boxes capable of providing interactive links to websites with the potential to support e-government development. Digital terrestrial set-top boxes containing MHP (Multi-media Home Platform) technology qualified, as did boxes for the Fastweb broadband service, but satellite receivers did not. Sky Italia complained. The European Commission ruled the subsidies unfair and this judgement was upheld by the EU Court of Justice (Wheeler, 2012).

RAI and Mediaset became leading members of the Association for the Development of the Digital Terrestrial TV, which collaborated with the government in planning the full transition to digital on a region-by-region basis. The initial target date chosen for completing analogue switch-off was 2006. This was postponed first to 2008 and then to 2012.

By the end of 2012 analogue terrestrial switch-off was complete, though with outbreaks of interference requiring case-by-case resolution. The release of analogue terrestrial spectrum will allow further digital terrestrial multiplexes to be allocated and the Berlusconi government had envisaged this being done by 'beauty contest'. Opponents who regarded this approach as potentially too favourable to incumbents argued that an auction could generate substantial revenue which, in the light of the country's economic crisis, the Italian government sorely needed. Following Berlusconi's fall at the end of 2011, Italy's new technocrat Prime Minister, Mario Monti, confirmed an auction as the course to be followed.

Once the full complement of digital terrestrial TV multiplexes is in place, a regulatory restriction will prevent any one single media content provider from being authorised to broadcast more than 20% of the total digital terrestrial television national programming. The intention is to reduce the dominance of the RAI-Mediaset duopoly. However, the definition of total programming excluded time-shifted repeat channels and pay-per-view, thus softening its impact and leaving Francesca Fanucci and Benedetta Brevini to conclude that

> Despite the promise of the technological change being able to bring more pluralism in Italy, the Italian broadcasting market is today still dominated by the long-lasting duopoly of RAI and Mediaset.
>
> (Fanucci and Brevini, 2013: 14)

## Portugal

Portugal is a small TV market of 3.9 million households, over 60% of which received digital television from satellite, cable or IPTV. Analogue terrestrial TV, on which the remaining households relied for their primary reception, offered four services, two public channels from the public broadcaster RTP and two commercial channels, SIC and TVI.

Portugal took an early initiative to launch digital terrestrial television in 2001, allocating a licence to a broadcasting–telecoms consortium, but, observing the disasters overtaking the early digital terrestrial ventures in Spain and the UK, the consortium delayed its launch and its licence was then revoked. No further action was taken until the European Union named 2012 as its recommended date for analogue switch-off. In response the government and regulator formulated a plan to launch six digital terrestrial multiplexes, for which the licences would be awarded via two separate tenders. Multiplex A would simply simulcast the free-to-view terrestrial channels (to which it was envisaged that a fifth service would be added), while Multiplexes B, C, D, E and F would provide a new range of pay-TV services in competition with the other pay-TV platforms. In 2008 Portugal Telecom (PT) won both tenders, beating a Swedish rival for the pay-TV award. As Denicoli and Sousa observed, while PT had been privatised, the Portuguese government still held 'golden shares' in it at that time (Denicoli and Sousa, 2012).

Following the economic crisis which began in 2008, Portugal then had a change of plan. In 2009 the proposed fifth terrestrial channel was cancelled. In 2010 PT requested the revocation of its licence for the pay-TV multiplexes, to which the regulator agreed. The result was a launch of digital terrestrial television on one multiplex only, carrying essentially the same national channels as analogue plus some ancillary services and an Electronic Programme Guide.

On this basis Portugal committed to the switch-off of analogue terrestrial transmissions in 2012. PT was obliged by its licence to provide support – of up to 50% of the cost of a receiver – to low-income households and viewers with special needs. Since digital terrestrial coverage was limited to 87% of the population, the other 13% would need to access the former analogue services by satellite. This proved to be a source of some consumer resistance (DigiTAG, 2011a) and in January 2012 PT announced an increase in its subsidy for satellite reception. Switchover was implemented in phases and was completed in April 2012. Portugal provides a case study of the implementation of digital switchover in a contracting economy.

## Ireland

Ireland, which has an extensive cable network and is also served by BSkyB's satellite service, together bringing digital television to around 60% of its 1.4 million TV households, had a series of failed attempts to launch digital terrestrial TV into the small residual market (Murphy, 2010).

Early abortive initiatives involving the public service broadcaster, RTE, were followed in 2008 by a scheme to launch free-to-view and pay-TV services on a new digital terrestrial platform. The infrastructure would be provided by RTENL, the transmission provider for RTE. The government legislated to give RTE a 2012 deadline for completing digital switchover, in line with the recommended EU target, and RTE collaborated with Ireland's commercial channel, TV3, and the Irish language network, TG4, in planning a free-to-view multiplex. The competition for the pay-TV licence was won by Boxer TV Ireland (a joint venture with the Swedish Boxer company). However, Boxer was unable to agree terms with RTENL and withdrew. The runner-up was a consortium called One Vision but it too withdrew, as did a third contender Easy TV. It was clear that starting a pay TV business in the small niche market for digital terrestrial TV left by the satellite and cable platforms, during an economic recession, was not going to work.

With the 2012 deadline looming, the government announced that the digital terrestrial platform would be free-to-view only, at least until analogue switch-off had been completed. In conjunction with the commercial channels RTE set up a digital terrestrial service branded *Saorview*, simulcasting the public and commercial analogue services and adding an RTE News service, an RTE daytime children's channel, digital teletext, radio and an Electronic Programme Guide. It would have 98% coverage, backed by a Saorsat satellite service for areas where terrestrial reception was difficult. By 2011 only around 250,000 households were still dependent on analogue terrestrial: their least expensive option would be to purchase a 50 euro MPEG-4 set-top box.

The analogue switch-off operation was coordinated with the UK's switch-off in Northern Ireland, so the Republic of Ireland completed its switchover process at the same time as the UK in October 2012. Ireland then swiftly auctioned its cleared 800 MHz spectrum.

### Slovenia

Slovenia, formerly a republic within the federal state of Yugoslavia, was admitted to the European Union in 2004. It is a tiny nation with just 700,000 TV households. Less than 25% of these relied on terrestrial reception, with cable and IPTV the two dominant platforms.

Digital terrestrial television was planned on the basis of two national multiplexes, the first run by the public service broadcaster, RTV SLO, and the second by Norkring, a subsidiary of the Norwegian telecommunications company Telenor. The intention was for the first multiplex to carry RTV's expanded public services and for the second to carry the national commercial channels, POP TV, Kanal A, TV3 and Pink.si, and the major regional ones. The legislative framework restricted the scope for the development of new thematic commercial channels by requiring a broad range of content.

In the event the first multiplex found itself with spare capacity which legally it could rent out. When the digital terrestrial commercial services leased capacity on this public service multiplex, Norkring struggled to make the second multiplex financially viable. Slovenia postponed its original analogue switch-off date from 2010 to 2011 but then completed the process.

However, in 2012 Norkring announced that it was withdrawing from the market. Neither the government nor the regulator was happy with this outcome and began a search for a different long-term solution. By the end of 2012 Slovenia was therefore investigating the possibility of a new DVB-T2 multiplex with fewer restrictions on pay-TV formats and to which all-digital terrestrial commercial services would be obliged to migrate. Slovenia's difficulties, like Ireland's, illustrate the problems of devising strategy for a minority platform in a small market.

## Croatia

Croatia's digital transition, from legislation to set the framework in 2008 through to completion by the end of 2010, forms a contrast with the experiences of Portugal, Ireland and Slovenia. A former Yugoslav republic with around 1.5 million TV households of whom just over a million depended on terrestrial reception, Croatia judged its strategy skilfully. It was substantially helped by the rapid growth of IPTV from 3% to 18% between 2007 and 2010, reducing the terrestrial platform from 75% to 58% of households over that period (DigiTAG, 2011b). Perhaps the most crucial factor was Croatia's political determination to burnish its credentials for joining the European Union by demonstrating that it could beat the European Commission's recommended 2012 analogue switch-off deadline.

Digital terrestrial services were initially developed on three multiplexes, with Multiplex A simulcasting the two public and two commercial analogue terrestrial channels. Initially, this was all that was available, with new national and local services only coming on-stream from 2010 onwards. So the concept had to be marketed on the basis of what viewers could expect to receive as much as on what they actually would receive at the start.

Multiplex A was required to have coverage of over 98%. The first three multiplexes used the well-established MPEG-2 compression system to help keep down the cost of receivers, but the possibility of using MPEG-4 for a fourth multiplex was kept open.

Analogue switch-off was planned on a region-by-region basis between January and December 2010, with plenty of targeted publicity and advice. The key feature of Croatia's switchover, however, was the availability of a generous subsidy towards the purchase of a receiver for all terrestrial households. This was similar to the American model of vouchers but very unusual in Europe, where the norm was to assist a minority of households with a defined group of needs. This scheme enabled the government to procure receivers from a range of suppliers via a public tender which detailed the switchover information required to be given to the public at specified points of sale. Digital terrestrial set-top boxes were priced at around 25 euros but terrestrial householders could use the vouchers (worth 10 euros) for receivers for any digital platform (in line with the EU's policy of platform-neutrality) – they simply had to use them before the end of 2010.

This state-run switchover operation was successfully completed on time – and Croatia duly welcomed as an accession state to the European Union at the end of 2011. By 2012 plans were being formulated for a fourth multiplex using DVB-T2 and MPEG-4, and including pay-TV services.

### Hungary

Hungary shed its Communist past with a new republican constitution in 1989 and became a member of the European Union in 2004. Its former state broadcasting organisation, Magyar TV, had been joined by a second public TV provider Duna TV, aimed at Hungarian minorities, in 1992 but the big change in television was the arrival in 1997 of two major German-owned commercial broadcasters, RTL-Klub and TV2, which swiftly captured the bulk of the audience. Additional satellite and cable competition has subsequently trimmed their audience shares but they remain the main players.

Cable accounts for over 60% of Hungary's 3.7 million TV homes and, together with satellite, had reduced the number of analogue terrestrial households to around 900,000 by 2007 when the European Union's recommended timetable for analogue switch-off prompted the Hungarian government to adopt a National Digital Switchover Strategy. Digital transition policy was developed on an axis of the Hungarian Parliament and the communications regulator, the NHH. The separate media authority responsible for broadcasting policy, the ORTT, was sidelined after it renewed the analogue licences of the two main commercial broadcasters for a further five years following their expiry in 2007 without imposing any new conditions relating to switchover. The commercial broadcasters were not keen to see their large audience shares diluted by the move to digital – and the ORTT was perceived as aligning itself with a go-slow attitude (Rozgonyi and Lengyel, 2010).

The Hungarian Parliament set the start-date for digital terrestrial broadcasting as 2008 and the deadline for the completion of switchover as 31 December 2011 (Urbán, 2008). Tendering for the role of managing the digital terrestrial multiplexes was undertaken by the NHH and a Parliamentary Committee. They awarded the job to the organisation responsible for terrestrial transmission, Antenna Hungária (AH), which had been privatised and acquired by the former French transmission provider, TDF. On a first multiplex AH would offer a service of simulcasts and new free-to-view channels, which it branded *MinDig*, and these would be complemented by *MinDig Extra* pay services on the second (and later a third) multiplex. MPEG-4 compression was adopted with HDTV in mind. AH's licence terms included a range of provisions relating to switchover management and communications.

Progress was slow for a number of reasons, including the macroeconomic climate. AH had difficulty finding new free-to-view services. Negotiations to bring RTL-Klub and TV-2 proved protracted and the two companies had little regulatory scope for introducing attractive new digital channels (Rozgonyi and Lengyel, 2010). So the *MinDig* free-to-view TV offer consisted of simulcasts of the public and commercial analogue channels plus different language versions of Euronews. In 2010 Viktor Orbán's new right-wing government introduced a major reform of Hungary's media creating a new media authority to replace the NHH and ORTT, but sparking a major row over government control of the news media.

By the end of 2011, when digital switchover had been scheduled to be complete, *MinDig's* digital transmission coverage had reached an impressive 98%. Consumer take-up of receivers in the market, however, lagged: only around 35% of the households dependent on terrestrial reception were equipped. For both practical and political reasons the analogue switch-off date was postponed to 2014.

### Russia

Russia is both a huge television market, with around 50 million TV homes, and a very complex one with a diverse population spread across nine time zones. The country is divided into five broadcasting areas, with time-shifted national services. While satellite and cable subscription services have proliferated in recent years, the great majority of households still rely on analogue terrestrial television, either with their own aerial or via a collectively funded mast. However, not all such homes receive the same number of analogue channels. There are significant differences according to geography: while 98.8% of the population receive one channel, only 33% can receive five (J'son and Partners, 2011).

While free to choose whatever set of technical standards for digital terrestrial television it wished, Russia selected the European DVB system: its analogue technology used the French SECAM system and its European neighbours were all committed to DVB. As a relatively late starter it was able to adopt the newer DVB-T2 standard (with MPEG-4 compression), giving greater multiplex capacity and facilitating HDTV (Broadband TV News, 2011a).

Russia's approach to digital switchover was first mapped out in 2007–2008 with the publication of a 'Concept Paper for the Development of TV and Radio Broadcasting in the Russian Federation in 2008–15'. The target was to achieve digital switchover by 2015 in line with the deadline agreed for ITU Region 1. The conceptual strategy led to a National Programme for the Development of Television and Radio Broadcasting in 2009–2015 whose objective was to create an integrated information environment to cultivate intellectual and cultural development and stimulate the economy, as well as to maintain social stability and advance civic society. Commenting on these aims Vlad Strukov added:

> The implementation of this programme was prompted not only by ideology but also because of national security reasons, particularly by the need to compete for broadcasting frequencies in borderline regions: the document overtly refers to a threat posed to Russian national interests in frontier territories, naming such former Russian adversaries as Ukraine, China and the Baltic States.
>
> (Strukov, 2011)

Under the national strategy there would initially be three digital terrestrial multiplexes. The first would be developed over the period 2009–2013 and the second and third would follow. Transmission would be the responsibility of the Russian Television and Radio Broadcasting Network (RTRN), a federal state enterprise.

The key political decision, made by a Decree of the President, was the content on the first multiplex which was to be broadcast on a mandatory basis throughout the country, free of charge to households, and transmitted on a 'must carry' basis by satellite and cable services. The detailed composition of this multiplex changed somewhat between 2009 and 2012 as eight channels expanded to ten but the grip of the state was clear. Four TV channels (covering news, information, culture and sport) would be provided by the state-owned media conglomerate VGTRK (All-Russia Government Television and Radio Company) and a further VGTRK channel, Karusel, would provide a service for children and young people. Two additional channels named were Pervyi Kanal (51% owned by the government) and NTV (owned by Gazprom-Media which in turn was owned by Gazprom, in which the state had a 51% holding). A further channel owned by the city government of Moscow was named later.

Thus the mandatory free-to-view channels were essentially subject to Russian state control and the decision-making process by-passed the semi-independent Federal Competition Commission (Richter, 2010). Ensuring that information and culture are state-managed remained as central to Russia's digital broadcasting future as it was to its analogue past. Legislative changes in 2011 tightened government control of the licensing process in a number of respects but a 2012 decree set out a legal framework for establishing a 'Public Television of Russia' which was added as a tenth service to the list of mandatory national channels (Richter, 2012).

While the firm hand of the state is shaping digital switchover, digital technology will bring an increase in the total number and range of other services. Satellite and cable subscription continues to grow. The second digital terrestrial multiplex will contain ten national channels and this time the channels were selected by the Federal Competition Commission. The third multiplex will include municipal channels with regional service areas. The selection of channels to be licensed will be made against a set of criteria including ratings, 24-hour service and 'social importance'. While the full picture has yet to emerge, in 2012 Andrei Richter judged that:

> Based on current evidence, television policies in Russia tend to consolidate the power of the executive to rule the broadcasting spectrum and 'make order' in the array of broadcasters that exist at national and especially regional level.
>
> (Richter, 2012: 283)

The Ministry of Communications and Mass Media has said that, if 95% of the population are not equipped to receive digital television by 2015, then analogue transmissions will continue in parallel. Given the sheer scale of the switchover task and the low consumer purchasing power among some sectors of Russian society, this is thought to be a very possible outcome (J'son and Partners, 2011). Securing the right frequencies for the post-analogue era and avoiding cross-border interference in frontier areas is much more important than tidily switching off every analogue home across the huge Russian land-mass.

## Europe heads for 2015

Across Europe as a whole, however, national governments have committed to meeting the ITU Region 1 deadline of 2015. The great majority of the European Union's 27 full member states met the EU's recommended target of the end of 2012, with Slovakia managing it just at the last minute. The exceptions were Hungary, Poland, Romania, Bulgaria and Greece, all of whom aim to complete before the end of 2015. Elsewhere, Iceland has a digital MMDS (Multi-channel Multipoint Distribution Service) in the Greater Reykjavik area serving around 80% of the country's households, plus two digital terrestrial television multiplexes, and analogue terrestrial switch-off is planned for the end of 2014. Ukraine experimented extensively with DVB-T technology before opting for DVB-T2 and planning a phased analogue switch-off ending in 2015. Belarus and Moldova are both targeting 2015, with much still to do.

Progress also proved patchy in the Balkans, with Macedonia on course for analogue terrestrial switch-off, Albania following but Montenegro and Bosnia struggling to put practical plans in place. While its neighbour Croatia decided on a rapid transition based on DVB-T and MPEG-2 technology, Serbia decided to adopt DVB-T2 and MPEG-4. It devised a switchover strategy underpinned by a legal framework but implementation proved slow, partly due to the difficulty of imposing digital order on the chaos of its analogue spectrum management. For most countries digital switchover represented an opportunity to increase the number of broadcasting services: for Serbia, which had allowed an uncontrolled and unregulated growth of channels in the 1990s, the challenge was how to reduce them. A slow build-out of the transmitter network and delays in settling the subsidy policy for receivers also contributed to Serbia's decision to postpone analogue switch-off until 2015. In 2011 a trans-national cooperation programme for South-East Europe, co-funded by the European Union, was initiated to help shepherd the Balkan countries towards a successful completion of switchover by the ITU deadline.

Albeit with a few stragglers, Europe has broadly achieved a well-coordinated approach to digital switchover. In terrestrial television the countries of Western Europe which embarked on the transition first are moving to the second generation of technology, DVB-T2 and MPEG-4 with HDTV, while several of the later starters have been able to go straight to this point. Television viewing showed increases not only in the UK but in Italy, Spain, Germany and France too.

In Western Europe 4G mobile broadband has been established in the 800 MHz band spectrum freed by analogue terrestrial switch-off. At a high-level of simplification the spectrum divide in terms of use which is beginning to emerge in the UHF band in Europe can be represented in the Figure below:

| TV broadcasting | Shared telecoms & TV: used for 4G |
|---|---|
| Channels 21–60 (470–790 MHz) | Channels 61–69 (790–862 MHz) |

*Figure 4.1* Emerging pattern of UHF spectrum use in Europe

However, as we shall see, a further ITU Region 1 conference scheduled for 2015 could start to take the switch of spectrum from broadcasting to telecommunications further still, opening the 700 MHz band to wireless broadband.

# 5
# The Wider Global Picture

## Summary of the chapter's argument

In contrast to Europe's digital switchovers coordinated around the ITU Region 1 deadline of 2015, the rest of the world is making the transition over a much more protracted period. In ITU Regions 2 and 3 the advanced economies of Canada, Japan, South Korea, Taiwan, Australia and New Zealand have completed, or will complete, their transitions in parallel with the Region 1 timetable. China and India, for different reasons, have both concentrated in the first instance on digitising their cable TV infrastructure. For countries which are still at a relatively early stage in the process a major issue has been the choice of technical standards, with competition between the American ATSC, the European DVB, the Japanese ISDB (Integrated Services Digital Broadcasting), the Chinese DTMB (Digital Terrestrial Multi-media Broadcasting) and a Brazilian variant of Japanese technology, SBTVD-T. A pattern of regional groupings has emerged: South-East Asia, Australasia and Africa have broadly adopted the DVB standard while South American countries have coalesced around Brazil's SBTVD-T. Central America and the Caribbean countries are being tugged in different directions.

Many ITU Region 2 and 3 countries will not complete the digital transition for many years – thus switchover will have a 'long tail'. Region 1 countries in the Middle East and Africa who miss the 2015 deadline, when protection of analogue terrestrial transmissions from interference will cease, will be able to cope. In the Middle East terrestrial television has a limited role and the dominant platform is satellite. In Africa bilateral agreements can resolve any cross-border interference problems.

The Middle East and African countries have pressed for the 700 MHz band to be made available for wireless mobile in Region 1, in line with the emerging pattern in Regions 2 and 3. They see mobile as their main route into broadband. While developing countries with relatively few TV channels may well be able to secure enough spectrum to expand wireless mobile without having to switch off analogue terrestrial first, in the end digital TV will displace analogue TV across the globe.

## Outside Europe

Across the wider globe the pattern of digital switchover, not surprisingly, is more varied. ITU Region 1 is not confined to Europe: it also includes the Middle East, Africa and Mongolia. Their characteristics, economically and in respect of television, form a contrast both with Europe and with one another. Several, possibly including Mongolia, will achieve switchover by the ITU Region 1 2015 deadline; others have started but will find they have not allowed enough time; while a third group have yet to complete their planning. However, the implications of missing 2015 are less serious for the Middle East and Africa than for Europe. Television in the Middle East is predominantly satellite-based and, while African countries attach more importance to terrestrial transmission, the number of TV channels and the level of penetration are limited. Cross-border interference from one country's digital services to another's analogue could probably be managed by bilateral discussions.

ITU Region 2 (the Americas and Greenland) and ITU Region 3 (Asia and Australasia) are both very diverse. Advanced economies – including Japan, South Korea, Taiwan, Canada, Australia and New Zealand – have completed, or will complete, their transitions in parallel with the Region 1 timetable. China and India, for different reasons, represent special cases. A cluster of developing countries have embarked on switchover with the probability of completing it before or soon after 2020. Finally, at the far end of the spectrum lie under-developed countries for whom digital television yet has no priority but who will ultimately be drawn into it.

Outside Europe (where the DVB standards were adopted universally), the wider globe, especially ITU Regions 2 and 3, has seen technological and commercial competition between the purveyors of rival technical standards. The biggest countries, in terms of their domestic TV receiver market, were able to formulate their own standards, which they then sought to sell to others in competition with America's ATSC and Europe's DVB systems, in order to enlarge their markets for transmission and reception equipment and attract royalties. Meanwhile, the DVB, to be followed later by the ATSC, developed second generation standards with improved performance. Smaller countries, unable to support technical standards of their own but with an increasing choice of others, found they could gain negotiating power as buyers by collaborating in regional groupings.

## Japan

Japan had been wrong-footed by the American development of digital television and Europe's decision to follow suit. It had achieved its original national goal – jointly pursued by the government, the consumer electronics companies and Japan's national public service broadcaster, NHK – to develop high-definition satellite television, but it had done so in analogue. NHK was broadcasting two 24 hour analogue satellite television channels, funded by a supplementary viewers' fee, and they had been joined by a commercial pay-TV service with the brash name of WOWOW. Together these services successfully drove take-up in the market. But Japan's ambitions for this achievement to become the foundation for a global HDTV standard were in ruins. Japan had tried hard to sell the Americans its analogue Hi-Vision system, modified for terrestrial transmission, in preference to the fledgling digital prototypes they were testing, but to no avail. Commercially, analogue HD was now a cul-de-sac and Japan's massive investment in analogue Hi-Vision had proved a false start.

Japanese receiver manufacturers, with their multi-national global businesses, swiftly positioned themselves to manufacture digital receivers for the United States and European markets but Japan was too proud a country to adopt either the American or the European technical standard itself. With some 48 million TV households and over 100 million TV sets, and as home to leading consumer electronics giants, it could support a separate set of standards of its own. So, with government encouragement, Japan's broadcasters and manufacturers developed their own set of digital television technical standards, called ISDB, embracing digital satellite, digital cable, digital terrestrial, data-casting, multi-media and mobile services. The Japanese maximised the technical compatibility of their standards for digital satellite (ISDB-S) and digital terrestrial (ISDB-T) television, to facilitate the manufacture of HDTV sets which could handle both forms of reception. Their digital terrestrial technical design also supported mobile television, with reception on hand-held mini-TVs or on mobile telephones.

Digital satellite grew up alongside the analogue satellite services, first on an international communications satellite from a pay-TV venture called Sky PerfecTV, and then, from 2000, from Japan's direct-to-home satellite, with services from NHK and a range of commercial broadcasters. An open market in digital satellite receivers developed, with tuners either built into, or sold to accompany, large flat-screen TVs. However, by the time these government-licensed digital satellite services were launched, NHK had built up over 10 million supplementary fee-paying households on analogue satellite, so Japan now faced a legacy problem here. Analogue satellite services continued until 2011.

Meanwhile, starting in 2003, Japan launched digital terrestrial HDTV and committed to analogue terrestrial switch-off in 2011 as well. Since it was initially impractical to find new frequencies for digital terrestrial television, a government-financed scheme had first to be implemented to reorganise the current analogue terrestrial frequencies: over 4 million homes need to be visited for TV retuning (Starks, 2007: 166). Digital terrestrial licences were awarded to NHK and the incumbent terrestrial broadcasters with an obligation to simulcast 85% of their analogue output and provide 50% of their services in high-definition. HD was, of course, an attraction to the consumer electronics industry and it also required so much spectrum that no new broadcasters could enter the market at that stage.

The commitment to accomplish digital switchover by 2011 was ambitious. Japan's population is densely crowded, with a high level of communal reception via cable and master-antenna relay systems. Moreover, the terrain is mountainous, requiring some 15,000 small relay transmitters. Receiver take-up was initially slower than planned, partly because of HD set costs. However, the combination of government leadership, cross-industry collaboration, a receiver promotion scheme and some subsidising of communal aerial systems brought progress back on target – until the earthquake and tsunami disaster of March 2011. At that point completion of switchover had to be postponed in three prefectures but, across the rest of the country, it was achieved according to plan (Kumabe, 2012a).

Full completion followed in 2012. The released spectrum was in both the VHF and UHF bands and its new uses included multi-media broadcasts to mobile devices. Japan marketed its ISDB technology to South America and to the Philippines and Maldives. Its next ambition is to launch Super Hi-Vision, with a resolution 16 times higher than HDTV, initially for large-screen public viewing. Another development is Hybridcast, a system for combining digital terrestrial television and Internet sources on a 'smart' (or Connected) TV set (Kumabe, 2012b). 3-D television is also being researched. Japan may have entered the field of digital television later than other leading countries but it has returned to the forefront of technology innovation – as it needs to, given the challenge to its consumer electronics companies from China, South Korea and Taiwan.

## China

China provides one of the most interesting case studies of digital switchover on account of its distinctive combination of market-led growth and political control. Its motives for switching its television services to digital technology stemmed both from its broader industrial policy and from its desire to manage the information and communication flows among its people. Releasing analogue terrestrial spectrum for other purposes was not initially a priority.

China's dramatic growth over the last quarter of a century, critically linked to its export market, has increased per capita income hugely, raising hundreds of millions of people out of poverty. It has also stimulated a massive migration from the countryside to the country's burgeoning cities, increasing inequalities between urban and rural areas. While Maoist egalitarianism has been overturned, the Communist Party's grip on broadcasting and communications remains strong, as it strives to perpetuate its role and safeguard the national integrity of an increasingly diverse 1.3 billion population against the kind of centrifugal forces which broke up the Soviet Union.

China has over 380 million TV households, with television reaching around 97% of the population, and around 2000 TV channels, largely financed by advertising, but with one owner, the state. Supervision is carried out by the State Administration of Radio, Film and Television (SARFT), which also licenses programme production companies. Central China Television (CCTV) is the dominant force at national level with a dozen channels. Then every province and autonomous region mounts its own broadcasts, including one satellite channel available for distribution across the whole country. In addition cities have their own local TV channels and county stations act as relays.

Television transmission relies on a mix of technologies. Satellite technology is extensively used for distributing services to cable head-ends and terrestrial transmitters, but direct-to-home satellite reception (DTH) is limited in scope. DTH services began to be beamed into China from abroad in the 1990s but, since direct reception of foreign broadcasts would threaten state control of television content, China's response was a regulation banning the ownership of DTH reception satellite dishes without a special licence. Licences were in practice largely restricted to hotels and foreign compounds, though in many rural areas without an alternative way of receiving Chinese domestic services the regulations were not seriously enforced.

Cable reception of satellite services, however, provided a filter between the broadcaster and the viewer through which control could be exercised. So when Hong Kong-based Phoenix Television, partly owned by STAR, launched a range of Mandarin services in 1996, it was able to reach agreement for these to be received via cable in neighbouring Guangdong province. Since then cable TV has blossomed in China and is now the norm in most Chinese cities, accounting for over 150 million households. Elsewhere in China, among the rural households which account for the majority of the population, reception comes mainly from terrestrial transmitters and small local relay systems fed by satellite distribution.

Since the switch to digital television significantly increases the number of programme channels, the Chinese government faced the question of how to expand TV content on such a scale without losing political control and, in the absence of latent consumer spending power among the great majority of Chinese households, how to pay for it. Indeed, given that access to released spectrum was not such a strong driver as in many other countries, why would China adopt a digital switchover policy at all?

Part of the answer lay in Chinese ambition to modernise the economy and acquire new competencies in the high-tech field: this is the country which in 2008 put men into space. More specifically, digital television is strategically important to Chinese industry. China had become the world's largest manufacturer of TV sets and the global switch to digital transmission was transforming this business, as analogue TV sets became obsolete in the advanced economies of the world. China's major players in the industry – such as TCL Group (a joint venture partner of the French company Thomson), Changhong Electric, Konka Group and Xiamen Overseas Chinese Electronics – could ill afford to fall behind. Remaining with analogue technology for the long term would have meant being tied to a shrinking market. On the other hand, digital switchover around the world represented a beckoning export opportunity, since countries planning their national transitions endeavoured to minimise the compulsory cost to their citizens and looked to China as a prime source of low-cost mass production of receivers.

The Chinese swiftly acquired the skills to make set-top boxes incorporating American, European and Japanese technical standards. However, with its own huge domestic market in mind, China decided to develop its own set of technical standards for digital terrestrial television which, unlike satellite and cable technology, is normally integrated into TV sets. As well as deterring rivals from seeking to enter China's domestic market, this would reduce the need to buy intellectual property from foreign companies. Designing the Chinese standard involved some rivalry between initially incompatible systems developed by Qinghua University in Beijing and Jiaotong University in Shanghai, which had to be incorporated into a combined Chinese DTMB standard.

However, replacing analogue terrestrial by digital terrestrial television was not China's main focus. Instead, it concentrated on converting its metropolitan and urban cable systems from analogue to digital, for which 2015 is the completion target. Here the motive was to increase, and also to control, the dissemination of information in the interests of creating and guiding a 'harmonious society' (Starks, 2010). The Communist Party leadership appreciated that a policy of withholding information from China's huge population of increasingly well-educated urban citizens could never work, yet it set its face against the conflict and discord which it associated with an open market in information and opinion. So it aimed to manage the public communication process – for which cable television, where the services supplied to every home can be identified and monitored, was well-suited.

Analogue cable systems in major cities could carry as many as 40 TV channels, including satellite channels from provinces right across the country, for a low basic subscription, though programme content was thin, with a lot of duplication between services (Chin, 2007). New digital cable services added a locally relevant government data channel providing public service information – covering topics like transport, health and social services – but not a whole range of new content from new sources, so cable households did not rush to sign up for new digital set-top boxes at higher subscription rates. Additional pay-TV options were available but were specialised and of limited appeal since the content potentially most attractive for a premium pay tier, sport and movies, remained part of the basic subscription service. Otherwise digital cable mainly meant more channels from the usual sources. So the pre-conditions for a market-led switch to digital through voluntary consumer spending were lacking.

An ambitious national timetable was nonetheless set. The major cities, including all the provincial capitals and all the cities in the east, were given a switchover deadline of 2005. Counties in the east, and the cities and most of the counties in the central region, as well as some cities in the west, were expected to switch by 2008. The target for the remaining counties in the central region and most of the counties in the west was 2010, with 2015 as the date for completion in the remaining counties in the west.

Slippage soon began. The 2005 target was missed and the government response was to begin making digital switchover compulsory, starting in small cities. Instead of being sold a new service package, consumers were informed that their systems would be modernised with a modest increase in the charge. The basic idea was to install one new digital set-top box per household for free and to control subscription increases strictly to guard against any significant consumer revolt. Cable companies were offered the regulatory carrot of a subsidy or soft loan and urged to invest, with a hint that the alternative could be an end to their monopoly status. Different forms of incentive were offered in different cities and provinces but, essentially, a major part of the cost was carried by the state and/or state-owned banks.

Meanwhile China had streamlined its telecommunications industry by reducing the number of operators from six to three, as the government began showing increasing interest in technology convergence. In 2010 the idea of 'three-network convergence' – enabling providers to offer television, telephony and the Internet services over a unified network – became a policy goal, with 12 cities and regions selected for trials (Hu and Hong, 2011). The government envisaged the prospect of telecommunications and cable operators entering one another's markets. While the telecommunications industry had been consolidated, the cable industry was fragmented into over 1000 decentralised companies. Frustrated by their patchy progress to full digitalisation and aware of the potential telecoms competition, SARFT proposed the creation of a national cable TV network with funding coming from both the government and the companies (China Daily, 2010). The government's goal is to combine television, telecoms and Internet networks by 2015.

Digital terrestrial television had none of the prominence it acquired in western countries and in Japan, except in Hong Kong where, for historical reasons, terrestrial reception was much more important, accounting for the majority of the 2.3 million households. Here implementation of digital terrestrial began in 2008, ahead of the Chinese Olympics The two main terrestrial broadcasters, TVB and ATV, started simulcasting their analogue services and added new digital-only channels, including HDTV. The services were free-to-view. Two types of set-top box were marketed with no subsidy: the cheaper version offered standard definition and the more expensive could display high-definition on an

HDTV-ready flat-screen TV set. Take-up rose rapidly from 9% to 20% over the summer of 2008. On the mainland only a showcase multiplex, managed by SARFT, was available during the Beijing Olympics.

Digital terrestrial implementation subsequently began in earnest, as did mobile digital transmissions, but terrestrial reception is seen as in decline. China has some 60,000 transmitters, many in mountainous terrain, and the prospect of converting them all is daunting. While direct-to-home satellite might seem a more appropriate technology for some rural areas, technology policy is subject to political considerations.

A state-owned DTH digital satellite company, offering a service of 25 TV channels and excluding foreign stations, was set up to provide digital TV to remote areas without TV coverage and may become the basis for a wider policy. The set-top boxes cannot receive signals from other satellites and the signals will not be available in urban areas where they could further threaten the economics of digital cable.

China's digital television switchover process thus shows a number of distinctive characteristics, including the transfer of political control from the analogue to the digital framework. The policy has also entailed an extensive use of state resources, disproportionately benefitting city dwellers and compounding the risk of an urban–rural 'digital divide'.

## South Korea

With Japan and China both promoting rival sets of technical standards, no clear regional pattern was likely to emerge in Asia, but South Korea is the only Asian country to have opted for the American ATSC technology. South Korea's analogue TV system was based on American NTSC analogue technology and it launched digital terrestrial television in 2001 (the first Asian nation to do so) before either the Japanese or the Chinese standards had been finalised. Its technical choice back then was essentially between ATSC and the European DVB system.

Having opted for ATSC, the country began to have second thoughts. Doubts about whether the ATSC system might prove technically inferior to DVB technology led to a prolonged period of debate, comparative tests and trials. At the time very few ATSC receivers had been sold but Korean receiver manufacturing companies, such as LG, had made a major investment in ATSC technology, so the outcome after much delay was a decision to stick with it. Only in 2008 did the full digital transition policy take shape, with the passage of the Digital Switchover Act setting the deadline for analogue terrestrial switch-off by the end of 2012 (Jung, 2010).

Since cable accounted for the great majority of Korean TV households and less than 10% of homes relied on terrestrial reception, the timetable was a feasible one. The Korea Communication Commission was formed as a converged regulator and drew up the Basic Plan. An Implementation Committee for Facilitating Digital Switchover was formed. The government took initiatives to mandate digital tuners in TV sets and to provide assistance to the elderly, disabled and low-income households. It also encouraged the digitisation of South Korea's extensive cable network on a voluntary basis.

Terrestrial households grumbled that they were not being offered an attractive new range of services. Concerns were also expressed about reductions in the digital switchover budget and concerns about the costs and logistics of converting multi-occupation housing (Jung, 2010). Nonetheless, South Korea duly completed analogue terrestrial switch-off at the end of 2012.

## DVB adoption in Asia

South Korea's neighbour Taiwan also started from an American NTSC analogue base. At the outset, in 1998, the government therefore selected ATSC as Taiwan's digital standard. However, the Association of Terrestrial Television Networks in Taiwan commissioned Tatung University to conduct tests in 2001 on the ATSC's and DVB's comparative technological performance. The verdict was that the ATSC system experienced interference problems both in the highly urbanised cities and remote mountainous regions of Taiwan. The government adopted a technology-neutral stance and left the decision to the broadcasters and the latter opted for DVB-T (Ko, Chang and Chu, 2011). Trials began in 2002 and a free-to-view digital terrestrial television service was launched in 2004. Helped by a rapid expansion of cable TV and the arrival of IPTV, both of which helped reduce the number of analogue terrestrial homes requiring conversion to digital terrestrial, Taiwan completed analogue switch-off in 2012.

Elsewhere in Asia, DVB terrestrial technical standards have been widely adopted. While the Philippines were attracted by the Japanese ISDB system, the Association of South-East Asian Nations (ASEAN) as a group selected DVB technology. Thus it has been embraced by Indonesia, Malaysia, Thailand, Singapore, Burma, Brunei, Cambodia, Laos and Vietnam, with the first five of these countries all deciding to adopt DVB-T2. Meanwhile Brunei aims to complete analogue switch-off in 2014. Most other ASEAN countries have named dates between 2015 and 2017.

## India

In South Asia DVB standards have been chosen by India, Sri Lanka, Bangladesh and Nepal. India has its own distinctive approach to digital switchover. Since the 1990s the country has seen a huge burgeoning of satellite TV channels and it now has around 500. Backed by strong advertising revenue, they provide news services in a range of languages and entertainment channels reflecting synergies with the Bollywood film industry. Only the public broadcaster, Doordarshan, uses analogue terrestrial transmission.

Around three-quarters of Indian households are served by cable and satellite (and satellite dishes can be seen atop the corrugated iron roofs of Mumbai's slums), but that still leaves a daunting 40 million households, predominantly poor, relying on terrestrial reception for Doordarshan (Bhat, 2012). While the transmission implications of ending analogue terrestrial are relatively straightforward, funding the reception side presents a major difficulty.

However, turning off analogue terrestrial is not the Indian government's priority. Its focus is on converting its sprawling analogue cable industry to digital. The motive here, at least in part, is to keep up with modern technology: India has been looking over its shoulder at the spread of digital cable in China. However, another factor is a desire to impose order on the country's 50,000 or so cable operators. The operators are obliged to pay revenue to the broadcasters and taxes to the government based on the number of their subscribers. Analogue cable is fed unencrypted straight into the back of TV sets, with no set-top boxes, so no check can be made on cable operators who under-report their subscriber numbers. The addressable digital cable set-top box is therefore expected to provide benefits not only to the cable viewer but also to the broadcasters and government.

The cable companies themselves proved less highly motivated. The government required the operators in the major metropolitan areas of Delhi, Mumbai, Kolkata and Chennai to switch fully to digital distribution by the end of June 2012 but by May only about 25% of cable homes in the four cities had been converted, so the deadline was postponed.

## Australia

Australia's initially unsuccessful foray into digital television, using DVB technology but following a strategy modelled in many respects on the early American approach, has already been described in Chapter 2.

Only 28% of Australian homes had switched to digital by 2007 and the Australian government had to abandon its 2008 switch-off date. Nonetheless, it retained the goal, not least because financing the simulcast transmissions of the public services was expensive for the government. A new Digital Action Plan was drawn up to address the problem of lack of attractive content. This allowed the broadcasters to use their HDTV channels for broadcasting new material. Moreover, the commercial broadcasters would each be permitted to launch an additional standard definition channel from 2009. Content restrictions on the public service digital channels would be eased and new data-casting and mobile developments licensed (García Leiva and Starks, 2009).

The aim was for new content to drive the set-top box market. Coincidentally, HDTV was coming of age with the growing popularity in the market of new large-size flat-screen TVs. Ownership changes in one of the major commercial broadcasters helped create a shift in attitude and, where previously commercial TV had dragged its feet on digital promotion, business strategies now began to be based on the expectation of analogue switch-off. In 2008, having observed the rapid recovery of digital terrestrial TV in the UK, Australia's free-to-view broadcasters formed a *Freeview* consortium (Given and Norris, 2010). The period 2009–2010 saw a blossoming of new public and commercial services:

> Ten launched a dedicated high-definition sports service, One HD, in March 2009, Nine an entertainment service, GO!, mid-year and Seven a second channel in November. The ABC had re-launched a second channel in 2005 and got special funding in the 2009/10 budget for a third, a children's channel. In January 2010 it announced plans for a fourth, a news and current affairs service. The SBS relaunched its second service, the World News Channel, as SBS 2 in June.
>
> (Given, 2010: 232)

New content and lower prices for attractive flat-screen TVs drove take-up in the market. By early 2009 47% of homes had switched and, having seen the progress in other countries, the government felt able to reschedule analogue switch-off. The process started gently in 2010 with the major regionally phased switch-offs scheduled over 2011, 2012 and 2013. Government assistance was provided to the elderly, veterans and the disabled who could receive a free installation and demonstration of an HDTV set-top box. A government-funded satellite service provided digital services to those outside digital terrestrial coverage areas. Take-up rose steadily with 82% having converted by March 2012

(Australian Government, 2012a). When Sydney and Melbourne complete the switchover process in December 2013, Australia's transition will have taken 13 years – not quite as long as the UK's.

## New Zealand

New Zealand initially left digital technology to the market. New Zealand's Sky satellite service adopted it and, armed with key sports rights contracts, built up a very successful pay-TV business, penetrating over 40% of the country's 1.6 million households. Since the Sky satellite service also carried the main public service and commercial terrestrial channels as well, it in effect commenced the process of digital switchover (within the limits of consumers' willingness to subscribe).

For the government and the terrestrial broadcasters the prospect of digital TV in New Zealand becoming synonymous with Sky satellite TV rang alarm bells. A Cost–Benefit Analysis was commissioned to examine the case for introducing digital terrestrial TV. It showed that the benefits could only justify the costs if analogue terrestrial switch-off followed.

Opting for DVB technology, the government offered digital terrestrial spectrum, without charge until analogue switch-off, to the public service broadcaster TVNZ, to the commercial analogue terrestrial broadcaster Media Works, and to the transmission provider Kordia (who would offer carriage to other terrestrial broadcasters including Maori Television). The government also provided some public funding towards the digital terrestrial simulcast costs of national free-to-view channels and towards two new public service digital channels, TVNZ 6 and TVNZ 7. A *Freeview* consortium was formed, again broadly modelled on the UK concept, to create a single marketing package of free-to-view digital TV and radio services (García Leiva and Starks, 2009).

Terrestrial coverage was initially restricted to 75% of the population, with the possibility of moving up to a higher figure later (Norris, 2010). However, extending digital terrestrial transmission even as high as 90% would clearly have been uneconomic in such a thinly populated and mountainous country. Accordingly, a complementary *Freeview* satellite service was planned from the outset and launched in 2007. Digital terrestrial services were then launched in 2008. By starting late, New Zealand was in a position to use MPEG-4 compression technology and incorporate some HDTV into its *Freeview* digital terrestrial proposition. Analogue switch-off, while a firm goal, was to be when digital take-up reached a threshold of 75% (with free-to-view and pay TV figures combined) or in 2012, whichever came first, with a target date to be named when 60% take-up was achieved.

2008 saw a change in government, from Labour to National, and a very different political attitude towards TVNZ, diminishing its public service role and affecting the funding and nature of its new digital channels (to be discussed further in Chapter 9). On analogue switch-off the new government chose not to set a hard date until 2010 by which time digital take-up had reached 70% (Norris, 2013). At that point the government announced a regionally phased timetable starting in September 2012 and finishing in December 2013. Terrestrial coverage would be extended to 86% and a Targeted Assistance Package provided for elderly and disabled households.

By mid-2012 86% of New Zealand homes had converted to digital TV, with 35% relying solely on *Freeview*. As Paul Norris has noted, this represents a substantial achievement within an analogue switch-off process which has been well-handled (Norris, 2013). It is planned to use spectrum freed in the 700 MHz band for mobile broadband (DigiTAG, 2012a), in line with practice in Japan and the United States.

## Canada

In ITU Region 2, the Americas, Canada followed hard on the heels of the United States. The American ATSC technical standard was adopted. A Task Force looked at digital switchover policy in 1997 and in 2001 the Canadian Radio-television and Telecommunications Commission (CRTC) began a process of consultation. It was never a question of whether Canada would go digital, just how and when:

> The switch was essential to broadcasting policy because if Canada lagged behind, broadcasters risked the loss of viewers tuning into American channels, particularly along the US border.
>
> (Bonin, 2010: 137)

There were a number of differences from the United States transition, however. August 2011 was selected as the completion date but the obligation to replace analogue terrestrial with digital terrestrial applied only to the major transmitters serving Canada's main areas of population (the mandated markets). This reflected the fact that terrestrial reception in Canada accounted for less than 10% of households, and also the sparse population of great tracts of the Canadian land-mass. Outside the mandated markets broadcasters were free to turn off analogue terrestrial, leaving small clusters of viewers to migrate to satellite or cable, or to continue using it until it ultimately withered on the vine. No subsidies were offered to the public. The Canadian transition in this sense was more market-driven than its United States counterpart.

Switchover was completed according to plan, accompanied by a marked shrinkage in terrestrial transmitter coverage, with terrestrial television serving only 5% of Canadian households by 2012. Released spectrum in the 700 MHz band was scheduled for auction in 2013.

## Technology rivalry in the Caribbean

When Mexico too adopted ATSC technology North America formed a coherent regional bloc. Although Mexico chose its technology early, not least because it is a manufacturer of TV sets for the North American market, it was initially in no hurry to complete the digital transition. In 2004 the government allocated digital terrestrial frequencies for simulcasting to the analogue terrestrial incumbents while extending their analogue licences to 2021. In 2010 switchover was brought forward to 2015 but this was later made conditional on 90% digital penetration of free-to-view households (Gómez Garcia and Sosa Plata, 2013).

The ATSC digital standard has also been adopted by Guatemala, Honduras, El Salvador, Puerto Rico and the Dominican Republic. European influences have also been felt in the Caribbean, however. When France switched fully to digital television, so did its overseas territories, including Martinique, French Guiana, Guadeloupe and St Martin. They all used the DVB standard. For the former Dutch territory, St Maarten, on the same island as St Martin, DVB was a natural choice. Curaçao, also a former Dutch territory, and Trinidad and Tobago, a former British colony, adopted DVB technology. A number of other Caribbean countries have yet to decide and can see the attractions of acting as a regional group, through the trade association Caricom. While the obvious choice is between ATSC and DVB, South America has thrown up another contender.

## South America

In technology terms, South America was initially fragmented, torn between the gravitational pull of North America on the one hand and the continent's European heritage on the other. Exploratory moves were made in the 1990s and Argentina's President Menem announced in 1998 that his country would adopt the ATSC standard. However, stakeholder support for this evaporated a few years later when the Spanish telecommunications giant Telefónica began to take an interest in the South American market (García Leiva, 2010). In 2006 Colombia selected DVB and Uruguay looked set to follow.

Brazil, which with some 60 million TV households was an attractive market for receiver manufacturers, was courted by both China and Japan, as well as by American and European interests. The government consulted widely and the newly created regulator ANATEL then supervised the conduct of a series of technical tests from which the Japanese ISDB system emerged as the winner. ISDB-T's suitability for reception on mobile devices was a factor. No decision was taken at that point though and, after the election of President Lula in 2002, another possibility – that of constructing a separate Brazilian standard from scratch – opened up and, with government funding, R&D centres began design work on this. Finally, in 2006 Brazil plumped for a Brazilian variant of Japan's ISDB, to be called SBTVD-T (Brazilian System of Digital Terrestrial Television). Brazil undertook to contribute the interface between the hardware and the software, named Ginga, but otherwise the system was very similar to the parent ISDB. Keen to win its business, Japan had offered to exempt Brazil from royalties and Japan's Bank for International Cooperation volunteered to provide a start-up loan (García Leiva, 2010). The first SBTVD-T digital terrestrial service was launched in 2007 and an analogue switch-off target of 2016 was set.

Brazil's South American neighbours then began to rally to this system, giving South America a coherent regional approach. Argentina had already called a halt to ATSC and Uruguay now backed away from DVB. They both adopted SBTVD-T, as did the previously uncommitted countries of Chile, Peru, Paraguay, Bolivia, Ecuador and Venezuela. With Costa Rica's decision to do likewise, Brazil's hybrid standard spread northwards into central America. Colombia, however, having originally chosen DVB, decided to adopt DVB-T2. Few of these countries pictured themselves switching of analogue terrestrial at an early date. Some, including Brazil, are serious about doing so within the period 2015–2020 but Peru has named an analogue switch-off date of 2023 and Bolivia 2024.

## The Middle East and Africa

Back in ITU Region 1 Israel, Turkey and Iran have all adopted the DVB standard. Israel completed switchover in 2011 and Turkey plans to do so in 2015. The Arab nations of the Middle East, because of the predominance of satellite TV, have for the most part given digital switchover low priority.

Africa shows a wide range of approaches and timescales, though generally DVB technology has been selected, with the DVB's second generation terrestrial standard DVB-T2 emerging as the norm. Mauritius has very largely carried out its switchover and is due to complete in 2013. Other countries making a serious effort to meet the ITU Region 1 2015 commitment include South Africa, Ghana, Nigeria, Kenya, Tanzania and Namibia.

South Africa's original plan was to begin digital simulcasting in 2008 and then switch off analogue terrestrial in 2011. However, in 2010 Brazil attempted to persuade South Africa and its neighbours to overturn their selection of DVB-T and join South America's ISDB-based system (Armstrong and Collins, 2011). In 2011, after much deliberation, South Africa and the Southern Africa Development Community finally settled on DVB-T2. A 'ceremonial launch' took place in 2012 and plans were laid to provide the country's 5 million poorest households with a 70% subsidy of the receiver cost from a fund into which a levy on telecommunications is paid. Meanwhile the South Africa-based company Multichoice is offering pay TV services, both on satellite and digital terrestrial television, widely across the continent.

Ghana investigated a different business model – the idea of a joint venture under which an external partner provides infrastructure investment for digital television transmission in return for access to spectrum benefits. The Chinese pay-TV company Star Times has worked with state broadcasters on digital switchover in a number of countries, obtaining enough channel capacity to launch low-cost pay-TV bundles. In Kenya the Chinese owned firm PAN (Pan-African Network) is constructing the country's second multiplex alongside the state-owned Kenya Broadcasting Corporation's first multiplex.

Television is relatively under-developed in Africa. While there are estimated to be 60 million TV households, around 700 million Africans do not yet have access to the electricity grid (Stirling, 2012). Where prosperity is increasing the market is growing but, perhaps of more significance, so is the market for mobile telephony. By 2011 Africa had over 620 million mobile telephone subscribers and had overtaken Latin America to become the second largest mobile market in the world (after Asia), with an average growth rate over the preceding ten years of 30% p.a. (GSMA and A.T. Kearney, 2011: 5). African countries were quick to see the potential of this market, not just for telephony but also for mobile broadband:

There is scope for developing wireless broadband services, particularly as smart-phones and tablets become more affordable to African consumers. As in other developing markets, wireless technologies are enabling broadband services to be made available far faster than through deployment of wired, fixed networks. Fixed networks are still required, to provide backhaul for the wireless access, but the fixed element of the deployment can be much sparser. Wireless broadband access networks, combined with the falling prices of smart mobile devices, create an excellent opportunity for under-connected Africans to share in the benefits of digital communications and enjoy the transformative effects of the Internet on their economies and societies.

(Stirling, 2012: 340–341)

Since the Middle East and African countries had only modest numbers of analogue terrestrial television channels, and therefore spare spectrum capacity even ahead of digital switchover, and since mobile telephony was already such a growth sector, the idea of transferring spectrum from broadcasting to telecommunications was an appealing one. Africans saw no need to wait till they had completed analogue terrestrial switch-off, nor to limit the potential wireless mobile spectrum to the 800 MHz band. Observing that the 700 MHz band was emerging as a home to mobile broadband in North America, Japan and other countries in ITU Regions 2 and 3 (albeit with different and incompatible band plans), they made a surprise bid at the 2012 World Radiocommunication Conference WRC-12 for ITU Region 1 to open its 700 MHz spectrum to mobile telecommunications (DigiTAG, 2012b). This could potentially harmonise mobile telecoms spectrum across the globe, allowing global roaming and facilitating a cost reduction in the production of handsets. Their proposal – that the 700 MHz band should be open for either broadcasting or mobile use – was accepted in principle, but with an implementation date only after 2015, the practical implications to be worked out in the meantime.

| TV broadcasting | Shared telecoms & TV | Shared telecoms & TV |
|---|---|---|
| Channels 21–48 (470–694 MHz) | Channels 49–60 (694–790 MHz) | Channels 61–69 (790–862 MHz) |

*Figure 5.1*　Long-term goal for UHF spectrum use across the globe?

The complications of relocating television services below 790 MHz in Europe would be challenging, not just in terms of broadcaster resistance and cost but also the avoidance of interference in such a crowded environment. Global harmonisation is therefore unlikely to be achieved swiftly. However, many developing nations now see wireless mobile as their most promising route into broadband (in contrast to the fixed line delivery of most broadband in North America and Europe). They are making their voices heard in international spectrum planning forums and a long-term goal may perhaps be beginning to take shape.

## Completing digital switchover worldwide

Given that developing countries may be able to secure the spectrum they require for mobile telecommunications ahead of switching off their analogue TV, the global digital switchover process will have a 'long tail'. ITU target dates notwithstanding, countries will proceed at their own pace, in tandem with their neighbours when necessary or advantageous. The path will not be smooth: the planning process may turn over stones beneath which lie unlicensed frequency use and copyright infringement, perhaps by politically well-connected broadcasters, leaving regulators daunted and tempted to procrastinate.

However, the technology switch is unlikely to halt. Analogue television transmitters and equipment are becoming obsolete in the developed world: while developing countries may find it easy to acquire them through dumping or one-off sales of redundant stock, in the long run analogue equipment will become more difficult and more expensive. Moreover, countries with very little television at present may well choose to 'leapfrog' into digital technology rather than extend an obsolescent analogue system and build up a legacy problem. The first phase of digital switchovers can be pictured as encompassing the years 2006 to the ITU Region 1 deadline of 2015. The next phase may cover a period as far ahead as 2030 but in the end the digital TV revolution will be worldwide.

# Part II
# Shaping the Outcomes

# 6
# How to Switch Off Analogue TV

## Summary of the chapter's argument

With the vital caveat that there is no 'one-size-fits-all' tool-kit, it is possible to draw out principles from the diverse national experiences described in Part I.

The starting-point for a digital switchover policy should be a wide-ranging public consultation and any necessary legislation, which could include creating a 'converged' regulator responsible for both broadcasting and telecommunications.

Even in countries where terrestrial reception has a very modest role, the policy is likely to include the launching of digital terrestrial television and the simulcasting of the analogue terrestrial services due to be withdrawn. To facilitate analogue switch-off, consumers need to be offered a free-to-view option, with receivers available at affordable prices in the open market. Notwithstanding the early crises in the UK and Spain, hybrid systems of digital terrestrial TV including both free-to-view and pay-TV can work.

In countries where terrestrial reception is dominant, high digital penetration achieved during the period of voluntary take-up is important as a pre-condition of switchover, since this reduces the number of households whose main TV set is likely to be analogue at the point of compulsion. Such take-up does not have to be exclusively digital terrestrial: other platforms can contribute if they carry digital versions of the analogue terrestrial services to be shut.

A Cost–Benefit Analysis can illuminate the funding issues. Subsidy can play a contributory role, especially in the closing stage of compulsory switchover, though it needs to be carefully designed to avoid unfairly favouring the terrestrial platform. A 'pure market' model without any subsidy is likely to prove elusive. Ingenuity is needed to incentivise those incurring most cost with least benefit.

Close collaboration between the principal stakeholders – the government, regulators, broadcasters, transmission providers, receiver manufacturers and retailers, and consumer representatives – is essential in order to reduce the risks to all parties.

## Learning from experience

Having recounted the saga of different countries' quests for a successful route to full digital switchover and noted the global trend, can we now answer the question 'How does a country carry out digital TV switchover?'

Part I of the book has revealed huge differences between countries. The most obvious commercial variables include market size, market maturity, the balance between terrestrial and satellite and cable platforms, latent consumer demand for new TV services and the pressures on spectrum. Relevant political differences include the nature of the government and the degree of its involvement in broadcasting, regulatory readiness, the role of publicly funded television and the attitude towards public expenditure in this field. Moreover, the pioneers were in the advanced and relatively wealthy economies of the United States and Western Europe, which limits the applicability of their learning points to less developed countries. The latter, however, starting later, can benefit from more mature higher-performance technology.

Any attempt to produce a step-by-step handbook would risk oversimplification but, that said, there is a need to codify some broad principles, both to guide policy-makers and to provide civil society with an informed level of understanding.

Digital switchover cannot be designed by following precedents from other cases. It is different from the switch to the 625 line system and colour television: in that case, retention of the old 405 line technology was not a barrier to the spread of the new and the timetable for completing the process was very gentle. It differs from the national programme to install North Sea Gas in every household in the UK in the late 1960s because that job was done by a central body which supplied and installed the consumer equipment without charge. It is not like the replacement of leaded petrol with unleaded, which was gradual, without a prominent switching date. Preparing all computer systems for the Year 2000 (Y2K) had a common date and an onus on every system owner to take remedial action, but the date was set by the calendar and not by politicians risking their popularity. Digital television switchover policy is, therefore, *sui generis* and the main source of learning for the next wave of countries has to be such principles as can be derived from the first wave.

## The starting-point

The starting-point in formulating a national digital switchover policy should be a wide-ranging consultation, explaining the issues and the implications and inviting responses. Key industry stakeholders, whose cooperation is essential, will welcome the opportunity to express their concerns and suggestions at the outset. So too will the viewing public, whose cooperation is equally essential and who in practice will probably collectively bear the lion's share of the cost. Every household wishing to continue to watch television after analogue switch-off will have to acquire, willingly or unwillingly, a digital set-top box (as a converter) or a new digital TV set. The consumer costs could extend well beyond a requirement to adapt the main TV set: all the additional analogue TV sets in the home are affected, as are the capabilities of analogue video-cassette recorders. In some cases new aerials could be required: the digital signal may be robust but at the margin it is less forgiving than analogue, so a ghostly analogue picture might be replaced by no picture at all. Communal systems, whether in blocks of flats, hotels, schools or prisons, all need to be converted.

Given the political and practical difficulties, it is only natural to ask 'why have a policy at all?' and this is perhaps the first question the public consultation process needs to address. Why not leave the transition entirely to the market? This is likely to be the perspective of many consumers, of commercial TV companies who see no advantage in it, and perhaps of politicians in countries where digital television, compared to much more pressing economic and social needs, seems an unimportant luxury.

It is indeed an option not to have a switchover policy, but simply to allow broadcasters and the receiver industry to make their own transitions to digital at their own pace, without any political coordination and without any hurry. The main drawback of this course is the postponement of spectrum release. There could be an excessively long period of inefficient spectrum use, with an open-ended long-term problem of protecting analogue terrestrial transmissions, so far as international developments permit, with corresponding constraints on digital development.

Also, under this 'do nothing' scenario, digital television will in practice arrive from internationally based satellite TV, broadcast direct to the home or delivered by cable, leaving domestic (including public service) television declining with an obsolescent analogue infrastructure. While for some policy-makers this may be entirely acceptable, others, wishing perhaps to safeguard their national language, their domestic TV production base and/or the educational and cultural contributions made by their national public service television, will want to see their own national broadcasting system updated.

A third consideration is the inevitability of the technology change now that so many countries have adopted it and with ITU Region 1 deciding to withdraw protection from analogue terrestrial TV in 2015. Mobile telephony and wireless broadband are growing apace, pushing for more frequencies and for standardised bands of spectrum across the world. Analogue terrestrial transmission networks wear out and, when they do so, replacing them with more analogue equipment will seem short-sighted – and very possibly more expensive than switching to digital transmitters. Since the change is coming anyway, it is generally better to manage an orderly transition. *Ad hoc* development through uncoordinated commercial initiatives is likely to lead to the breakdown of interoperability, so that different receivers are required to view the services of different broadcasters.

So the desirable outcome of an initial phase of explanation and consultation is a recognition that a digital television transition is going to happen anyway and that there are political, social and economic gains to be had in making it orderly, well-managed and fair. That clears the way to consideration of the next issues of 'how?' and 'when?'.

## Legislative and regulatory framework

In most countries some form of legislation will probably be required, depending on the legal basis for broadcasting: the end-dates for analogue terrestrial licences may need to be amended. Some initial reform of the regulatory organisation may also be advisable. Many countries at the start find themselves with separate regulatory bodies for broadcasting and telecommunications – the United States being a long-standing exception with its Federal Communications Commission (FCC) covering both. With the two technologies now converging, it is increasingly common to create a single 'converged' regulator, as the UK did in creating Ofcom in 2003. Since the switchover process involves some switch of spectrum from television to telecommunications, having one regulatory body to judge the balance, establish fair criteria and procedures and handle international negotiations is logical.

## Platform issues

The scope of media digitisation needs to be decided. A nation committed to keeping its electronics industry in the vanguard of technology will be more ambitious than one which simply wants to avoid cross-border interference.

The basic level of switchover, exemplified by the Netherlands, involves launching digital terrestrial television in order to switch off analogue terrestrial television and reclaim the spectrum, without attempting to convert analogue cable systems to digital on a similar timescale. A higher level of ambition entails converting all television platforms to digital technology, as Finland has done. In theory (though only the UK has talked seriously, and perhaps confusedly, about this) a higher level still would involve converting all radio, as well as all television, to digital transmission.

In practice the commercial providers of satellite television services are likely to switch fully to digital, on their own timescales, well before national digital switchover policies are completed. The same principle applies in theory to the cable industry. However, in a very large and/or fragmented and decentralised cable system, given the scale of the rein-vestment, the transition is likely to be staggered over a much longer time period and, if there is no public policy intervention, some analogue cable systems could well outlive analogue terrestrial.

If the principal policy goal is to be able to utilise terrestrial spectrum much more efficiently, then the continuation of pockets of analogue cable is not of major significance. The crucial need is for the whole cable system to carry new versions of the main analogue terrestrial services which are being withdrawn. Ideally these would be carried in their new digital form but a pragmatic solution for a period may be to permit analogue cable companies to down-convert the digital feeds at the cable head-end and distribute them in analogue form. Digital broadcasters will not like this approach, especially if analogue cable customers then miss out on extra services or extra features being provided to digital audiences. However, governments may not want to wait until 100% conversion of the cable system can be achieved before securing the analogue terrestrial spectrum saving.

In countries where the Negroponte switch is well-advanced, there may be scepticism about the need for digital terrestrial at all. Why not switch all viewers to satellite, cable or broadband? As high-speed broadband spreads and a growing number of households receive IPTV (Internet Protocol TV), it is easy from a North American or northern European perspective to postulate the idea that TV and the Internet will in future just arrive down the same 'pipe'. The concept of one service which can deliver all the attractions of high-quality broadcasting coupled with the rich content and interactive potential of the Internet sounds a winner.

However, TV via broadband is still at an early stage of development, with capacity issues an economic constraint on simultaneous mass viewing. In the UK BT pragmatically opted for its hybrid service, BT Vision, combining interactive services received by broadband with the *Freeview* digital terrestrial television service received via a terrestrial aerial.

Moreover, requiring reluctant viewers to buy a piece of consumer equipment they may not want is difficult enough; attempting to persuade everyone to pay a subscription for their digital television would be politically impossible. For the compulsory element of digital switchover, retaining a free-to-view option is important – and neither cable nor broadband offer that.

Could digital satellite, on its own, provide the free-to-view option? In the Middle East perhaps – but generally persuading reluctant terrestrial viewers to acquire a set-top box and install it between their existing aerial and their existing analogue TV set is simpler than persuading them to jettison their terrestrial aerial and buy a satellite dish and set-top box installation at, normally, a higher price.

Introducing digital terrestrial TV as a prelude to switchover is, therefore, usually the route of least political resistance. It provides an obvious transition for incumbent analogue terrestrial broadcasters, for whom a switch from one form of terrestrial transmission to another, using the same transmitter masts, is less disruptive than abandoning terrestrial broadcasting altogether. Even in countries where dependence on terrestrial reception for the main TV is very low, terrestrial TV's role in serving second and third TV sets may ensure that it is maintained. Technology development could alter the picture in future but meanwhile the basic approach is to launch digital terrestrial TV, simulcast the analogue terrestrial services due to be withdrawn, develop a digital consumer proposition strong enough to drive the widespread take-up of digital receivers, and then, when enough people have switched, close down analogue terrestrial transmission.

## Spectrum planning for the transition period

Spectrum planning work will determine how the launch of digital terrestrial television can be made compatible with the protection of analogue transmissions during the transition period and how many digital terrestrial multiplexes might be possible pre-switchover. It is essential to decide whether provision will be made for high-definition terrestrial television at the outset, since HD services require greater capacity, putting a constraint on the total number of channels.

Another fundamental decision is the level of digital terrestrial coverage desired post-switchover. Some countries, such as the UK, decided to match the near-universality of analogue terrestrial transmission, which is simple from the consumer point of view, but expensive in terms of transmitter investment. Other countries, such as Germany and New Zealand, decided to limit coverage to a lower figure, to rely on free-to-view digital satellite elsewhere, and thus to withdraw terrestrial TV from some rural areas. Different coverage targets may also be chosen for different services, with higher coverage for public service television than for commercial channels.

The other main spectrum planning issue is whether the plan should be based on the principle of using temporary frequencies for digital terrestrial television initially and then switching the digital services to the old analogue frequencies at the point of analogue switch-off. The alternative, adopted in Japan, is to bring up the new digital terrestrial services on the frequencies where they will remain for the long-term – and publicise them to encourage viewers to migrate from the analogue frequencies due to be closed down. While this latter approach reduces viewer disruption at the point of switchover, it could well entail disruptive and expensive frequency changes for some analogue services before digital terrestrial TV can be launched.

## Technology choices

The digital television pioneers have standardised and documented the technology of digital television transmission and reception in rival international families of standards known by their acronyms – ATSC, DVB, ISDB, DTMB and SBTVD – developed respectively by the United States, Europe, Japan, China and Brazil. Few other countries constitute a big enough market to make it feasible to create their own standards, so the issue now is generally choosing to which of the 'big five' to pay royalties. As we have seen, regional blocs have emerged facilitating economies of scale in the receiver market, so newly embarking countries should certainly consider joining the appropriate regional group.

Technical performance in the nation's own terrain should be evaluated, and comparisons now need to include the emerging second generation standards like DVB-T2. The analogue legacy system is a factor – ATSC presents itself as a successor to NTSC, and DVB as a replacement for PAL and SECAM – but is not critical. Compatibility between the terrestrial technology and that used for other platforms is more relevant. ATSC was designed essentially as a terrestrial system, as was China's DMBT. DVB has DVB-S standards for satellite, DVB-C for cable, and DVB-H for mobile (or handheld) TV. Japan's ISDB system is more fully integrated, facilitating joint satellite–terrestrial receivers and the use of the terrestrial technology for mobile TV.

Within a selected set of technical standards, more specific choices need to be made on the trade-offs between quality, predicted coverage and channel capacity. Improved compression techniques, specifically the use of MPEG-4 technology rather than MPEG-2, help reduce HDTV's requirement for large amounts of spectrum.

For pay-TV (and sometimes for copyright protection on free-to-view TV) conditional access technology will be required. There are key regulatory issues here and in relation to the selection of an API (Application Programming Interface) and the design of Electronic Programme Guides. The judgment is how far to leave these choices to the market, resulting in different organisations adopting separate proprietary technologies – and how far to aim for open standards and interoperability within any one platform or even between platforms. The European Union framework of regulation permits diversity, including proprietary technology, but requires the owners of proprietary set-top boxes to offer fair and reasonable terms of access to other broadcasters – and a common interface for conditional access is mandatory on integrated digital TV sets.

Consultation with all the relevant interested parties, including informed consumer groups, is advisable in advance of making technology selection decisions. Smaller countries especially will want to take account of the expertise of receiver importers. Low receiver prices are a product of manufacturing volumes: specifying a receiver which is unique to a small market is likely to prove a mistake.

## Funding options

It is possible to do a Cost–Benefit Analysis for digital switchover and, while the results will be only as reliable as the inputs (and probably only a very rough guide), the exercise does focus the mind on some important truths:

• There are costs for the broadcasters, in content creation for new channels and in transmission infrastructure and operations, which for commercial TV companies relying on advertising may exceed any increased income the new channels will bring (simulcasting, of course, is essentially a cost without additional income).

- Less visible because more diffused, but almost certainly greater, are the consumer costs of investing in new reception equipment – and there are no income benefits to consumers (only value for money in the new receivers and programme services).
- Spectrum release brings long-term benefits to the end users of the reallocated spectrum – and meanwhile there may be a windfall benefit, via an auction process or through spectrum pricing, to regulators and governments. These financial benefits are predicated on the successful completion of analogue switch-off.
- The financial costs – for broadcasters and consumers – are incurred well ahead of the generation of revenue to regulators and governments from spectrum efficiency benefits.
- The spectrum-related benefits are very unlikely to be so great – and reliably predictable – as to warrant the government covering all the broadcasters' and all the consumers' start-up costs.

Given this analysis, funding strategy is a conundrum. Without the right pattern of incentives digital switchover can easily stall, trapped in a vicious circle of limited expenditure on content, lack of consumer appeal, low receiver volumes, high receiver prices and low take-up.

A range of approaches is possible, with a strong market role at one end of the spectrum and a subsidy-led model at the other. In the market model the costs are borne primarily by the broadcasting industry, the receiver industry and the consumer. Public expenditure is limited to the role of government and regulators in facilitating the change and to any subsidy for specific groups. The timing of switchover is determined primarily by the market and politically announced deadlines may have to be postponed.

In the subsidy-led model the government decides the timing of switchover, regardless of the level of market demand for new services and new receivers and therefore has to provide a substantial part of the funding, either directly or indirectly. The decision to subsidise raises two major questions:

- deciding on the level, which needs to be justified both in relation to the expected benefit and in relation to other competing calls on public expenditure;
- designing a subsidy which can support the goal of analogue terrestrial switch-off without being platform discriminatory, either at the

transmission or the receiver end, and which is therefore proof against a legal challenge, for example from a cable or satellite company alleging unfair support for terrestrial television.

In Europe early subsidy schemes were controversial and gave rise to legal challenges and European Commission investigations. Significantly, even when it found fault in particular cases, the European Commission recognised that subsidies may need to have a role in digital switchover policies. Following some case history, it set out guidance on how to design public subsidy schemes without falling foul of competition law. The principles to be followed, it advised, are transparency, necessity, proportionality and technological neutrality. Specifically, it declared it would view favourably:

- funding for the roll-out of a transmission network in areas where otherwise there would be insufficient coverage;
- financial compensation to public service broadcasters for the cost of broadcasting via all transmission platforms in order to reach the entire population, provided this forms part of the public service mandate;
- subsidies to consumers for the purchase of digital decoders as long as they are technologically neutral, especially if they encourage the use of open standards for interactivity;
- financial compensation to broadcasters which are required to discontinue analogue transmission before the expiry of their licences, provided this takes account of granted digital transmission capacity (European Commission, 2005b).

Hybrid models involve using public policy to influence the market. The main public broadcaster can be given additional funding and required to play a central role. Also the regulator can reduce the licence charges paid by commercial analogue terrestrial broadcasters as digital take-up grows, recognising that the increase in the number of broadcasters reduces the value of their franchises and, at the same time, incentivising them to assist, rather than resist, the switch to digital. In hybrid models the switchover date, at least initially, may be made dependent on a consumer take-up threshold.

No pure market model seems feasible. While a Cost–Benefit Analysis can show that the economic benefits exceed the costs at the 'big picture' level, the cost–benefit balance for every stakeholder making up this 'big picture' is unlikely to be positive. In cash terms, the main start-up costs fall on broadcasters and the main cash benefits come to regulators and governments, via the sale of spectrum, towards the end. Broadcaster end benefits include new subscription and advertising revenue from new digital services, but for an advertising-funded analogue terrestrial broadcaster facing increased competition in a larger digital market, the sums are tricky. Just being able to stay in business through a major technology shift may be a much more significant benefit than any extra revenue.

A successful national funding policy is therefore likely to involve some element of *finesse* on the part of the regulator, whereby some part of the potential spectrum benefit is transferred to those bearing the start-up burden. This could be achieved by a grant of digital terrestrial spectrum on advantageous terms, by some legitimate form of subsidy, by a reduction in broadcaster licence charges, or by some other regulatory change such as easing the constraints on advertising and product placement. Another approach which, post-switchover, the FCC is exploring in the United States is to offer broadcasters who surrender spectrum some share in the proceeds from its sale to the telecommunications sector.

## Competition, choice and the consumer proposition

Closely related to funding strategy is the structure of competition envisaged during switchover:

- how many platforms are in direct competition with one another?
- is the digital terrestrial proposition designed to be wholly or largely free-to-view, in order to complement other platforms which are primarily subscription-based?
- if the digital terrestrial services do include pay-TV, are they differentiated, for example by target market segment and price, from other pay-TV propositions?

The aim should be to widen competition and choice without undermining financial viability. It is tempting to view the launch of digital terrestrial television as an opportunity to bring in new broadcasters and new channels, strongly differentiated from those on offer by satellite and cable. However, the inherent appeal of pluralism and choice needs to be tempered by an awareness of the impracticability of simultaneously launching too many new channels with high start-up costs and no audience. In practice some of the new channels on digital terrestrial TV are likely to be services already established on multi-channel satellite and cable.

That said, the digital terrestrial consumer proposition needs to be distinctively attractive. Since subscription cannot easily be made compulsory, a free-to-view option is required, and since the economics of free-to-view digital television do not permit the providers to give away free digital receivers, consumers need to be willing to buy (or rent) the digital receivers required. Why should they? To launch a digital switchover policy without adequate prior analysis of the receiver retail market is a recipe for expensively broadcasting digital programmes into the ether with no one on the receiving end.

The consumer motive for buying a new digital receiver could be:

- directly related to the equipment, for example improved picture and sound quality, greater portability/mobility, widescreen, or easier navigation and recording
- more incidental to the receiver and primarily a function of the new services it provides, whether new channels or interactive features.

In reality, the consumer proposition could be based on some combination of these factors but there is a distinction between

- a consumer strategy based solely on features, such as HDTV, which essentially require the purchase of a new TV set (or equivalent in terms of a new display monitor as well as a set-top box)
- a consumer strategy based on services, such as extra channels, which can be based on the purchase of set-top boxes working with existing analogue TV sets.

The latter involves a smaller consumer outlay and a switchover policy based on it should generally be achievable over a shorter timescale.

Research has a role. While public understanding may be limited at the outset, public awareness and attitudes can be surveyed and possible elements of the consumer proposition tested in focus groups. Consumer costs of conversion can be estimated and assessed in relation to 'willingness to pay' for the consumer proposition. The art is to match the value of the free-to-view proposition to the cost involved in receiving it.

The bodies to whom digital terrestrial spectrum licences are granted will probably be the managers of individual multiplexes who will combine a number of different channels and services technically. In creating the framework for multiplex licences, the regulator starts to shape the mix of channels and services – for example, by specifying the balance between national, regional and local services and between scheduled channels of programmes, on the one hand, and on-demand data and interactive features, on the other. The balance envisaged between free-to-view services (publicly financed and/or supported by advertising) and subscription-funded pay-TV channels will also be part of the framework. The multiplex licensees could be multi-channel broadcasters or they could be separate organisations which make their own contractual arrangements with more than one broadcasting organisation, perhaps multiplexing together the signals of rival broadcasters. Ownership restrictions related to broadcasting dominance or cross-ownership with other media may apply. Licensees may be appointed or selected by 'beauty contest' against a set of criteria, including the range and quality of the broadcast channels they propose to carry. In some cases the regulator may specify, or play a role in the selection of, the channels. Multiplex licence applicants also need to have sufficient financial strength to sustain their investment.

The task of selecting the multiplex licensees and, either directly or indirectly, determining the make-up of the services they will carry is, from the public's point of view, at the heart of the digital switchover policy. The 'citizen interest' has a vital place here alongside consumer appeal. Publishing the bidders' proposals and consulting on them prior to the formal selection gives civil society a voice in the process at a critical point. Public deliberations should also encompass the regulatory obligations and commitments in the field of subtitling, signing and audio-description which will make the digital services accessible to those with hearing and sight impairment. Advisory consumer groups can help articulate both needs and solutions here.

## Regulatory requirements

There should be a regulatory obligation on the multiplex licensees to collaborate in various respects, achieving sufficient technical commonality to ensure that all their free-to-view services can be received on the same digital receiver as one another. This may involve ensuring that transmission organisations, if there is more than one that could be contracted by different multiplexes, also collaborate.

The design of the digital terrestrial licences granted to existing analogue terrestrial broadcasters should have the switchover goal clearly in mind. For example, spectrum for simulcasting could be treated as a loan. An obligation to cease analogue broadcasting within a certain timeframe could be incorporated in the digital licences, subject to certain caveats. An obligation to publicise, and participate in, the organisation of switchover at some later date could be made explicit at the point when the licence is first granted.

Regulation also extends to relationships between platforms. Policy decisions on 'must carry' obligations for cable and satellite bear directly on the ease and cost of switchover. If cable and satellite relay the services which will cease to be broadcast on analogue terrestrial, then cable and satellite households – at any rate in respect of their main TV sets – will not be deprived at analogue switch-off.

One other tool available to governments and regulators is to require manufacturers, from a particular date, to include digital receivers in any integrated TV sets they bring to market. The purpose is to curtail the continuing sale of analogue TV sets and to ensure that the TV set replacement market becomes a driving force in delivering digital switchover.

The principal arguments in favour of mandating integrated digital TV sets are that it:

- provides evidence of the seriousness of the switchover commitment
- takes full advantage of the TV set replacement market and boosts the volume production of integrated digital TV sets, bringing down consumer prices and providing further impetus to switchover.

The principal argument against mandating is the imposition of an unnecessary cost on TV set purchasers who rely on set-top boxes for their digital technology (including, of course, most pay-TV households).

Either to complement mandating, or as an advisory alternative, labelling digital TV sets so that consumers can readily identify them is a further policy option. A corollary is to place warning labels on analogue TV sets, as the Japanese did. The practicalities of implementing and enforcing a labelling policy require the full involvement and commitment of manufacturers and retailers. It needs to be backed by a comprehensive system of conformance-testing.

The transition to digital television may well be accompanied by an increased take-up of pay-TV options, given the greater opportunities – on all platforms – available to pay-TV operators. The move of major sports events (and feature films) to pay channels, depriving free-to-view only households of these familiar attractions, could well be part of this shift. A further regulatory issue, therefore, is whether to intervene here, imposing restrictions to protect free-to-view access for certain major national sporting events, or whether to let the market take its course, leaving the sport organisers to decide how best to market their TV rights.

## Key relationships underpinning digital switchover policy

Switchover cannot be achieved by a simple political *diktat*. A framework of collaboration is required – between political and market stakeholders, and among market stakeholders. At the centre of it are two fundamental relationships.

The first is the relationship between the government and regulator, on the one hand, and the incumbent analogue terrestrial broadcasters on the other. To achieve switchover without a consumer rebellion, the government and regulator need the incumbent terrestrial broadcasters to use their scheduling and marketing skills to persuade their audiences across from their analogue to their digital transmissions.

The broadcasters will look for incentives, such as free spectrum for developing new services, increased funding (for public broadcasters) or a reduction in licence costs (for commercial broadcasters). Commercial broadcasters in particular will be keen to restrict the number of new entrants to their market. Indeed one attraction to incumbents of introducing HDTV as part of the switchover strategy is that it may require so much digital spectrum as to exclude new digital terrestrial entrants during the transition period. Governments and regulators, however, also have to consider how much political importance they attach to bringing in new broadcasters, either for social and cultural reasons or to help boost the attractiveness of the digital television consumer proposition, and they have to be fair to satellite and cable broadcasters with different commercial interests. While switchover may rest on a shared strategic understanding between government/regulator and incumbent terrestrial broadcasters, the relationship should not be a cosy one.

The second key relationship is between multiplex licensees, broadcasters and the receiver industry (manufacturers, importers and retailers). Digital switchover policy will not advance far simply by creating the preconditions for broadcaster investment unless, at the same time, consumers have access at an acceptable cost to new digital receivers.

Vertically integrated pay-TV broadcasters generally provide receivers to their customers at no or little extra cost as part of the subscription service. Here the broadcaster specifies the receiver technology and probably underwrites the cost of manufacturing, while the retailer sells subscriptions (perhaps with a staff commission on every successful sale). The risk is largely carried by the pay-TV broadcaster, who needs deep pockets.

The free-to-view sector generally retains the traditional division between broadcasters, who are responsible for programme content and transmission, and receiver manufacturers and retailers, who sell direct to consumers. To avoid the risk that the receivers might be unable to display, or navigate between, all the different terrestrial services, close technical collaboration is needed between the broadcasting and the receiver industries. The market can only function smoothly if all, or virtually all, broadcasters collaborate both with one another and with all, or virtually all, receiver manufacturers on all the detailed practicalities of interoperability, from conformance-testing to the service information which populates Electronic Programme Guides.

## Switching off analogue terrestrial TV

With a long transition period the process of analogue switch-off can be designed several years after digital terrestrial switch-on, as a separate step. Alternatively, with a shorter timescale, it can be part of an integrated digital switch-on/analogue switch-off strategy.

It makes sense to separate the two stages in a large country with a high dependence on terrestrial television, with sufficient spectrum for a prolonged period of simulcasting, and where some commercial and political uncertainty may surround the switchover timing. That way, the effectiveness of the launch of digital services and the speed of take-up can be assessed before analogue switch-off is firmly timetabled. A shorter timescale is more appropriate where the number of terrestrial households to be switched is small, terrestrial spectrum is scarce, and subsidy has a significant role.

Timing is essentially a political judgment. How many households could analogue switch-off deprive of television (a) in respect of their main TV set (b) in respect of secondary sets and recording equipment? By modelling growth in the satellite and cable markets alongside realistic expectations of digital terrestrial take-up, it is possible to judge how long it might take for the number of households in danger of deprivation to be reduced to a politically acceptable small minority.

Politicians may initially choose to base the timetable on a threshold for digital take-up. This helps avoid the risk of announcing a date and then having to postpone it, losing credibility both with the industry and with consumers. However, in the end, both for credibility with investors and to help consumers to be ready, a hard date has to be named.

The 'hard date' could be a set of hard dates – for switching-off region by region, as many European countries have done, rather than switching the whole country on a single day. Adopting this approach, however, requires an understanding of the interference implications of each regional change of frequencies. This is easier in countries whose transmission patterns have been designed and managed as national networks, rather than those where locally managed transmitters have grown up on a commercial basis.

An essential requirement at this stage is a spectrum plan for terrestrial broadcasting's post-switchover requirements and an operational plan for implementing it. The latter will need to be coordinated with a strategy of public communication and viewer support.

Operational responsibility can be entrusted to a regulatory body or, alternatively, some specially constituted body, with strong links to broadcasters, transmission providers, retailers and installers, could be appointed to coordinate the various bodies involved and spearhead consumer communications. In the latter case, the body could be appointed by the relevant government department, as in Sweden, or else, on the UK model, the government and regulator could ask the broadcasters to appoint it in conjunction with the receiver industry. Governments and regulators will nonetheless retain some direct implementation responsibilities of their own.

Further policy issues linked to the preparation for analogue switch-off include:

- undertaking any switch-off pilots to test feasibility and readiness
- identifying any groups for whom analogue switch-off could be seriously difficult and assessing what measures to take to assist them
- setting or amending the broadcasters' licence conditions and clarifying responsibility for switchover operations at the transmitters
- deciding whether some cable transmissions can continue in analogue, using down-converted digital inputs
- checking that the industry will meet consumers' recording needs (e.g. with hard-disc recorders)
- ensuring sufficient advance training within the industry, especially of retail and installation staff
- ensuring sufficient advance financial and practical planning by social and private landlords and by a wide range of institutions from hospitals to hotels and from pubs to prisons.

The communications strategy needs to provide as much local and individual focus as possible, with practical back-up advice and support. A viewer-friendly approach is to switch off one TV channel first, build in a pause to allow any remaining analogue viewers to make a last-minute purchase of a new receiver, and then, a week or so later, switch off the remaining channels.

## Public persuasion

Throughout the whole switchover policy process, public explanation and persuasion play a central role. In a field like television reception, compulsory policies have to have a wide measure of public support in order to be enforceable.

If the strategy is to allow an extended period of time for voluntary migration before the compulsory timetable starts to bite, it may make sense for the initial communications drive to come primarily from broadcasters, retailers and the receiver industry, engaging with the public as consumers, without complicating commercial marketing with political arguments. The benefit of a 'softly, softly' approach from a political standpoint is that it can help avoid a major storm of adverse publicity of the kind that might trigger a mass consumer revolt. The drawback, however, could be a continuing low level of public awareness.

Switchover cannot in the end be implemented without high public awareness. Everyone has to buy, or have already bought, a digital receiver in order to continue receiving television at the point at which the analogue signal from their local transmitter is switched off. So a gear-change in communications is required when the timetable is named. The arguments deployed to encourage digital take-up will probably be insufficient to sell the concept of a compulsory analogue terrestrial switch-off. The long-term and social benefits of utilising spectrum more efficiently need to be explained.

In the later stages the focus will be less on those who have already converted their main sets voluntarily and more on those – especially the elderly, the disabled and the poorest households – for whom switching presents serious difficulties. Targeting such groups with advice and information, practical help and charitable or publicly financed assistance is the key both to helping the groups themselves and to winning the consent of the wider population who would otherwise be concerned on their behalf.

Research in the UK highlighted the point that, for those most reluctant to convert, cost was not necessarily the issue. Receiver design and installation instructions were an issue. The complexity of the technology – in terms of choosing it, installing it and operating it – can be daunting and help could be required with the practicalities here.

The public awareness and understanding of digital switchover need to be measured and tracked, stimulating new publicity initiatives if necessary. Then the final stages of public communication must be closely linked to the practicalities of the transmitter switching operations, informing consumers what exactly will happen in their local area and when, explaining what to do, for example if manual re-scanning is required, and offering sources of help. As well as leaflets, posters and other forms of advertising, public information spots and on-screen captions giving a point of contact for more detailed advice are likely to play a major role. While some of them may have dragged their feet earlier, at this point analogue terrestrial broadcasters have every incentive to inform their audiences of how to continue to watch their programmes after switchover without disruption or aggravation.

## Investment and risk reduction

Digital switchover essentially revolves around two major investments designed to trigger a third. The first is in digital transmission infrastructure – from production facilities through to multiplexing equipment and transmitters – and the second is in attractive new content and services. When these two interact successfully they stimulate the third investment – by consumers in new digital receivers. When all three interact successfully, full switchover, implying analogue terrestrial switch-off, becomes feasible.

This pattern of investment is not under the management of any one party, nor can it work without the right framework of public policy. The risks involved cannot all be managed by the individual investors or groups of investors.

Governments and regulators cannot easily switch off analogue terrestrial broadcasting without migrating existing terrestrial broadcasters to digital terrestrial – and that migration is too risky for the broadcasters unless there is public policy support, in terms of spectrum allocation and financial regulation, allowing a viable free-to-view market to develop alongside pay-TV. Broadcasters cannot embark upon the transmission investment and new content creation without some assurance from the receiver industry on the supply and marketing of digital receivers.

Neither broadcasters nor the receiver industry will switch out of the analogue market fully without some announcement from government of a firm and reliable switchover timetable which will be enforced. However, governments will only commit to a firm timetable if the consumer proposition of the broadcasters' services and the industry's receivers is strong enough to carry most analogue terrestrial households across to digital TV of their own volition and to minimise the risk of a consumer–voter revolt.

Consumers will only accept the policy without rebelling if they understand the reason for it, if the consumer proposition offers real benefits (one measure of which is the level of voluntary take-up), if the element of compulsion is relatively low, and if help is provided to those who will find switching most difficult. Governments and the industry need to deliver those assurances.

National switchover policy only becomes workable when, in effect, the various stakeholders help to reduce one another's risks as well as their own. Collaboration between public policy and the market needs to provide a sophisticated form of mutual risk reduction.

# 7
# Converged Communications

## Summary of the chapter's argument

The digital switchover process, though for most countries focussed on analogue terrestrial TV switch-off, has a much broader character stemming from television's convergence with telecommunications and computer technology. From the start digital television sought to offer interactive services by linking television and telephony.

Early ventures into interactivity proved frustrating. Hopes that the digital TV set-top box might function as a surrogate computer were misplaced, as access to interactive services via the Internet developed apace. However, television came to be viewed on the Internet, providing On-Demand Catch-Up TV, liberating viewers from the constraint of time. Mobile technology offered television freed from the constraint of a fixed reception place and, because of the camera feature in the mobile handset, facilitated contributions to television by members of the public. Connected TV then brought the Internet to the main TV screen alongside broadcast programmes. Meanwhile, radio was readily available and commonly accessed on the Internet, as well as shifting slowly from analogue to digital broadcast transmission. Broadband developed as a platform alongside satellite, cable and terrestrial. Broadcasting was subsumed into a wider world of digital communications.

These developments have stimulated a debate over whether we are witnessing 'the end of television'. The technology is evolving towards a hybrid broadcast–broadband TV. With greater viewer choice, audiences are fragmenting but still spend most time watching the programmes of established TV channels. Major content providers are diversifying across multi-media and consolidating into conglomerates. Convergence is radically altering the context of communications regulation.

## Digitisation and convergence

Convergence is not an entirely new phenomenon but digital coding and compression technology, the development of the Internet, high-speed switching and broadband networks have undoubtedly accelerated the process (Iosifidis, 2011b: 170). At the heart of convergence is the fact that the digitisation of video and audio signals is common to all three technologies. Digitally coded content can be replicated, manipulated and transferred between different producers and distributors, crossing traditional communications boundaries. IPTV (Internet Protocol Television) has become a way of distributing both the Internet and TV services – and, as speed and penetration increase, the broadband platform could become one of the principal means of distributing digital television.

Revolutions can be divided into phases, with each phase containing the seeds of the one to follow, and the digital television revolution is no exception. In their study of the economics of the business, Patrick Barwise and Robert Picard picture a digital switchover stage preceding a digital convergence one. They see analogue terrestrial switch-off as the culmination of an evolutionary expansion of TV channels and the growth of subscription which started with analogue satellite and cable. They view digital convergence as a more distant but 'potentially even more revolutionary change' when nearly all homes could have a broadband connection fast enough to deliver television programmes in real time (Barwise and Picard, 2012). This categorisation is relevant to their focus on the impact of technology on funding options, with the advent of conditional access the key change of importance.

However, the transition from analogue satellite, cable and terrestrial TV to digital satellite, cable and terrestrial TV was not just an evolution in the number of channels and the role of subscription. It constituted a dramatic step-change in channel provision and, with analogue terrestrial switch-off, the move of whole nations, not just willing subscribers, into multi-channel television. Moreover, it brought, from the outset, interactive services based on linking broadcast distribution to a telecommunications 'return path' which had not been generally feasible before. The first explicit convergence business alliance in the UK, involving BSkyB and BT, began in 1998. Technology convergence has been part of the digital television revolution from the start – and continues to shape content design, reception devices and the means of distribution.

## Early interactive services

In the UK first BSkyB's satellite operation and then, on a smaller scale, ONdigital's terrestrial venture adopted the idea of a telephone 'return path', enabling the viewer to send back simple signals from the digital set-top box to the broadcaster or another organisation linked with the broadcaster. BSkyB's digital satellite service was launched with a receiver subsidy financed by a consortium of BSkyB, BT, the Midland Bank (later part of HSBC) and the Japanese electronics giant Matsushita (manufacturer of Panasonic consumer equipment) who reckoned their payback would come from a set of 'Open...' interactive services offered via the telephone. To receive the subsidy the subscriber had to agree to have the set-top box linked to a phone line which could then be used for interactive banking, travel booking and pizza ordering, for example. ONdigital marketed an interactive service option, ONnet, based on a telephone line link, including Internet access using a laptop keyboard pointed at the set-top box.

The political rhetoric around convergence at that stage envisaged interactive digital television as a surrogate computer. PC penetration in the UK was still limited and largely confined to middle class homes, while digital satellite television in particular, greatly assisted by its Premier League Football contract, had spread its dish aerials across the nation's council housing estates and was perceived as having much broader appeal. A 2001 Department of Trade and Industry White Paper enthused:

> Digital television will transform the communications services available in the home. Using technology that people understand and are comfortable and confident with, we will be able to provide a learning resource and communications centre in every living room. It puts control of viewing in the hands of viewers rather than broadcasters. Choice will increase, and the potential of teletext will be unleashed by use of graphics and high-speed updates. Combined with a phone line, it can give everyone access to the Internet in their living rooms, stimulating computer literacy in the population as a whole. It will offer new Internet-based learning opportunities and interactive services, making e-shopping and e-banking more attractive for many people and opening up new opportunities for business products and services.
>
> (DTI, 2001)

However, although branded 'Open...' BSkyB's interactive services were a 'walled garden', separate from the Internet. Consumers found them slow and clunky and in 2001 BSkyB bought out its partners and closed the consortium. The ONnet service too proved cumbersome and, in its early years, *Freeview* neither offered return path services nor required a telephone return path in its receiver specification. When, for example, the BBC offered viewers the so-called 'red button' choices of which Wimbledon tennis game to watch, the TV set was receiving multiple feeds, some of which were hidden, so the *Freeview* viewer was selecting from among an extended number of channels on offer, rather than truly interacting with the broadcaster.

Interactivity at this stage therefore was rather limited. The reality was that, for services like electronic banking and shopping, using the Internet from a computer proved much more satisfactory than trying to operate via a television set-top box. In the UK the number of households with a broadband connection to the Internet rose from 19% to 59% between 2003 and 2005 (Dutton, di Gennaro and Millwood Hargrave, 2005), bringing the Internet 'centre stage' and deflating early notions of the TV set-top box as the gateway to e-commerce. This led to the distinction between the 'lean-forward' technology of the computer on a desk, where the user was actively engaged in purposeful actions using a mouse and keyboard and the 'lean-back' technology of the TV set, where the viewer conceptually relaxed on the sofa and consumed entertainment passively.

## Television on the Internet

However, an interface between TV, radio and the Internet was being constructed. Radio services from around the globe were carried on the Internet and people could work at their computers and listen either to their favourite domestic radio network or to a radio station from another continent. The broadcasters, public and commercial, built their own online services, carrying news and information as well as a range of entertainment items. The BBC was an early and internationally successful entrant, with the BBC News website a prestigious complement to BBC TV and Radio news. As media players became a more standard feature of personal computers, online video features were included on broadcasters' websites and news channels carried in full.

Meanwhile the Press also grew online versions of their newspapers, with websites rapidly displacing the classified advertising print business.

Newspaper websites also started to include video interviews and short clips of sports and other news.

Steadily 'television' began appearing on the Internet. TV content, such as 'live' feeds of press conferences and speeches, could be streamed to specialised audiences of computer viewers at much greater length than broadcasting schedules would normally allow. A major landmark was the birth of *YouTube* in 2005 – a website designed for sharing videos, to which anyone, amateur or professional, could upload their offerings and from which anyone could select material to view. A further development was the Internet distribution of 'live' events, such as concerts and sporting competitions, for which the broadcasters had not sought the rights, perhaps judging the potential national audience to be too small, but which via the Internet could reach dispersed groups of enthusiasts across many parts of the globe.

As viewing 'television' on the Internet grew, the 'lean-back/lean-forward' distinction started to erode, but convergence stopped well short of a merger. Broadcasts remain essentially 'pushed out' simultaneously to everyone so that, within local reception constraints, all the channels are 'there' at the reception end (when viewers change channel, they are switching between different services which the TV set is already receiving). Video material viewed on the Internet, by contrast, is normally 'pulled' by the user. The programme content exists as 'packages' which are sent to the user when requested. This provides huge flexibility: while broadcasts are conceptually one-to-many communications, the Internet facilitates a multi-directional many-to-many pattern. TV on the Internet is thus well-suited to On-Demand viewing.

## Television anytime

Video-on-Demand (VoD), the supply of video content in response to a user's request, was one of the early selling propositions of the digital cable and IPTV television platforms, with their two-way communication capacity. An obvious application was the delivery of movies, providing an electronic substitute for the video rental store. The satellite platform initially had to be content with the compromise concept of Near-Video-on-Demand (NVoD), using its huge channel capacity for parallel transmissions of the same film with staggered start-times. A subsequent development both in digital satellite and digital terrestrial television was the downloading of a range of films and archive TV programmes to a hard-disc digital recorder from which viewers can retrieve and watch content at their convenience.

TV broadcasters, however, were aware of a slightly different demand – for a chance to see TV programmes yet to be archived, within a short period after their 'live' transmission. Although digital recorders provided increasingly sophisticated functionality for this, the viewer still had to know about the programme in advance and set a recording. Many viewers, though, found their interest kindled in a programme only after its transmission, through reading a review or talking to friends, for example.

Using Internet technology the BBC developed its iPlayer to make newly transmitted BBC programmes available via broadband for 'Catch-Up' viewing. They could be viewed free of charge within the window of a week. After a series of trials, including monitoring its effect on other Internet traffic, the service became generally available in 2007 and was widened in 2008 to provide a bigger window for access to previous episodes in a series. The iPlayer swiftly proved a huge success. Most viewers accessed it on their computers, but cable customers could view it directly on their TV sets and the extra popularity of this was striking. Other UK broadcasters launched their own equivalent services and parallel developments took place in several other European countries, Australia and North America. Since the Internet is international, these Catch-Up TV services were not confined technically to national markets, though rights negotiation, marketing and payment system issues had to be addressed.

The advent of digital television has not just been a matter of hugely increased channel choice, therefore. Taken together, sophisticated digital recording equipment and the Video-on-Demand services facilitated by convergence have given digital television viewers one of the great benefits of the digital television revolution. They free the viewer from the 'tyranny of the schedules' and allow self-scheduling to suit one's convenience. In that sense the digital television viewer has been freed from analogue television's constraint of time.

## Television anywhere

Another major strand in convergence has been the development of what is often now termed 'mobile TV'. The term hides a distinction between broadcast and telecommunications distribution to portable or mobile reception devices.

After the technical standards for digital satellite, digital cable and digital terrestrial television had been devised, broadcasting technology experts began work on related standards which would be suitable for transmission to portable and mobile receivers. They had in mind transmitting TV programmes for reception on small sets in caravans and boats and on receivers for commuter-train, bus or back-seat car passengers, but they also envisaged the possibility of small hand-held portable devices. The Europeans designed a DVB variant called DVB-H (hand-held); the Americans developed ATSC-M/H (Mobile/Hand-held) and MediaFLO (Forward Link Only); the Japanese included a mobile TV capability within their ISDB standard; while South Korea decided to use the DMB (Digital Multi-media Broadcasting) technology also in use in some countries for digital radio.

These broadcast technologies have had varying levels of success in different markets. Broadcast mobile TV has flourished in Japan and South Korea, where mobile telephone hand-sets were designed to incorporate it, and is growing in China, India and Brazil. Japan's approach of integrating mobile transmission into its digital terrestrial TV system meant that the Japanese commuter could continue to watch the same programme when moving from the home TV to the mobile handset or vice versa.

By contrast, broadcast mobile TV has tended to flop in Western Europe and North America. DVB-H services have been closed in Germany and the Netherlands. The explanation for this is both technical and content-related. Technically, the wide range of different hand-sets and the high cost of transmissions have been a factor. Made-for-mobile content proved expensive for a relatively small market, while conventional linear TV programmes were found to be too long (de Renesse, 2011). Additionally picture resolution on small screen sizes and sound quality in noisy environments caused frustration (Goggin, 2012). As a result the business case for broadcast mobile TV failed to add up.

Instead smart-phones using 3G telecommunications technology became the route into TV on the move. Not only can smart-phones provide Internet access, enabling users to manage their e-mails and listen to radio services, but they can also handle TV Apps offering tailored services of news and sport, including video:

> This simple add-on of television to the near ubiquitous cellular mobile sets the scene for the second coming of mobile television – at a time when full-blown digital terrestrial broadcasting to handhelds is still far away from becoming an affordable and profitable reality.
>
> (Goggin, 2012: 130)

The launch of the Apple iPad and other tablet devices has greatly widened the range of devices on which 3G and 4G television-related services can be viewed. Watching Catch-Up TV proved to be a very popular use of the tablet. Mobile TV in its various and evolving forms, coupled with this increased choice of hand-held and portable receivers, offers the digital TV viewer increasing freedom from the constraint of location.

However, while broadcasting and telecommunications technologies have converged to facilitate mobile TV, an element of divergence has also developed here. TV content has to be refashioned or 'versioned' for telecommunications (as distinct from broadcast) distribution to mobile devices. For broadcasters, already adapting their content for online publication, this added a further process of versioning to the production process.

## User-generated content and audience involvement

Not only has convergence reduced constraints of time and place on television viewing, it has also created a complex and intricate pattern of multi-directional communication – in which the boundary between broadcasters and their audiences has become blurred.

In the mid-twentieth century the only people who normally made television programmes were the employees, on staff or contract, of an established TV broadcaster. Then the business opened up to a wider 'magic circle' encompassing independent producers. With the birth of *YouTube*, low-cost digital video camcorders, and easy-editing computer programmes, the circle started to dissolve – enabling anyone to become a producer and make a programme.

The camera functionality of the mobile telephone handset introduced a new pattern of contributing to television. Taking photos – and e-mailing them – was found to be the second most widespread use (after texting) of smart-phones in the UK (KPMG, 2012). Members of the public able to take stills or video in unexpected circumstances when no professional camera team was present could offer them for broadcasting. Material could be uploaded to *YouTube* or sent to major news organisations like CNN and the BBC. In this way citizens became news-gatherers, especially at accident or natural disaster scenes and in demonstrations or civil conflict.

News editors now regard UGC (User-Generated Content) as a key source. Its role has been critical during the series of events in the Middle East – from the Iranian election protests of 2009 through to the Arab

Spring upheavals in Tunisia, Egypt and Libya in 2011 and the conflict in Syria from 2011 where conventional journalistic access was prohibited or severely restricted. The reliability of UGC may be difficult to verify, and need qualification, but, in the absence of better sources, it has become mainstream news bulletin material.

The dramatic growth of social media, most famously *Facebook* (with over 800 million users worldwide) and *Twitter* (with over 100 million tweets posted daily) has added to this proliferation of news sources. Social media can be used both to organise and to publicise protests and other events. Journalists now scan them on a routine basis for leads to stories.

With so many people linked together in networks which reflect their sets of interests, broadcasters have new tools with which to reach out to their audiences, build a fan base or connect with potential new viewers. Viewers are urged to text, e-mail, cast their vote in talent and reality shows, and access websites where they can 'play along' with quiz and other entertainment programmes. TV shows have their own *Facebook* pages. TV journalists supplement their TV appearances with blogs and tweets. Analogue television, of course, had its own forms of viewer feedback but the ethos of digital television is different. Digital broadcasters are engaged in fostering relationships with communities of interest and building brand loyalty among identifiable groups in the crowded and competitive digital marketplace.

## Radio goes digital (slowly)

The invention of digital radio preceded that of digital television. Much of the R&D work was done in Europe in the late 1980s and Digital Audio Broadcasting (DAB) became an internationally recognised technical standard in 1995. However, while it was internationally recognised, it was by no means universally adopted. The American radio industry had other ideas from the start and investigated the idea of carrying a digital signal within analogue radio channels (now marketed as HD Radio), while satellite digital radio offered another development option (Stoller, 2010: 276–277). Japan used its ISDB technology.

Even within Europe the industry became technologically fragmented. While several countries followed the UK in adopting DAB, France chose the rival system DMB, with video and multi-media capabilities, and in 2005 a new improved version of DAB (DAB+) arrived and was taken up in Germany and central Europe. So, while analogue AM and FM radio services remain global, and analogue radio sets carried (or driven) from one country to another continue to work, digital radio has little chance, at least in the immediate future, of providing comparable international operability. While there are aspirations to market receivers capable of decoding DAB, DMB and DAB+ (O'Neill and Shaw, 2010), the only real global digital distribution system for radio is the Internet.

The UK launched DAB back in 1995 but the service initially consisted largely of simulcasts of the BBC and commercial analogue stations. Receiver costs remained high and manufacturers were dubious about committing to high volume production. From 2000 onwards the prospects improved. Both the BBC and the commercial radio sector introduced new digital-only stations, receiver prices fell below £100 and the broadcasters collaborated to fund and organise marketing and promotional activity (Lax, 2011). The UK became the world leader in digital radio take-up and by 2010 some 11 million DAB radios had been bought by 35% of its households (DCMS, 2011b).

Consumer interest though remained modest. In 2011 over 70% of all listening was still to analogue and the sales of analogue radios continued to outstrip digital radio sales. Neither the technical quality nor the additional stations constituted a totally compelling digital radio proposition. As Tony Stoller, former Chief Executive of the UK's Radio Authority, observed:

> DAB proved to be as good as properly installed fixed FM, but not that much better. It had the advantage of maintaining that quality when mobile, unlike FM, but the power demands of the earlier generations of DAB microchips made this difficult to exploit. Battery use remained a problem into 2009. Ease of tuning, and the ability to provide text alongside audio data, were useful add-ons, but it was pretty obvious that DAB lacked a 'killer application' to drive it into the market.
>
> (Stoller, 2010: 279)

In its *Digital Britain* report of 2009 the UK's Labour government decided to commit to switching off analogue radio on the television model. The notional timing of this was to be 2015, but a two-year notice period for the date was made subject to two criteria: (a) improved digital coverage and (b) digital radio listening reaching a 50% target (BIS and DCMS, 2009). The succeeding Conservative–Liberal Democrat Coalition government established an Action Plan in support of this goal. The driving force came from the broadcasters who wished to limit the number of years during which they simulcast their analogue services, with the government and regulator feeling an obligation as a result of the licensing incentives the commercial radio stations were offered in return for committing to DAB.

However, a House of Lords report noted that, in contrast to the television position, 'the spectrum which will be released by the majority of the stations ceasing to broadcast in analogue has little alternative use or value' (House of Lords, 2010: 30). Given the continuing role of analogue radios in cars, the existence of 150 million or more analogue radio sets, and potential resistance by the public, the feasibility of analogue radio switch-off in the short term has been regarded with some scepticism. Nonetheless, the migration of radio listening from analogue to digital will continue – with listening to radio services on the Internet and on digital television playing a part in the process. Radio too is part of the digital multi-media communications picture.

## Connected TV

A rapidly growing manifestation of convergence is now Connected TV – the concept of watching the Internet on a TV set. Households served by IPTV, of course, have this facility already and games consoles linked to TV sets can also deliver Internet viewing. However, what is now developing and targeting a much bigger market is a hybrid TV-Internet proposition, also sometimes known as Smart TV.

The central idea is not to use the TV set for services like home banking or e-mail which are best left to the computer or the mobile handset, but rather to use it to bring On-Demand TV programmes and feature films distributed over the Internet to the large flat-screen HDTV sets. Access to *YouTube* and to social media is also provided. Viewers can then move seamlessly between broadcast content and Internet-delivered content, with the means of distribution irrelevant from the consumer perspective.

This can be achieved either by building Internet access into TV sets or by the marketing of hybrid set-top boxes. Some leading TV manufacturers are marketing Connected TV sets using proprietary technology to give access to a limited range of Internet TV services for which an agreement is in place. One of their options is to include Google TV technology, as Sony, Samsung and LG have done, for example (*The Times*, 2012a). Viewers can look for programmes here by entering words into a search bar though, at the time of its launch, Google TV's access to the websites of the United States networks NBC, CBS and ABC was blocked for commercial rights reasons. Connected TV sets made a big publicity splash at the 2011 NAB (National Association of Broadcasters) show where it was predicted that they would account for 50% of flat-panel digital TV sets sold by 2015 (Seel, 2011).

Open technical standards for Connected TV have been developed but different answers are being adopted in different places, even within Europe. The most widely supported standard here is HbbTV (Hybrid Broadcast–Broadband TV), the product of Franco–German R&D collaboration, which has been selected by Germany, France, the Netherlands, Austria and Spain. However, Italy uses MHP (Multi-media Home Platform) technology and the UK has a system based on MHEG (Multi-media and Hypermedia Experts Group) in the interests of compatibility with hardware–software interface choices which have already been made.

The main initiative in the UK, branded *You View*, began as Project Canvas, a partnership between the BBC, ITV, Channel 4, Five, BT, Arqiva and Carphone Warehouse. The BBC was particularly keen to bring the BBC iPlayer to the main TV set. The venture was controversial (BSkyB criticised the BBC's use of public money) and followed the cancellation of an earlier scheme on competition grounds. The proposal was closely scrutinised by the BBC Trust, the regulator Ofcom and the UK's Office of Fair Trading but passed muster. Important commitments were that the provision of services would be open to third parties and that the technical specification for receivers would be published and available for any manufacturer to adopt. *You View* set-top boxes were launched on the market in 2012. Once connected both to a TV aerial and a broadband connection, they provided a combination of *Freeview* channels and free Catch-Up and On-Demand services to the TV screen.

Hybrid TV content can be free-to-view, as Catch-Up TV is within its time window, or carry a charge, for example, for a movies-on-demand service. The latter has already emerged as an area of keen competition: BSkyB launched its Internet TV service of film and sport, NOW TV, in 2012. The market hold of national cable and satellite operators is under challenge from major international players such as Netflix and LoveFilm which are shedding their origins as DVD postal businesses and fanning out across the Internet. In the United States Netflix was able to claim 24 million customers watching films and TV shows online in 2012, compared with 14 million customers for its DVD service (*The Times*, 2012b). As hybrid TV technology spreads, these and other 'Over the Top' services, piggy-backing on equipment and connections already installed in the home, are predicted to become an integral part of the television viewing patterns of the future. 'Companion apps' like Zeebox allow you to combine social networking and TV viewing.

Other Connected TV features include increasingly sophisticated Electronic Programme Guides (EPGs), offering a scroll-back to past programmes as well as a scroll-forward function, and equipped with search engines for finding programme categories and specific programmes. The industry is already working on the viewer's central question: 'How will I know what I want to watch when my TV set offers not just hundreds, but thousands of choices?' One of the answers is to monitor your viewing habits, process your personal data and then offer you choices you can be expected to like. Another is an EPG that can tap into social media and provide you with the recommendations of your electronic friends. The EPG could appear on your portable handset and work in sync with your large HDTV screen. The relationship of 'second screen' use to TV viewing is already the subject of audience research.

The full implications of the advent of Connected TV are still a matter of speculation (and the subject of much industry hype). The market for feature films and high-investment TV drama has long been an international one. However, the viewing rights have been sold on different time 'windows' for different forms of distribution and viewing (e.g. DVD and TV) and different launch dates for different countries. The ability of audiences around the world to view the same production simultaneously via the Internet in future is likely to put pressure on this pattern of marketing, one symptom of which could be an initial increase in piracy. The long-term effect may be to shift content owners' marketing strategies towards global, rather than national, launches to pay-TV audiences.

## Infrastructure transformation

This emerging vision of a new era of interchangeable content between broadcasting and the Internet is predicated, however, both on the continuing improvement of digital compression technology and on continuing investment in the infrastructure of high-speed broadband.

Historically, broadcasting has been recognised in many countries, especially in Europe, as a public service to which, as far as practicable, every citizen should have access. Universal or near-universal coverage was a public policy requirement for transmission and, as we saw in Chapter 3, the UK went to the expense of providing 98.5% digital terrestrial coverage, matching the earlier analogue terrestrial, as part of its digital switchover policy.

Telecommunications policy ensured a universal service for telephony but, with the rise of the Internet, new communications infrastructure policy issues have arisen. Once simple dial-up access to the Internet became frustratingly inadequate, and the demand for broadband grew, judgments had to be made about whether simply to leave infrastructure investment to the market or whether to formulate a public commitment to provide a specified level of broadband performance to every household within a regulatory framework that would subsidise uneconomic areas.

For the UK, the question came into sharp focus after the late twentieth century dotcom and telecommunications bubbles burst and investment in the fixed telecommunications network slowed, leaving Internet traffic bottlenecks between networks and local telephone exchanges (BIS and DCMS, 2009). A further issue was the delivery of a satisfactory quality of service over the 'last mile' to the individual home. While cable customers were reasonably well-served, around half the country lay outside the cable infrastructure and depended on BT's copper wire network, utilised either by BT or by an alternative provider.

Internet performance is denoted in bits per second (expressed in Kilobits and Megabits) which are a measure of speed (normally download speed) which in turn is a function of bandwidth capacity. In its early days the Internet ran largely on telephone modems delivering data at 14.4 Kbps. By 2005 broadband networks were providing an average of 512 Kbps and this rose to an average of 3.3 Mbps in 2009. However, these averages concealed very varying levels of performance, with major weaknesses in rural areas.

In its *Digital Britain* report of 2009 the UK's Labour government therefore committed to delivery of a Universal Service Commitment of 2Mbps (BIS and DCMS, 2009: 51–53). In 2010 its successor Coalition government, noting that over 70% of UK households had broadband access, identified some 2 million homes which could not access a good level of service and undertook to ensure that 'virtually all homes will have access to a minimum level of service of 2Mbps by 2015' (BIS and DCMS, 2010: 4). Public money would be invested in broadband delivery from the Licence Fee, where an under-spend on the Digital Switchover Help-Scheme was anticipated.

However, minimum service levels were only part of the story. For the future the real requirement, agreed by both the Labour and Coalition administrations, was for superfast broadband at downstream speeds of at least 30Mbps, which Virgin Media was already beginning to provide. The 2009 *Digital Britain* report declared:

> Next generation fixed fibre and cable networks offer not just conventional high-definition video entertainment and games, but

potentially more revolutionary benefits for our economy and society – telepresence, e-healthcare in the home and, for small and medium-sized businesses, access to cloud computing (which substantially cuts hardware and application costs and allows much more rapid product and service innovation). And next generation broadcast will move us into a new era of interactivity and high definition services.

(BIS and DCMS, 2009: 48)

The Coalition government's 2010 policy paper, entitled *Britain's Superfast Broadband Future*, argued that:

Superfast broadband will provide the foundations from which the UK economy will grow and recover from the recession. It will change the way we do business, how we interact with people and how we access entertainment. It will offer better and more efficient channels for delivering public services, making them more accessible. It will reduce costs for consumers and enhance the capability of businesses to communicate and exchange information with their customers and suppliers. This is fundamental to our future prosperity.

(BIS and DCMS, 2010: 7)

Delivering superfast broadband can be done by fixed broadband or by wireless technology. A high capacity fixed network based on fibre optic connections either to the home (FTTH) or to a nearby cabinet (FTTC) generally needs to be a core part of any national strategy, and can be coupled with mobile networks offering very high bandwidth – often using spectrum released through digital television switchover.

The UK's political rhetoric reflected an awareness of infrastructure initiatives and targets in other advanced economies. Japan, South Korea and Singapore are in the vanguard, with 40% of Japanese homes already served by superfast broadband (Ofcom, 2011: 10). Singapore has committed to a Next Generation Nationwide Broadband Network involving a fibre optic connection for superfast speeds into every home. In the United States the FCC has developed a National Broadband Plan with a long-term goal of at least 100 million United States homes having affordable access to actual download speeds of at least 100 megabits per second and actual upload speeds of at least 50 megabits per second (FCC, 2010). Already, post-switchover, the FCC has consulted broadcasters on the notion of releasing additional broadcasting spectrum for broadband purposes in return for an opportunity to benefit financially.

Australia initially announced an ambitious universal fibre optic commitment but scaled it back to a plan for fibre-to-the home for 90% of homes with the remaining 10% served by wireless technology providing up to 12Mbps. Broadband targets in Europe include Germany's goal that 75% of households will have download speeds of 50 Mbps by 2014, Spain's plan to make 100 Mbps broadband available to 50% of its population, and France's aim of 100% access to very high-speed broadband by 2025 (Ofcom, 2011: 229).

Promulgating a strategy, and setting target dates in the middle distance, is much easier than delivering implementation. The closer to 100% the superfast broadband coverage target, the less likely it is to be delivered by the market – and the more likely that the public expenditure implications will be challenged, as they were in the case of Australia's original scheme. Nonetheless, the direction of telecommunications infrastructure development is clear. The question is not whether we shall have superfast broadband; it is, rather, who will get it when?

The authors of *Digital Britain* opined that

> In Digital Britain, with the Universal Service Commitment delivering video quality bandwidth and most households having much greater bandwidth, streamed, downloaded or searched-for content will become the norm.
>
> (BIS and DCMS, 2009: 109)

A House of Lords report in 2012 put the case for a national broadband network as a fundamental strategic asset and saw Internet access as 'a domestic essential' and 'key utility' (House of Lords, 2012: 5). It also pictured the possibility of television moving to Internet distribution in the long-term and argued that, in that event, a Universal Service Obligation for broadband would need to mirror broadcasting's obligation. A Universal Service Obligation for broadband Internet has already been adopted in Finland (Levy and Nielsen, 2010).

## The 'end of television?' debate

Are we witnessing the beginning of the 'end of television', as broadcast and broadband media move beyond convergence and fuse, leaving 'television' an ill-defined sub-set of a larger communications industry, in which 'one-to-many' schedules of programmes broadcast at fixed times for fixed place reception are a fading memory? This is a debate which has sprung up in academic journals and on media industry conference platforms as the digital television transition has progressed. Much depends, of course, on how you define 'television'. What makes it distinctive? Is it the technology for distributing it, its content, its 'live' schedules, or the receiver the viewer uses? Here we look at the means of distribution and then at audience usage.

## Distribution

Some very early signs of what ultimately may prove to be a long-term reduction in broadcasting transmission can be detected. According to Nielsen figures, the number of Internet-only TV homes in the United States is growing significantly, though still accounting for less than 5% of the total number of TV households (Advanced Television, 2012a). Could this be the beginning of a trend of 'cord-cutting' – disconnecting from cable and satellite to rely wholly on broadband Internet for video content? In its Consultation on a strategy for spectrum management over the period 2012–2030, Ofcom envisaged broadcast television continuing to play a central role, but added:

> Over a much longer (post 2030) timeframe the universal take-up of superfast broadband could enable IPTV services to provide a viable substitute for the DTT [digital terrestrial television] platform, enabling a potential future DTT switch-off scenario.
>
> (Ofcom, 2012b: 4)

Broadcast engineers have started to feel the pressure. They recognised that one of broadcasting's weaknesses, compared to the Internet, was its splintering into rival, incompatible technical standards. In 2012 a group of senior industry experts, representing the ATSC, DVB and key organisations in Japan, China, Brazil, Korea and Canada, signed a Future of Broadcast Television (FOBTV) memorandum of understanding, reasserting the importance of terrestrial broadcasting and making a pledge to work towards a global digital terrestrial television standard. Given that digital terrestrial television was originally invented to torpedo Japan's quest for a global analogue standard, as we saw in Chapter 1, the wheel could turn full circle.

The FOBTV initiative also included a commitment to collaborate with other transmission systems:

> Today, technological innovation may be able to break down many of the long-standing barriers that have prevented common systems. This could enable removing the gaps between the different television

signal formats and transmission systems used around the world. The 21st century is an era of integration of broadcasting, internet and communications, all of which have evolved in parallel. Consumers are calling for more convenient and user-friendly services. The development of digital technology opens the possibility of cooperation among all the different networks and transmission systems.

(FOBTV, 2012)

In Europe researchers at the University of Braunschweig in Germany, sceptical about the continuing need to devote so much spectrum to terrestrial television, have developed the concept of Dynamic Broadcasting, combining terrestrial TV, broadband and hard-disc recording technology in a 'dynamic' receiver which manages itself to ensure that TV reception is only used for 'live' viewing and that all other material is delivered by broadband to the recorder. The broadband connection then monitors the pattern and the idea is that this could enable the service provider to predict and modify the TV transmission parameters to improve spectrum efficiency (DigiTAG, 2012c).

To the question 'are we witnessing the end of television?' the technical answer is: No, but we are seeing the beginning of a hybrid broadcast–broadband system of distribution.

## Audience usage

However, distribution shifts are not what most participants in the debate have in mind when they discuss the 'end of television'. In an Issue of the Annals of the American Academy of Political and Social Science devoted to this topic in 2009, Elihu Katz pictured television, like print and radio before it, as evolving along a content axis of 'same' to 'differentiated' and a consumption axis of 'together' to 'alone'. He continued:

> Is television really dying? For the television some of us knew in the 1960s and 1970s, the answer is 'yes'. The television of 'sharedness' – of nation-building and family togetherness – is no longer with us, having made room for a television of hundreds of channels, of 'niche' broadcasting, of portability, one that is part of a system that integrates with the Internet and other new media.

He linked this with a loss of public faith in professionals and regulators 'who claimed to know, better than we do, what's good for us' and diagnosed, if not the end of television, at any rate the end of 'classic television' (Katz, 2009: 7).

In the same Issue Amanda Lotz argued that television, while continuing to exist, was evolving into a post-network era where content breaks free of the schedule (Lotz, 2009a) and, in *Beyond Prime Time*, she observed:

> For the better part of twenty years, the industry succeeded in incrementally adjusting old practices but, by the early twenty-first century, the technologies and opportunities to create and share video became too preponderant for 'further adjustments' and a whole-scale revolution began to take place.
>
> (Lotz, 2009b: 7)

José Alvarez-Monzoncillo, author of *Watching the Internet: the Future of TV?'*, also sees an unprecedented shift in television with major ramifications both for business and for viewers:

> The social functions once fulfilled by TV are in crisis, while new ones have yet to be defined. Whereas the analogue business was based on advertisers and audiences, it is now Internet users who will influence the growth of new and digital media markets. Until now, we watched media only on one screen; now we watch it on several screens. Before, we watched media with our family; now watch it alone. Network coverage spreads beyond the nation-state; plural, egalitarian access has led to a new hyper-segmentation; content is shaped around 'lifestyle', shattering the logic of the homogeneous, cross-class family audience.
>
> (Alvarez-Monzoncillo, 2011: 26)

For others, television looks to be in much better health. Australian academics Jinna Tay and Graeme Turner have argued that the American perspective needs to be challenged and, providing a wealth of data about the strength of broadcast television in the Asian market, question any assumption that the American market represents a model which the rest of the world will follow. In *Not the Apocalypse: Television Futures in the Digital Age*, they conclude that, while viewing practices will change,

> We should not lose sight of the continuities with aspects of the broadcast regime nor assume that we are awaiting the same process of evolutionary change in every market as a result of a shift in technological capabilities. Nor, and most importantly, should we overlook the notable and highly contingent national, regional, political and

cultural differences which need to be factored into any genuinely international and comparative account of the possible futures of digital television.

(Tay and Turner, 2010: 47)

Australian data at the end of 2011 showed 'traditional TV viewing on the rise' (Advanced Television, 2012b) and, as we have seen, TV viewing has risen in the UK and other European countries. In the UK, despite the rise of On-Demand services and new recording technology, the vast majority of TV viewing remains 'live', though spread across more channels. Even within homes equipped with digital video recorders, time-shifted viewing accounted for only 15% of all viewing hours in 2011 (Ofcom, 2012a: 170). Patrick Barwise has argued cogently that time-shifted viewing from recorders and Catch-Up TV of programmes drawn from the TV schedule need to be seen as an integral part of linear TV. The *Digital Britain* idea that 'streamed, downloaded and searched-for content' will provide the bulk of the viewer's TV diet once we all have access to high performance broadband is, in his view, fantasy (Barwise, 2011).

Certainly viewing habits have remained conservative in the face of the more melodramatic forecasts of a transformation. Even Alvarez-Monzoncillo concedes that Internet users currently spend fewer than six hours a month watching videos, whereas average television viewing in most developed countries is three hours a day (Alvarez-Monzoncillo, 2011: 66). The persistence of traditional viewing patterns may, of course, be attributable to the 'legacy' viewing habits of the older generation brought up on analogue television and the incomplete state of the broadband infrastructure – and therefore temporary. On this argument viewing behaviour will only fully reflect all the new opportunities created by technology convergence after a generational lag. However, a significant part of the explanation for viewer conservatism is that, even with an abundance of channels and content, the established broadcasters remain the main source of high-quality original TV production. Digital technology may allow anyone to become a producer but digital TV economics restrict the production companies able to make major investment in top-quality content.

## Content provider concentration

Convergence is altering the business economics of media content provision. Growing usage of the Internet has attracted advertisers who, in varying degrees, have migrated there from the traditional outlets of newspapers and commercial television. The switch of classified advertising away from newspapers has been particularly marked, leaving the local newspaper industry struggling, but the impact on broadcasting has also been significant. The size of the Internet advertising market surpassed the television advertising market in 2011, as advertisers chased the younger audiences using social media and watching online videos (*Times*, 2011a).

New Internet businesses have flourished and new commercial giants have appeared but as intermediaries, rather than content producers:

> Google and Yahoo own no news, Amazon owns no publishers, iTunes own no record companies, YouTube owns no television producers, PayPal has no liability side, and Skype and Facebook own no networks.
>
> (Alvarez-Monzoncillo, 2011: 13)

For the established content providers the convergence of technologies created a conundrum. They needed to move into multi-media in order to maintain their appeal – hence TV broadcasters developed online sites and versioned their content for different devices (and newspapers produced online editions) but diversifying involved costly new investment. Some revenue could be secured from Internet advertising but websites and mobile phone apps were often free to users: indeed the ethos of the Internet was free access to anyone to almost anything from anywhere in the world. Constructing 'pay walls' around quality content was difficult when competitors' material was available for free.

On the other hand, established content providers had a major advantage over new entrants: they already had content, most obviously in broadcasting, films and publishing, which could be adapted, extended and versioned, so they were not 'starting cold'. Their most promising strategy was to leverage their existing investments as much as possible, exploiting synergies and spreading overheads. Archives could be mined and successful formats marketed. This could be done on both a trans-national and a trans-media basis. The vertical integration of content production and distribution service provision was another strategic option.

Accordingly, while the number of channels, Internet sites and receiving devices multiplied, the trend among major content providers has been towards concentration, with 'mergers, acquisitions and other business alliances between previously separated media companies' (Iosifidis, 2011b: 69). While the Internet has seen a huge expansion of suppliers of content produced at relatively low cost, the sources of major invest-ment in high-quality production for what we still call 'television' have become consolidated.

In the UK the former analogue channels have developed new TV, online and On-Demand services and the BBC has expanded its com-mercial business, BBC Worldwide. ITV has been transformed from a federation of regional companies into ITV plc. Channel 5, previously owned by RTL (Radio-Television Luxembourg), was bought by North-ern and Shell, owners of the *Express* and *Star* newspapers, in 2010. BSkyB, part owned by Rupert Murdoch's multi-media News Corpora-tion, acquired the telecommunications company Easynet in order to enter the broadband service market. BT conversely began buying sports rights with the aim of competing as a major player in content as well as distribution.

In Europe the giant is the German Bertelsmann group, a major pub-lishing company and now the majority owner of RTL, which in turn owns TV stations in several European countries, including groups of channels in Germany and the Netherlands and M6 in France. The French pay-TV group, Canal Plus, is owned by the multi-media con-glomerate Vivendi, which acquired Universal Studios in 2000 and found that it had over-expanded.

In the United States the buying, selling, merging and de-merging of media businesses between powerful conglomerates is a way of life. Gen-eral Electric (GE), owners of NBC, formed NBC Universal jointly with Vivendi to run the NBC TV network, Universal Studios and a range of cable channels. Then, in 2013 GE sold its stake in the venture to Comcast, America's biggest cable operator. The CBS TV network was acquired by the media giant Viacom in 2000 but Viacom then sep-arated it out again. The ABC TV network is now owned by Disney. America's fourth network, Fox, is owned by News Corporation, along with Twentieth Century Fox, the publisher Harper Collins and a portfo-lio of newspapers in the United States, the UK and Australia. However, the separation of the TV and film business, to be known as the Fox Group, from the News Corporation publishing business was announced in 2012. Time-Warner, the product of a merger between the Time maga-zine publishing house and Warner Bros film business, having shed AOL, runs HBO (Home Box Office) and CNN among a range of other inter-ests. Liberty Media, a multi-national cable business with other interests including the QVC shopping channel and the book retailer Barnes and Noble, acquired the UK's Virgin Media in 2013.

With technology convergence accompanied by media corporation convergence, the shape of the all-digital communications industry is emerging. The picture is of an abundance of channels and services, new reception and recording devices, a blurring of the distinction between TV and other video content, the emergence of hybrid broadcasting–broadband distribution, the fragmentation of audiences across more channels (but remaining, for the most part, viewers of television), and a concentration of major multi-media content suppliers. It amounts to a transformation of the analogue broadcasting industry and sets a new context for communications regulation.

# 8
# Cross-Media Regulation?

## Summary of the chapter's argument

Governments constructed a distinctive regulatory framework for analogue television, reflecting (a) restricted market entry due to spectrum scarcity and (b) the mass audiences for TV programmes and their intrusion into the home. Broadcasters had to be licensed and the terms of their licence prescribed obligations and constraints on programme content.

During the digital transition this framework was adapted, to a limited extent, to encompass the convergence of television and Internet-based video. In Europe 'television' was no longer defined by its means of distribution or reception device but by its 'live' schedule of programmes. However, the digital revolution is undermining the analogue-related foundations of this regulatory framework: spectrum scarcity no longer restricts entry to the converging video production and distribution business, TV audiences have fragmented and viewers have much greater control over what they watch where and when.

Accordingly, it will become necessary (even if many governments opt for evolutionary change here initially) to re-examine the foundations of this broadcasting regulation. The first question is whether any special government-based regulation is needed at all, or whether, as for the Press historically in the UK, the United States and other liberal democracies, the public interest could be properly served by a combination of the law and self-regulation? In 2012 the UK concluded that the traditional Press model was flawed, to the extent that legally rooted independent regulation was proposed as an option for newspapers.

While there is a public interest in a framework of regulation for digital television and related online video services, the notion of basing this on licences for the use of spectrum is becoming an anachronism. With newspapers developing online versions with video content, the concept of three sets of regulation for 'television', Internet-based videos and the Press, with different standards, creates anomalies – compounded by the fact that the Connected TV set can display differently regulated services on the same reception device. The logic of convergence suggests a cross-media approach with recognition of the case for more demanding regulation of media organisations with a major market share and very substantial public influence, regardless of their means of distribution.

## Cultural differences

The context for regulation after digital switchover is being set by convergence, especially as broadcasters and newspapers both move increasingly into online distribution as multi-media content providers. However, different countries have historically developed regulation in different ways and, despite the commonality of the technology and business trends, are at different starting-points in facing the implications of digital convergence.

In the United States, whose culture still reflects an early history of dissent against seventeenth century European religious institutions and eighteenth century British rulers, freedom of expression is enshrined in the Constitution. Thus, in the First Amendment it passed in 1791, the United States Congress prohibited itself from making any law 'respecting the establishment of religion, or prohibiting the free exercise thereof' or 'abridging the freedom of speech or of the press'. Here, therefore, any form of media regulation which constrains liberty of expression is open to legal challenge.

The 'Old World', however, has a more ambivalent cultural heritage, encompassing the suppression of religious heresy and seditious libel, on the one hand, and the blows for liberty struck by Milton in the seventeenth century and Wilkes in the eighteenth, on the other. In 1798, just a few years after America had adopted the First Amendment, the British government, combating both the ideas and armies of the French Revolution, banned the import of foreign newspapers.

In the twentieth century the patterns of media regulation in the United States and in Europe diverged greatly. In the United States broadcasting, like the Press, grew up as essentially a commercial industry. In Europe, by contrast, while the Press was often only lightly self-regulated, broadcasting was placed firmly within the state's control – albeit within 'arm's length' public service broadcasting institutions with editorial independence in the UK and a number of other countries. Commercial broadcasting was admitted later within a purpose-designed regulatory structure.

The analogue television regulatory pattern, especially in the UK and Europe, rested, to a significant extent, on the assumption that spectrum was scarce. The reasoning here was that very few television broadcasters would be possible; those selected would therefore be 'privileged' and should be expected to meet high-quality standards and to provide a wide range of genres, from light entertainment to religion, designed to meet the needs of different audiences within the constraints of one, or at best, two channels.

A second assumption was that the viewer was relatively powerless. With mass audiences, television broadcasters were powerful and influential organisations, so, to safeguard the citizen, they should be required to show 'due impartiality' in matters of political and public controversy. Moreover, because they pumped their programmes straight into the intimacy of the home, leaving the viewer with far less choice than a newspaper reader, they were required to avoid giving offence and to shield children from unsuitable content before their presumed bedtime. This was a very different world from the campaigning, topless model-featuring, politically partisan Press.

In the United States, with many more analogue TV channels than most European countries, regulated fairness came to be seen as potentially in conflict with the First Amendment's protection of free speech. The 'Fairness Doctrine', which had obliged broadcasting licensees to present controversial issues of public importance and to do so fairly by airing rival views, was abandoned in 1987. However, although the great majority of Americans viewed television via cable and satellite, American regulation of taste and decency remained rooted in a licence to use spectrum for 'over-the-air' broadcasting. This was the basis for the FCC fining the broadcaster in the 'Nipplegate' episode of 2004 when Janet Jackson had a 'wardrobe malfunction' and bared a breast during the Superbowl coverage.

Different cultures and traditions have brought different regulatory systems from the analogue era into the digital age, though the European Union provides a degree of consistency within Europe. The general pattern is for media regulation designed within separate structures for the Press and broadcasting – and an underlying assumption that broadcasting is distinctively different and should be regulated more closely, using the state's licensing of spectrum as the basis for state-sanctioned interventions over content.

Digital television and convergence combine to challenge this. The advent of digital plurality in broadcasting has undermined the spectrum scarcity assumption – with UK viewers having upwards of 50 channels in place of five, for example. The multiplicity of choice combined with sophisticated recording technology has weakened the idea of the power-less viewer. The Internet arrived with yet another regulatory framework, that of telecommunications, plus a North American ethos of freedom of expression and an international dissemination which defied tidy national control. Internet video services and online newspapers, available alongside broadcast television on a Connected TV set, now blur the historic regulatory boundaries. An all-digital communications media pattern is emerging and eroding the intellectual pillars on which media regulation was constructed.

Regulatory institutions have sought to adapt as new forms of communication have developed. The UK's regulatory history provides an illuminating example, culminating in the integration of broadcasting and telecommunications regulation. However, as the case study reveals, it has yet to find a new intellectually strong framework for regulating digital media.

## UK regulation: a case study

### Press regulation

Newspapers are no longer licensed – the English Licensing Act lapsed in 1695 – but their governance has not been left entirely to the law and the market. In the UK, following a Royal Commission on the Press (1947–1949) and a subsequent threat of statutory regulation, a voluntary Press Council, funded by newspaper proprietors, was formed in 1953 to uphold ethical standards. It failed to command public and political confidence. In 1991, again in order to fend off government intervention, the industry formed a new non-statutory Press Complaints Commission (PCC) which drew up a code of practice and adjudicated on complaints. There were no quality standards (beyond adherence to the code), no barriers to political partisanship, no penalties for breaches of the Code (other than an apology and publication of the PCC's adjudication), no restrictions on entry to the industry and no enforceable obligation even to belong to the PCC. Editorial freedom and journalistic independence were paramount.

The PCC was widely criticised as being ineffective, especially when Northern and Shell, publishers of the *Express* and *Star*, withdrew from it in 2011. It came to the end of the road with the scandal later that year over illegal phone-hacking by researchers and journalists working for News Corporation's *News of the World*. The scandal was hydra-headed: the issues went beyond wide-scale journalistic law-breaking and newspaper management cover-ups into police corruption and uncomfortably close relationships between politicians and newspaper proprietors.

The government set up an investigative Inquiry under Lord Justice Leveson, in testimony to which the PCC proposed abolishing itself. Instead it proposed the creation of a new self-regulating body, resting on contractual commitments from its members. Newspaper owners and editors wished to avoid any structure which was statute-based. Lord Leveson's report recommended an independent regulatory body which could enforce a code of conduct, investigate complaints and apply sanctions. However, he argued, controversially, that this would require legislation to provide a statute-based higher body which could recognise and validate the independent regulator and perhaps act as a 'backstop' regulator for any major newspapers that refused to accept independent regulation (Leveson, 2012). The Press opposed any statute.

Newspapers' freedom to editorialise and champion one political party at election time, if it wished, had always been part of Press freedom. However, evidence to the Leveson Inquiry of the cosy relationship between Conservative politicians and the Murdoch Press, and memories of New Labour's not dissimilar relationship in the past, showed the political power associated with this freedom to be partisan. While some other newspapers, like the *Telegraph* and the *Mail*, tended to be consistent in their political support, the Murdoch-owned *Sun* had switched its allegiance more than once at critical points in the electoral cycle (after its Editor famously claimed 'It's The Sun wot won it' in 1992), causing politicians of both major parties to court its support. The extent to which politicians courted News Corporation contacts in order to secure their journalistic support both in fighting elections and in governing was exposed as unwise and unhealthy – but no one proposed requiring them to observe 'due impartiality'. Although Lord Leveson's candidate for the recognition and backstop body was Ofcom, politicians were opposed to that: Press and broadcasting regulation were to remain separate.

### Broadcasting regulation

The development of broadcasting regulation in the UK, starting in the 1920s, was shaped by the state. For its first three decades the BBC was an unchallenged public service monopoly. Commercial television was admitted in 1955. However, the ITV commercial companies were contractors who supplied regional and network programmes to a public body, the Independent Television Authority (ITA), under a set of regulatory obligations and constraints, and the ITA broadcast them via its own transmitters. The BBC's radio monopoly continued until local commercial radio was introduced in the 1970s, leading to the transformation of the ITA into the IBA (Independent Broadcasting Authority).

The BBC operated under a Royal Charter and licence, the IBA under a statute, and the governing bodies of each, while editorially independent, were government appointees. The IBA selected the programme companies, set the conditions of their franchises, and approved their senior management appointments and their schedules. The whole system – BBC and IBA – was termed 'public service broadcasting'. Content was to be of high quality and broad in range, serving both majority and minority audiences, with social and cultural purposes rising above the lowest common denominator of popular appeal. The BBC Governors and the IBA Members were trustees for the public, committed to pursuing the public interest, as distinct from political and commercial interests.

At the outset, the regulatory structure was a serious constraint. Clause 4 of the BBC's first licence required it to abstain from 'statements expressing the opinion of the Corporation on matters of public policy' and from 'speeches or lectures containing statements on topics of political, religious or industrial controversy'. The BBC argued fiercely and successfully against this 'ban on controversy' but the ban on editorialising remained (Briggs, 1965: 129). The government retained a reserve power to ban content but never used it in peacetime, though it did occasionally lean on the Board of Governors to try to stop a programme being broadcast. Alongside editorialising constraints, broadcasters also had obligations of 'taste and decency' and a scheduling duty to protect children from adult material.

With the arrival of commercial television and the stimulus this gave to the BBC, UK broadcasters managed to shake off political restrictions on news and current affairs coverage. Due impartiality on matters of controversy, though, became integral to their remits. For the citizen, due impartiality could be an advantage, with broadcast programmes eschewing the partisanship of the Press and ensuring that a full range of viewpoints was aired. An alternative perspective was voiced in 1973 by Anthony Smith who saw it as a kind of 'ideology' to help keep the institutions 'out of trouble' (Smith, 1973: Preface).

In 1982 Channel 4 was launched as an advertisement-financed public service body under the IBA with a remit focussed on minority interests. However, during the long period of Conservative government from

1979 to 1997, UK broadcasting was transformed from an institutional public service duopoly into a more pluralist analogue market. Channel 4 was designed as a publisher, whose programmes were supplied by independent producers and this opened up an independent production industry. It subsequently ceased to be a subsidiary of the IBA and became a separate public body. Cable and satellite services developed, creating a subscription TV market, and for a period cable had its own 'light touch' regulator. The IBA was broken up and its transmitter department privatised. Television came under the new Independent Television Commission, which was clearly a regulator, not a publisher. Commercial radio was expanded. Channel Five was created as a further competitor for commercial advertising revenue.

The trend was towards liberalisation and decentralisation, with a relaxation of 'positive' regulation for the commercial sector. However, 'negative' regulation, to address media abuses, was strengthened by the creation, first, of a Broadcasting Complaints Commission and then of a Broadcasting Standards Council, the two subsequently merging to form the Broadcasting Standards Commission.

## Impact of the Internet

Regulatory oversight of telecommunications came under another regulator, Oftel, which had been formed in 1984 when British Telecom was privatised and its market opened to new entrants. Its main preoccupations were issues of pricing and fair competition. Content regulation had not been a great telecommunications concern. The Internet was 'governed', in that interoperability and domain addresses were managed with discipline, but it was not regulated. With a background in research-sharing, its ethos was of a free exchange of ideas across frontiers.

However, the UK government did address issues of criminal online content, in particular child sexual abuse images and criminally obscene adult pornography. In 1996 the Internet Watch Foundation was established to work with Internet Service Providers (ISPs) and others, within a self-regulatory system. It developed a 'notice and take-down' system to try to ensure that such material was removed from the network. ISPs also offered their customers filters designed to assist parents to block their children's access to inappropriate content.

Different countries with different political systems and political concerns ranging from the suppression of dissent to the combating of terrorism made more extensive use of filtering and blocking techniques. The UK sought to suppress illegal activity, including copyright piracy, but generally it respected the Internet pioneers' commitment to freedom of information and expression. The Internet was more lightly regulated than the Press.

## The digital transition

In 2003, following the launch of digital broadcasting and with the prospect of increasing convergence, the UK established a new 'converged' regulator, Ofcom, to replace the Independent Television Commission, the Radio Authority, the Broadcasting Standards Commission, Oftel and the body which had previously managed spectrum, the Radio Communications Agency. It acquired some overlap of responsibility with the BBC Board of Governors (replaced from 2007 by the BBC Trust): while the latter was accountable for the BBC's adherence to standards of accuracy and impartiality, Ofcom was given broadcasting-wide responsibility for protecting audiences from harm and offence, plus a role in assessing the market impact of any proposals for new BBC services. It also had a remit periodically to review the effectiveness of public service television broadcasting as a whole.

So Ofcom found itself regulating in different ways and to different degrees:

- the BBC, Channel 4 and (for Wales) S4C public services, which were run by public bodies with specific remits of their own, going well beyond the obligations common to other broadcasters;
- the commercial broadcasters, ITV and Channel Five, with an analogue terrestrial history, which were still categorised as public services on the basis of obligations relating to their range of content;
- other commercial broadcasters with satellite and/or cable distribution or newcomers to digital terrestrial multiplexes with no analogue history.

All three sets of broadcasters had accuracy and due impartiality obligations, including services for UK reception originating outside the UK – for some of whom the UK obligation of due impartiality was a major source of contention.

Regulating Video-on-Demand also came within Ofcom's remit. The UK had favoured a minimum of regulation of the Internet except where content was in breach of the law but in 2007 the European Union replaced its 1989 *Television Without Frontiers* Directive with an Audio-Visual Media Services (AVMS) Directive spanning both broadcasting and the Internet and requiring some regulation by Member States of the latter. The Directive was technology-neutral, in the sense that it applied whether material was received on a computer or a TV set, but it distinguished between 'television broadcasts' delivered in a linear transmission schedule, simultaneously to all homes, and 'on-demand' services selected on a non-linear basis by the viewer. It excluded services which did not seek primarily to distribute audio-visual content, such as electronic versions of newspapers.

The regulatory constraints on On-Demand content were much lighter than for mainstream television. They focussed on prohibiting incitement to hatred and the risk of harm to children (including risks from advertising). Member States, whose job it was to enforce this lighter regulation, had until 2009 to transpose them into national law and could make lighter and more flexible arrangements such as self-regulation or co-regulation.

The UK Video-on-Demand industry initially set up a self-regulatory Association for VoD services originating in the UK. It had a contentious start and in 2010, to clarify its scope and strengthen its powers, it was converted into the co-regulatory Authority for Video-on-Demand (ATVOD). Under this arrangement Ofcom designated ATVOD with authority to regulate in accordance with the AVMS Directive but retained statutory 'backstop' powers, including the ability to impose financial sanctions (Mac Síthigh, 2011).

### Regulatory silos

Although, in forming Ofcom, the UK had integrated a number of previously separate regulatory bodies, the pattern of media regulation remained elaborate and complex. In particular, it retained separate silos for broadcasting, the Press and the Internet. Television was still assumed to require the highest level of content regulation, whether a major channel or an obscure import. Next came the Press – and finally, on account of its ethos and of practicalities, the Internet was treated with the lightest touch.

Having different regulatory rules related to different means of distribution creates anomalies. At the beginning of 2012 Ofcom withdrew the broadcasting licence of the Iranian English-language television channel, Press TV, after a long-running dispute. Press TV had been found in breach of Ofcom's requirement for due impartiality in 2009 and 2010 (Fielden, 2011) and was then fined for broadcasting an interview with an imprisoned journalist which had been conducted under duress. Press TV refused to pay the fine, so Ofcom revoked its licence (Guardian, 2012a) and the channel was taken off satellite television. Press TV transmissions remained on the Internet, however, where neither Ofcom nor ATVOD had the authority to stop them.

In 2010 Rupert Murdoch's News Corporation, owners of the *News of the World*, the *Sun*, the *Times* and *Sunday Times*, had been seeking to extend its 40% share ownership of the satellite broadcaster BSkyB in order to take full control. News Corporation's competitors objected, sparking an extended investigation and debate over media ownership concentration and plurality. When the *News of the World* phone-hacking scandal broke, News Corporation withdrew its bid in the face of public and Parliamentary ire. As evidence came to light of a management cover-up, Ofcom, cheered on by some Labour politicians, investigated whether News Corporation qualified as a 'fit and proper person' to hold a *broadcasting* licence. Ofcom has a duty to make 'fit and proper persons' judgments in licensing around 500 TV broadcasters and hundreds of radio stations, many of them tiny. In this case the professional integrity of BSkyB and Sky News was not an issue. What the public wanted to know was whether News Corporation was fit to run such a powerful group of *newspapers*, but neither the Press regulator nor Ofcom had the power to ask it.

Another anomaly lies in regulatory responsibility for online news. UK broadcasters had developed news services on the Internet which were a combination of text, still photos and video clips and these fell within the remit of the BBC and Ofcom. At the same time newspapers had moved onto the Internet, publishing electronic versions (some free, some for a charge) which could also combine text, photos and video clips. So *Telegraph* video news can be received on a Connected TV without any due impartiality obligation. Indeed it is thought to have dropped its original brand 'Telegraph TV' in order to avoid attracting broadcast regulation (Purvis, 2010).

Electronic versions of newspapers had been excluded from the scope of the European AVMS Directive, and hence from ATVOD's supervision, and left for the PCC to oversee. However, newspaper websites could be developed in ways going well beyond electronic versions of their print publications and in 2011 ATVOD declared that it viewed *News of the World* Video, *Sun* Video, *Elle* TV and the *Sunday Times* Video Library as On-Demand services (Fielden, 2011).

As television channels become super-abundant and television broadcasters turn multi-media, as online video services continue to grow, as newspapers slowly migrate to the Internet under commercial pressure, these divided responsibilities, with different regulators setting different standards and holding different powers, will appear increasingly anomalous. The point has been illustrated here through a UK case study but the principle applies much more generally. As Tim Suter has noted, audiences risk becoming confused when moving from one regulatory territory to another:

> This will be particularly sharp when the same content is available from different providers, with different degrees of protection or restriction, but via the same hybrid service and on the same device (for instance, films with a particular rating which either may be only permitted for broadcast after the watershed or behind some form of PIN protection if transmitted earlier in the day: but they may be freely available via an on-line film category at any time of day with either limited, or no, PIN or other restriction.

> (Suter, 2013: 76)

## Some fundamental questions

In the short term some national governments and regulators – and indeed the European Union – may prefer to try to evolve new patterns of regulation slowly, not least because audience behaviour is changing less rapidly than technology. However, to shape a regulatory framework appropriate to the steadily converging digital communications media, it is necessary to go back to some fundamental questions. Do we need special regulation for digital communications media?

Preventing monopoly abuses and ensuring competition are economy-wide issues, enforced by law and overseen by Competition Commissions. In addition, there is a body of media law dealing with essential issues for citizens – from the prevention of incitement to terrorism or racism through to remedies for libel and defamation. Phone hacking and bribery of the police are illegal. If there is a body of law dealing with essential issues for citizens, if the consumer has plenty of choice, and if the owners and managers of media organisations additionally set their own standards of quality and responsibility, why have any additional media regulation at all?

Economic liberals have argued that, with an abundance of digital communications media and a cornucopia of choice, the regulatory framework inherited from the analogue era should be dismantled. State-based media regulation, over and above legal requirements, is inherently contrary to citizens' best interests: for the digital future the less regulation, the better. This is widely perceived as the American 'First Amendment' model and it fits the ethos of the Internet. Within other cultures different perspectives can be found. In the UK Steven Barnett has pleaded passionately for a halt to the erosion of the UK's analogue TV regulatory framework, which he sees as having nurtured high-quality news and current affairs:

> As that protective regulatory framework diminishes, and as competition intensifies, great television journalism is under threat. It has already virtually disappeared in the United States, where the legacy of Edward R. Murrow and other revered journalistic voices from the past were long ago overwhelmed by an unregulated market that cared little for the democratic role of journalism. And now it is under threat not just in the United Kingdom but in many other developed and developing countries whose politicians are being seduced into believing that the market place is the universal panacea. History warns us – screams at us – that this is entirely wrong.... Thoughtfully constructed, responsibly implemented and genuinely independent regulation can promote the best journalism, not restrain it; regulation can liberate it rather than censor it.
>
> (Barnett, 2011: xi)

Why then might some form of regulation going beyond the law and the market serve the public interest in the all-digital era? The five areas of citizen concern listed below are not intended to provide a definitive answer (for a fuller analysis, see Suter, 2013) but they do capture the main issues which could justify the regulation of digital communications:

- Preventing the exercise of undue power, particularly political influence, by media organisations
- Prescribing high standards of quality and range of content for cultural reasons
- Protecting children from potentially harmful content
- Forbidding the publication of offensive content (explicit sex, gratuitous violence, unwarranted swearing or blaspheming)
- Ensuring accuracy, fair treatment and respect for privacy to safeguard individuals against misrepresentation and mistreatment by the media – complemented by rights of complaint backed by remedies and sanctions

## Preventing the exercise of undue power

Preventing monopolies and fostering competition are desirable policy aims across most of the economy but the media do constitute a special case because of their ability to influence public opinion and shape the agenda of politics and public affairs. However, the notion that broadcasting needs extra controls because of its traditionally bigger audiences is offset by the historically greater freedom of the Press to favour particular political parties – and the emergence of media conglomerates makes cross-media ownership a major concern. Regulatory policy here should span the communications media. The heart of any assessment of plurality, or investigation into prospective acquisitions and mergers, should not be the means of distribution – broadcasting, Internet or print – but the market share, especially of news services, held by any one entity, taking into account all media outlets of size and significance.

Should regulation require news and matters of political controversy to be presented impartially, without 'editorialising' or political partisanship? For public service broadcasters, with a public policy remit and/or supported by public funding, due impartiality is certainly an appropriate requirement but the economic liberal assumption has generally been that, once access to scarce spectrum no longer constrained market entry to broadcasting, this obligation could be lifted for commercial broadcasters. Like the Press, or for that matter like online video publishers, they could be free to decide for themselves whether to adopt a duly impartial stance or to be partisan. Under this assumption, the American decision to abandon the Fairness Doctrine in the twentieth century points the way forward for the rest of the world in the twenty-first.

Steven Barnett has argued strongly in favour of retaining the impartiality obligation in the new digital environment. It encourages serious journalism, as distinct from opinionated comment; it has the trust of viewers; and removing it, far from allowing a much fuller range of views to be voiced, could give undue influence to a relatively small number of wealthy media barons with their own political agendas (Barnett, 2011).

However, the task of content regulation across hundreds of different broadcasters is difficult in practical terms, anomalous in relation to other media, and, in theory, could place a lot of power in the hands of a state-appointed regulator to decide the politically acceptable agenda within which some form of impartiality is required over time. The policing of impartiality involves some very contentious judgments. The UK regulator decided in 2003 that Fox News – the 'voice of right-wing America' in Steven Barnett's term – could be broadcast by satellite in the UK without breaching the due impartiality requirement since its cultural origins were elsewhere and its audiences were tiny (Barnett, 2011: 218). However, Ofcom more than once found the Iranian Press TV in breach of its Code for broadcasting programmes in which the Israeli viewpoint was not given due weight and consideration. Press TV did not deny that it was biased but argued that it should have the right to be (Fielden, 2011). Surely the touchstone here is whether the restriction on partisanship is necessary to prevent undue political influence being wielded by a media organisation? Logically, such a test would apply to Press barons as well as to commercial TV moguls (and indeed to Internet News aggregators), though, if a media organisation has so much power as to warrant the imposition of an impartiality requirement, then its dominance raises the bigger question of whether it should be split up.

As the logic of convergence works its way through the regulatory debate, the media may in the end divide into:

- public institutions for which due impartiality is a requirement;
- commercial organisations which voluntarily choose it as a policy because it preserves their consumers' trust;
- other content providers, whether small TV channels, online services or print publications, which are unconstrained – provided they respect the fairness, accuracy and privacy obligations discussed below.

### Prescribing high standards of quality and range of content

Should media regulation prescribe high standards of quality, with conditions about the range and/or sources of content, in pursuit of cultural objectives which cannot be met by reliance solely on competitive market forces? Most countries would give a positive answer: even the United States has a small public broadcasting sector. Beyond the framework of public service media, there is also a case for setting certain national, regional or local content or language obligations on some media companies, perhaps with some form of subsidy or compensation. The approach here is likely to vary markedly from country to country (with some supra-nationally prescribed quotas in the European Union).

However, it is not desirable, or practical, to have prescriptive 'positive' regulation across the whole commercial media market or even across all 'television'. The question then becomes: on what basis should 'positive' regulation rest and whose job should it be to enforce it with what sanctions? In the UK case, why should all broadcasters who used to have analogue terrestrial transmissions be classified as 'public services', to the exclusion perhaps of other newer channels, and why should the 'public service' concept be exclusively identified with broadcast distribution? Evidence of new thinking is beginning to emerge here. Stewart

Purvis, a former broadcaster and Ofcom regulator and now an academic, has challenged the public service status of Channel Five (Purvis, 2010), while Ofcom itself once floated the idea of a new Public Service Publisher (PSP) designed on a multi-media basis (Ofcom, 2004b). While this particular proposal drew mixed responses, it was evidence that the logic of shifting regulation onto a cross-media basis was permeating regulatory thinking.

## Protecting children from potentially harmful content

Regulatory restrictions designed to protect children from pornography, unduly graphic violence, manipulative advertising, or other potentially harmful content are widely supported. Where serious harm is at issue, the law comes into play. In more discretionary areas, television broadcasting has a strong record of regulation. This includes the concept of the mid-evening 'watershed' after which young children are presumed to be in bed, allowing more adult material to be shown later at night – a concept likely to continue as long as the great majority of viewing remains to 'live' schedules, rather than to time-shifted programmes and online videos. The United States uses the V-chip ('V' for violence), now mandatory in every new TV set above a certain size, to facilitate parental blocking of violent programmes. Most television programmes are assigned a rating according to a system established by the television industry which is encoded before transmission. Parents can use the remote control to set the V-chip to block the display of programmes that carry particular ratings. Parental locks also block access to Video-on-Demand services.

However, the argument that television needs greater control than other media because it comes straight into the home uninvited has weakened. In practice parents' main concerns in this area relate to the largely unregulated Internet. The problem is not so much TV programmes coming *uninvited* into the family sitting-room as content children may *invite* on to their computers in the privacy of their bedrooms. While illegal material can be tackled further 'upstream', a complementary approach involves giving parents the tools to block sites with inappropriate content.

The way forward here – on a basis that encompasses both television and the Internet – is likely to consist of four elements:

- the law, in relation to advertising as well as programme content
- industry self-regulation by content providers and schedulers involving greater emphasis on a clear labelling of material and, where appropriate, using warnings

- a steady transfer of responsibility from central regulation 'down-stream' to parents and individuals, who will be expected to manage their consumption of video content in much the same way as they manage the consumption of print content
- media literacy initiatives in the field of education to help underpin this transfer.

### Forbidding offensive content

The idea of regulation to uphold 'taste and decency', historically embedded in broadcasting, is already hard to implement in any centralised top-down fashion. The blurred boundaries between different media forms are one problem. Changing standards – and the wide discrepancy of attitudes within the variety of diverse communities which make up many nations – are another. Again the trend is likely to be towards improving labelling and warning, so that those who wish to avoid being offended can do so readily – as they generally can with print media.

Noting the inappropriateness of current broadcasting restrictions for the Internet or current Internet *laissez-faire* for broadcasting, Roger Darlington has argued for basing a more converged system of content regulation on a 'test of harm', rather than the subjective test of offence against taste or decency. The definition of 'harm' he offers is:

> 'Content the creation of which or the viewing of which involves or is likely to cause actual physical or possible psychological harm'. Examples of material likely to be 'caught' by such a definition might be glorification or trivialization of violence, incitement to racial hatred or acts of violence, and promotion of anorexia, bulimia or suicide.
>
> (Darlington and Tambini, 2011: 289).

Looked at from the standpoint of different community and religious cultures, this test of 'harm' would be open to widely different interpretations if applied to material which was not actually illegal. However, it points to a core set of continuing concerns which include issues related to crime, such as payments to criminals or demonstrations of criminal techniques. While on matters of taste and decency, the way forward lies largely through advance warnings which help individuals to exercise choice and control at the user end, in respect of harm provisions will continue to be required in media codes of practice. Such provisions should logically apply across broadcasting, the Press and the Internet.

## Accuracy, fair treatment and privacy

Rules of accuracy, fair treatment and respect for privacy are needed to safeguard individuals against misrepresentation and mistreatment by the media. In the UK the Leveson Inquiry established beyond debate that voluntary regulation of the Press by the Press was wholly inadequate and the issue became how best to regulate the industry on an independent basis. The Leveson proposal to root Press regulation in legislation, however subtly, was heatedly contested, with fears about turning the clock back three centuries to a licensed Press, and the government proposed the alternative of rooting it in a Royal Charter.

It is hard to see, other than at a very detailed practical level, why regulatory approaches here should vary according to media distribution technology. From the individual citizen's standpoint all media should be subject to regulation relating, for example, to:

- factual accuracy
- explanation of the context in which media contributions will be used
- avoidance of harassment
- respect for privacy
- respect for grief
- misuse of irresponsible management of data.

What rights of complaint against the media, backed by what remedies and sanctions, should there be? The most serious grievances against media treatment will continue to involve recourse to the courts on matters of libel, defamation and breaches of privacy. However, the need for simple cost-free procedures for handling complaints about alleged breaches of a code of practice, with investigations and judgments made independently of the institution or industry involved, has now been fully recognised. The most obvious redress for an upheld complaint is a retraction and/or correction displayed with due prominence and accompanying a report of the investigation body's findings. Again the underlying principles here cross the media distribution boundaries: the wronged individual would expect the concepts of accuracy and fair treatment to be consistent across print, broadcast and Internet journalism.

## Towards a cross-media regulatory framework?

The 'silo' structure of regulation no longer fits the media environment. As communications on the Internet develop and convergence advances further, the argument will grow for a high-level set of principles – and institutions embodying them – which can span the communications media as a whole.

This is not to deny that some distinctions between media will remain significant for regulatory detail. Moving pictures can have a very different impact from still photographs and swear words impact differently in print and broadcasting with the different conventions for semi-disguising them. However, such differences arise also between television and radio and are not so great as to warrant completely different institutions and standards.

We shall still need a state-constituted regulatory body to have a continuing role in the field of spectrum management, across both broadcasting and telecommunications. It will issue licences to, and levy charges on, the primary users of spectrum. However, many TV broadcasters now gain access to their audiences via contracts with a satellite, cable or IPTV operator or with a digital terrestrial multiplex licensee. This tends to undermine the idea of using spectrum licensing as the basis for content regulation.

Cross-media content regulation does not necessarily imply the creation of an all-powerful agency enforcing a single set of rules: important distinctions exist between public and commercial media organisations, and between dominant players and others. Fear of an all-powerful single super-regulator and/or of a 'one-size-fits-all' set of uniform regulations tends to inhibit a radical breakaway from the inherited regulatory silos. New thinking is, however, beginning to emerge.

Drawing on some earlier work with Liz Forgan, Damian Tambini has proposed the idea of basing content regulation on a sliding scale of consumer expectation and market share, providing a rationale for different sets of standards which was not related to the means of distribution:

> The basic principle is simple. Where consumers expect regulation, for example when services receive public funding, and where audiences and therefore the impact of the media are largest, stronger content regulation should be applied.
>
> (Darlington and Tambini, 2011: 291)

While the context of his proposal was the convergence of broadcasting and the Internet, it is easy to see that the basic principle could be equally applicable to the Press.

Lara Fielden has proposed a cross-media regulatory framework with three tiers (Fielden, 2011). Tier 1 regulation would apply to cross-platform public service provision, would have a statutory basis and would include a due impartiality obligation as well as other 'positive' quality standards. Tier 2 would involve an independent regulator for 'ethical private media' who would set their own voluntary standards over and above the legal minimum. Tier 3 would be for 'baseline private media' and should have its own regulator ensuring compliance with essential legal requirements. This might sound rather like Ofcom, a reformed Press Complaints Commission and ATVOD each put onto a cross-media basis and thus embodying a transition process with a UK focus, but the underlying line of thought points a way of escape from the bogey of a super-regulator with a single approach.

Another formulation, ignoring transitional issues for the present, would be a cross-media framework consisting of:

- a statutory body, responsible for spectrum management and top-level spectrum licensing; for market analysis and assessments of media plurality; for media research; for consultations on matters of public concern; and for enforcing, either directly or through some form of co-regulation, media organisations' compliance with legal obligations
- self-regulation by the trustees of public bodies in respect of their specific remits, including due impartiality, paralleled by self-regulation by the company boards of commercial content providers who opt for a due impartiality policy
- an industry-wide independent Media Standards body, responsible for publishing a code of practice on fairness, accuracy, privacy and related matters and for administering an effective, sanctions-backed complaints procedure in the interests of the public.

The statutory regulator would use licences to manage spectrum, including continuing requirements for shifts of frequencies, as mobile telephony bands become more standardised internationally and expand while terrestrial TV benefits from technology improvements offering greater compression. However, licensing would cease to be a tool for the detailed content regulation of hundreds of broadcasters. In respect of content, state-based regulation would be restricted to taking appropriate action across all media to promote compliance with the law.

The much broader range of standards regulation, based on a code of practice, could be the responsibility of the separate independent Media Standards body which would neither be nominated by, nor funded by, the state. Membership of the Media Standards body would be expected of all media organisations above a certain size or market share (and should not attempt to encompass every parish magazine or Internet blog). Commitment to its standards and sanctions would be supported by a well-publicised kitemark denoting membership and verified conformance, so that the public would know whom and what to trust.

## A reality test

The ideas may be emerging but is there any sign of a cross-media approach taking root in practice? Lara Fielden has pointed to two examples. The first is Finland which retains a system of licensing for broadcasters but also has a Council for Mass Media which, having regulated news and current affairs in both print and journalism since its formation in 1968, now embraces regulation of online media as well (Fielden, 2012). The second is the work of a Convergence Review Committee in Australia which reported in March 2012.

In Australia the Press is regulated by the voluntary Australian Press Council while the statutory Australian Communications and Media Authority (ACMA) regulates broadcasting, telecommunications and the Internet and is responsible for spectrum management. The Convergence Review Committee was asked by the government to re-examine the country's media and communications policy framework in the light of technology convergence. Its report advocates a new 'principles-based' technology-neutral approach. Broadcasting licensing would end but some of the obligations imposed on licensees would continue for major 'content service enterprises' (Given, 2012).

Content service enterprises would be defined by their control over the professional content they deliver and by audience size and level of revenue – and regulated on a common basis regardless of their means of distribution. Thus newspapers and 'television-like' services would be brought within scope, but social media and user-generated content excluded. Regulation of these sizeable media organisations would cover ownership issues, content standards including the protection of children, and the production and distribution of Australian and local content. Smaller content providers, below the threshold set for content service enterprises, could choose whether to opt into the regulatory code of standards or to develop their own codes. Regulatory responsibility would belong to two bodies, a new statutory body to replace the ACMA and a separate industry-led body to oversee journalistic standards (Australian Government, 2012b).

The key point emerging from this and other analyses is that, in the design of a regulatory framework for digital communications media, the size and power of organisations is a much more significant factor than their means of distribution.

## Self-regulation by the consumer

Alongside the force driving towards a cross-media framework is another, however, driving towards more and more responsibility being taken at the reception end by the consumer. Reliance on central regulators of content will inevitably be reduced, partly because of the sheer volume of material available and partly because, with the growth of the Internet, of its increasingly global nature. As Lunt and Livingstone have noted in stressing the importance of media literacy,

> In the emerging global, technologically diverse and fast-moving markets for media and communications, individuals will have greater choice and will need to rely much more on their own judgments of quality, truthfulness and enjoyment.
>
> (Lunt and Livingstone, 2012: 16)

It is simply impractical for any regulator, even in closed societies, to monitor everything. So consumers will need to make their own judgments, assisted by labelling and warnings and armed with parental locks. Not only that but, where serious breaches of standards do occur, they will need to help the regulators by complaining – that is likely to be the only way many issues will come to a regulator's attention.

## Emerging outcomes?

The implications for regulation of an all-digital multi-media communications industry remain uncertain. The outcomes of the digital television revolution in this area are not yet known. The inconsistency of the inherited regulatory silos is becoming widely recognised but national decisions about what to do about them, and when, lie in the future.

Economic liberals still look forward to the withering away of regulation: the Press in the most liberal regimes was unshackled from the state long ago; the Internet is a free spirit which cannot practically be tamed; and, given the abundance of choice, top-down television regulation can now be dismantled, leaving viewers to self-regulate. However, this vision could prove a mirage. An alternative prediction is that television content will be freed from state control via licences tied to broadcasting spectrum, that self-regulation will increase but that key elements of regulation will remain at national level and be placed onto a cross-media basis. There will not be one set of rules for all: media organisations with the greatest market share and potential influence will, in some respects, be regulated differently from the myriad of small players. Moreover, a vital and distinctive element in the mix will be public service media, the subject of the next chapter.

# 9
# Public Service Digital Media

## Summary of the chapter's argument

Public service broadcasting has its roots in radio and, in its earliest incarnation, in monopoly. As it has evolved, encompassing television, facing commercial competition and adapting to social change, it has become harder to define: a core set of principles includes universality, independence of government and of commerce, serving minorities as well as majorities, reflecting national culture and identity and sustaining high quality.

In the 1980s and 1990s, as multi-channel subscription television arrived, market liberalism was in the ascendant in many countries and public service broadcasting on the defensive: its decline, in audience share at least, was seen as the fore-runner of its fall. However, it emerged in the twenty-first century in good health, albeit in a much more fragmented market. It reinvented itself for the digital age, stressed its distinctive public service character and spread into multi-media. Public service broadcasting morphed into public service media.

Of critical importance was public service television's role in assisting governments – indeed, almost partnering them – in implementing digital switchover. This brought additional public service TV channels and, temporarily anyway, extra funding. However, as switchover was completed, new pressures began to appear.

Governments reduced funding levels during the economic recession which began in 2008. Competitors challenged the degree to which public service broadcasting extended onto the Internet. Newspapers seeking to charge for their online versions resented the free availability of news on public broadcasters' websites. Tests were devised to control public service media's scope.

Technological convergence, especially the multiplication of reception devices, raised question marks over licence fee systems which had historically rested on possession of a TV set. However, the principle of citizen-funded public service media is more important than the administrative mechanism and, although technically broadcasting could be shifted wholly onto a commercial basis, financed by advertising and consumer charges, public funding is likely to survive in practice. Public service media re-established their value but their funding, and their standing, was reduced during the post-2008 economic recession.

The final outcome of public service media's place in the new digital environment will not be determined by technology, nor by economics, but by political choice – ultimately, citizen choice.

## The public service concept

The idea of public service broadcasting was developed in radio – or the Wireless, as it was commonly known. The BBC was the archetype, though it is far from typical today. The British Broadcasting Corporation, with John Reith as Director-General, was formed as a licence fee funded public service monopoly in 1927, replacing the earlier British Broadcasting Company. Its aims were to provide a service of information, education and entertainment. As it developed as an institution under Reith's leadership, guided by its Governors and by the recommendations of early external Committees of Inquiry, its central underpinning principles crystallised:

- funding from a compulsory licence fee linked to possession and use of a receiver
- independence from political or commercial influence on programmes
- governance by a board of trustees for the public interest
- political impartiality
- high-quality information, entertainment and education programmes
- a wide range of content, serving both majority and minority interests
- mixed schedules, to expose audiences to new (and improving) experiences
- universal access to the programmes.

In ethos it was the antithesis of the broadcasting market-place which was developing in parallel in the United States. Reith stood unashamedly for cultural elitism and viewed the monopoly as essential for its protection. In his era he was a giant, unafraid to lead:

> It is occasionally indicated to us that we are apparently setting out to give the public what we think they need – and not what they want, but few know what they want, and very few what they need.
>
> (Reith, 1924: 34)

While there may be some truth in this, these days very few are willing to leave the choice to a monopoly, however benign.

## Modern public service broadcasting

In more recent times the term 'Public Service Broadcasting' (PSB) has become notoriously difficult to define. It remains applicable to the large and well-financed public service broadcasters to be found in the UK and Japan, the BBC and NHK, but their positions of strength and global reputation in a pluralist commercial market are unusual. France dismantled the ORTF (*Office de Radiodiffusion-Télévision Française*) in the 1970s, leaving only a part of it to evolve into today's public service *France Télévisions*. Here, as in Germany, Spain, Italy and Ireland, the public service television channels were partially financed by advertising. In the UK the term PSB is also used not only to refer to the BBC and the publicly owned advertisement-funded Channel Four, but also to the terrestrial commercial broadcasters who have historically had public service obligations imposed by regulation.

In the United States a public service element was 'retrofitted' to the commercial broadcasting market at the end of the 1960s, aiming to boost programme content which the market was failing to provide. A Corporation for Public Broadcasting (CPB) was formed to channel a modest level of federal funding into a loose association of educational and community TV stations which were brought together in 1970 within a new Public Broadcasting Service (PBS). Unlike its CPB radio partner, National Public Radio, PBS does not produce its own programmes for national broadcasting but acts as a network for the distribution of programmes made by its members. Even allowing for federal funding, these 350 or so not-for-profit broadcasting stations remain very dependent on donations from foundations, sponsors and individuals.

In Canada, Australia and New Zealand public corporations based on the BBC model were founded, but have evolved in different ways. The CBC in Canada is supported by both federal funding and advertising.

ABC in Australia is now financed by the Australian government, as is a second public service broadcaster, SBS (Special Broadcasting Service), targeted on minority communities. New Zealand's public service television, TVNZ, was the subject of a radical commercial reform in the 1980s and is now largely dependent on advertising finance, but able, like other broadcasters, to bid for funds for specific programmes and projects from a public grant-making body, NZ On Air.

In many countries around the world the term 'public service broadcaster' is used to describe organisations which are essentially state broadcasters, lacking editorial independence from the government. In central and Eastern Europe post-Communist regimes have sought to transform former state broadcasters into politically independent institutions and found it to be a continuing challenge. In countries emerging from civil war and/or dictatorship – in the Balkans and the Middle East, for example – media reform with a similar aim is often part of the process of 'reconstruction'. In Thailand, which has been prey to political conflict, the Thai PBS, created in 2008, has emerged as 'the first and so far the only truly public broadcaster in Southeast Asia' (Open Society Foundations, 2010: 24).

At heart public service broadcasting serves a set of social purposes, determined with regard to citizen (as distinct from consumer) interests, and is editorially independent of political and/or commercial control. In a 2009 survey of six broadcasters across the four countries – the UK, Australia, the United States and New Zealand – Mary Debrett (adapting a definition originally developed by the UK's Broadcasting Research Unit back in the 1980s) adduced five key elements of public service broadcasting:

- universal service
- independence from government and from vested interests to enable the provision of fair and impartial news and current affairs
- the servicing of the interests of minorities including children, in addition to mainstream audiences
- the reflection of national culture and identity
- the provision of quality programming which encompasses a preparedness to innovate and not to be driven by audience size (Debrett, 2009: 809).

The modern context may be different, and the reliance on monopoly is long-dead, but these elements continue to reflect the founding principles of the BBC.

## 'Decline & fall'?

The trend towards pluralism and an abundance of TV channels and radio stations has in general posed a risk for public service broadcasting organisations. Their audience share declined, raising questions about the residual purposes of public service programming when so many other choices were available without any form of tax funding. In parallel, political, social and economic changes have radically altered society's relationship with its broadcasters, eroding the deference to authority and cultural prescriptions of the early twentieth century. In the UK the BBC television monopoly was broken by the arrival of the regulated commercial Independent Television service (ITV) in 1955 and the resulting 'duopoly' was then destroyed by the creation of Channel 4, Channel Five and the birth of satellite and cable multi-channel subscription TV.

The logic of where pluralism might lead UK public service broadcasting was pursued rigorously in the 1980s by the Peacock Committee, which had been asked by Mrs Thatcher to investigate the financing of the BBC. While the Prime Minister may have hoped for a proposal to replace the licence fee by advertising, what she received was a short-term recommendation to limit increases and impose a quota of independent production – and a radical long-term vision of an era of viewer and listener sovereignty, with an abundance of choice, a lowering of the barriers to entry and very little regulation. Subscription would replace the licence fee as the main source of BBC funding and the concept of public service would be separated from the BBC as an organisation. 'Programmes of merit', which might not survive in a competitive market, could be produced by any organisation, funded by a grant dispensed by a new Public Service Broadcasting Council.

Broadcasting, in the Peacock Committee's view, should therefore shed its history and evolve towards a fully developed consumer market:

The past effects of packaging and channelling in developing viewers' and listeners' tastes do not justify a paternalistic attitude which would prevent them from making less constrained choices in the future. In many walks of life it is possible to accept that earlier constraints and restrictions may have had beneficial side effects, while insisting that consumers should be regarded as the best judges of their own welfare in formulating future policy. (A historical analogy may be helpful: a social critic in the late 18th and early 19th century could pay sincere and generous tribute to aristocratic patronage in forming taste in painting, music and literature, while welcoming the greater freedom of choice offered both to artists and patrons by the wider bourgeois market that was beginning to develop.)

(Home Office, 1986: 132)

The last two decades of the twentieth century were characterised in television by liberal reform: the stimulation of competition, deregulation, the separation of commissioning and production, and the growth of a production sector which was independent of broadcasting organisations. Competitive forces and technology improvements reduced the cost of programme-making. The independent sector showed up public service institutions as cumbersome and inefficient and governments used comparative efficiency data to justify squeezing their public funding. The threat to public service television was not just an economic one, however: it was a philosophical one as well. Faith in the market was the prevalent ideology.

Writing in 1998 Michael Tracey diagnosed 'The Decline and Fall of Public Service Broadcasting'. The public service broadcasting model, he argued, was losing out to a market-based consumer sovereignty model, facilitated by cable and satellite technology, which rested on the idea that

in a democratic society the state has no right to make choices for its citizens in the audio-visual area any more than it has the right to tell them which books to write or read.

(Tracey, 1998: 11)

Dramatic illustration of the 'deconstruction' of public service broadcasting was provided by the commercialisation of TVNZ in New Zealand during the 1980s. The organisation was stripped of its public service objectives and left free to apply, along with others, for grants from NZ On Air for any public service programmes it wished to make in its new commercial guise. In Japan NHK's special status would, Michael Tracey predicted, be undermined by the spread of international satellite services, cable and audio-visual telecommunications. American public service television was outside the cultural mainstream and, while claiming to be local, was merely 'balkanized': it may broadly serve 'the needs and interests of those inside, and that tiny portion of the American public which attends to its offerings' but fails to serve the broader society (Tracey, 1998: 253–254).

Looking at how global market-based communications systems could erode the concepts of 'the nation' and 'the public' on which the idea of public service had rested, Tracey, though a strong believer in public service broadcasting himself, concluded that 'the game is up':

> Whatever the bravery and wisdom of public broadcasters who articulate serious principles and who keep the faith in difficult circumstances, in the end it is not possible to have a viable social institution which is out of step with the prevailing sociological realities.
>
> (Tracey, 1998: 279)

Yet, though its audiences declined with the advent of multi-channel and digital television, public service broadcasting did not 'fall'. Inspecting its health a decade later, Tracey's successors found it alive and well:

> In the twenty-first century, as public service broadcasters continue to fight for funding and audience in the fragmenting market-place, engaging with the possibilities of digital transmission and the World Wide Web, it is evident this system has survived the market liberal reforms of the late twentieth century.
>
> (Debrett, 2010: 15)

How do we explain this?

## Self-transformation

If we take the BBC as a case study, part of the answer is what I have described elsewhere as its 'skin-shedding' ability (Starks, 2011). While all organisations evolve and adapt to a changing environment, the BBC has twice transformed itself so radically as to warrant the description of the organisation shedding its skin. The first of these was in the 1960s when it managed the transformation from primarily a radio broadcaster to primarily a television one – simultaneously with the change from a former monopoly to a combative competitor in the television duopoly. The second was in the 1990s, when duopoly had given way to pluralism, and the BBC adapted, again simultaneously, to the challenges of multi-channel multi-platform television and of digital technology.

Responding first to the financial efficiency challenge and the need to embrace the independent production sector, the BBC introduced 'Producer Choice', a resource management reform which attributed full costs to each programme, allowed programme commissioners to compare BBC internal and independently produced programmes, enabled BBC producers to compare the costs of internal and external facilities, and permitted the purchase of the latter. The monolithic structure was opened up, releasing 'many *billions* of pounds', and enabling the BBC to claim that its efficiency was now transparent (Birt, 2002: 239). Its reward was to be able to reinvest the savings in programmes.

However, the reinvestment was not just in *any* programmes. It was managed within a programme strategy related to a major re-think about public service. The inherited ideology of public service as 'something for everyone because everyone pays the licence fee' would no longer wash: in the increasingly pluralist structure of broadcasting, why should it be the job of any one organisation to serve everyone and, post-Peacock, the licence fee was far from sacrosanct. The question the BBC now had to answer, in the context of the pre-1996 review of its Charter, was 'why, in a world of proliferating TV and radio networks, do we need a BBC *at all*?' (Birt, 2002: 343). The BBC's answer was to focus on areas where 'market failure' could be expected and to downgrade its investment in feature films and sports events, where pay-TV provided an ever-expanding service. In the context of a review of its Charter, it proposed its key public service roles as:

- providing the comprehensive, in-depth and impartial news and information coverage across a range of broadcasting outlets that is needed to support a fair and informed national debate
- supporting and stimulating the development and expression of British culture and entertainment
- guaranteeing the provision of programming and services that create opportunities for education
- stimulating the communication of cultures and ideas between Britain and abroad (BBC, 1992: 19).

Meanwhile, the corporation took full advantage of the emerging opportunities offered by new digital technology to transform itself into a multi-channel multi-platform broadcaster, seeing the satellite broadcaster BSkyB as at least as significant a competitor as ITV. It successfully bid for a multiplex on digital terrestrial television on which it developed new channels. It acquired satellite capacity both for its BBC-branded public services and also for a new set of archive-based subscription channels, run by the UKTV commercial joint venture, to provide supplementary revenue. In 1994, enterprisingly, it launched BBC Online and took the critical decision that its news and other public service content on the Internet should be offered without charge and without advertising, funded by licence fee money. Henceforth the public service BBC would be multi-channel, multi-platform and multi-media.

While the 1990s saw a step-change in the scale of activity of, and financial contribution made by, the BBC's commercial arm, the licence fee remained the bedrock of the BBC's domestic services. The public's blend of support and reluctant tolerance for this tax improved with a political decision to exempt the over-75 age group. Importantly, the BBC's size made its competitors wary: commercial television did not want an organisation that large as a rival for advertising, nor did BSkyB and cable TV want it as a head-to-head competitor for subscription revenue. So public funding underpinned the BBC's move into digital broadcasting. John Major's Conservative government privatised the BBC's transmission arm but allowed it to keep the proceeds of the sale; its Labour successor supported the BBC's move into multi-channel digital broadcasting in 2000 by agreeing a licence fee level of inflation plus 1.5% for five years.

The BBC thus reinvented itself for the digital age and, in doing so, shed many of its earlier characteristics. Around a third of its output was provided by independent producers and it was a buyer of external facilities and support services, so it ceased to be a self-sufficient organisation, doing everything with its own staff. More significantly it became a collaborator with, as well as a competitor to, its rivals. Digital terrestrial television multiplex management involved close collaboration with ITV, Channel 4 and Channel Five. The practicalities of satellite reception required reaching agreement with BSkyB – and, as we saw in Chapter 3, in 2002 BSkyB became a partner in the *Freeview* joint venture which the BBC spearheaded in order to rescue the digital terrestrial platform.

Despite the scale of change, however, the BBC had essentially retained the underlying principles of public service broadcasting. The old concept of mixed schedules which impelled viewers to watch programmes they would not have chosen for themselves was by now pretty weak. The schedules of the mainstream channels still contained a mix of genres, but alongside them were themed services aimed at specific audiences. Moreover, recording technology had advanced so far that viewers were increasingly able to arrange their own schedules with ease. The ethos of paternalism inherited from Reith had faded within the BBC as it had in the wider society. In a more democratic, pluralist and multi-ethnic society, the BBC could not act as a cultural Czar: consumer choice was now central to the whole broadcasting industry, public and private. But the BBC remained determined to offer viewers experiences it believed the market would not spontaneously provide and to cross-trail its programmes in order to publicise that choice. Like the licence fee, the BBC's independence and political impartiality remained intact, as did the principle of universal access to its programmes. With a new Charter, running from 1996 to 2006, the BBC appeared to have buried the Peacock Committee's vision of its future.

Other public service television organisations similarly transformed themselves into digital multi-channel broadcasters. The German public service television broadcasters, ARD and ZDF, were in the vanguard, initially launching new services on digital satellite. Following the BBC's example, Swedish and Finnish public broadcasters were quick to see the advantages of exploiting the opportunities for new services offered by digital terrestrial television. New 'niche' channels and online services were launched by *France Télévisions* and the Spanish national broadcaster TVE (Iosifidis, 2007). In Japan NHK had initially made the move to multi-channel TV via analogue satellite but then switched successfully to a digital multi-channel strategy, migrating its viewers to its new digital services and branching out into multi-media and mobile TV. Across a number of countries public service broadcasting entered the field of digital technology and emerged as public service media.

## Digital television switchover role

This brings us to the second part of the explanation of public service television's successful survival into the twenty-first century: governments needed them as partners in their digital switchover strategies.

Simulcasting public service, or state, television channels is one of the first steps governments take in embarking on the digital transition and strengthening their digital output normally helps consumer take-up. Public service channels also offer the ideal vehicle for publicising switchover to the public: they normally have near-universal reach and a campaign of public information messages can reduce the need for expensive paid advertisements on commercial outlets.

In the UK the government was particularly keen to see the public service broadcaster in the digital switchover driving seat. This was partly through fear of the potential unpopularity of 'turning off the nation's telly', partly through prudence following the near-collapse of the digital terrestrial platform with ITV Digital's bankruptcy in 2002, and partly because of the decision not to commit direct government expenditure to the switchover process. So the government looked to the BBC, using licence fee money, in collaboration with other broadcasters and with the wider industry, to lead the UK's digital television switchover. The purpose-formed broadcasters' company, Digital UK, which handled operations and communications, received the bulk of its funding from the BBC. The Help-Scheme, which the government designed to assist the elderly and disabled, was funded from a ring-fenced element of the licence fee.

The BBC thus became, in effect, the UK government's partner in managing digital switchover. The risks of the government using the BBC's Charter renewal of 2006 as an opportunity to begin dismantling BBC public service broadcasting and funding in line with the Peacock Committee's recommendations were minimal. The central role of *Freeview*, which would have near-universal coverage after analogue switch-off, further entrenched licence fee funding in the UK broadcasting market, as Greg Dyke, Director-General at the time, had foreseen:

> Freeview makes it very hard for any Government to try to make the BBC a pay-television service. The more Freeview boxes out there, the harder it will be to switch the BBC to a subscription service since most of the boxes can't be adapted for pay TV. I suspect Freeview will ensure the future of the licence fee for another decade at least, and probably longer.
>
> (Dyke, 2004: 187)

Under its 2006–2016 Charter the BBC's Public Purposes were defined as:

- sustaining citizenship and civil society
- promoting education and learning
- stimulating creativity and cultural excellence
- representing the UK, its nations, regions and communities
- bringing the UK to the world and the world to the UK
- in promoting its other purposes, helping to deliver to the public the benefit of emerging communications technologies and services and, in addition, taking a leading role in the switchover to digital television (DCMS, 2006).

In other countries too digital switchover also tended to reinforce, or halt any reduction in, the role of public service television. Governments valued their role in managing the transition. In Germany the public service broadcasters were 'instrumental in the successful switch-off of terrestrial analogue transmission' (Woldt, 2010: 175). Spain's re-launch of digital terrestrial TV after the collapse of Quiero was based on giving a greater role to RTVE. In Finland, when the initial switchover policy stalled, remedial action included giving the public service broadcaster YLE a licence fee increase of 1% above inflation. In New Zealand TVNZ was given back a public service Charter and it received additional public funding for six years to enable it to launch two new advertisement-free channels as part of a broader *Freeview* strategy (Norris, 2010). In the United States the Association of Public Television Stations played a constructive role in implementing the FCC's switchover policy and negotiated new agreements with the cable industry for the carriage of its stations' new digital services.

## Justification re-established

A number of European public service broadcasters had only started to face commercial competition in the 1980s and 1990s and, shocked into realising that they would have to fight to retain their audiences, some public service channels responded by becoming more similar to their commercial competitors, employing 'a strategy of subtle imitation in order to defend their market share' (Iosifidis, 2007: 64). The pressure was particularly strong where the public service broadcasters relied on advertising for a share of their funding.

However, public broadcasters looking to safeguard their future while assisting governments with digital switchover swiftly realised that content convergence with commercial channels was not a viable public service strategy for securing new digital channels. They sought to sharpen their distinctiveness and re-establish the intellectual case for sustaining and cherishing public service media in the environment of an expanded market. They aimed both to puncture the idea that the advent of digital television would enable nearly all tastes and needs to be met by the market and to make the case for an expansion of their own remits. Broadly they succeeded: new public service channels providing news, children's programming and international services were launched in a number of countries.

The gloss was coming off the image of the market. It had produced an abundance of channels but not necessarily a significant increase in the number of mainstream providers: with the consolidation of powerful transnational multi-media corporations the market tended towards being 'oligopolistic' (Helm, 2005: 7). Even in pluralist markets advertising revenue was being spread more thinly. Competitive pressure here was intensified by the shift of some forms of advertising to the Internet. In respect of the UK, Patricia Hodgson, a former Chief Executive of the

ITC (the television regulatory body which preceded Ofcom in the UK), noted in 2008 that:

> Individual broadcasters spread a diminishing pot (of advertising) across more services, so even the most popular channels and stations find income static or falling. Revenues for ITV1 are down 20% over five years. Not surprisingly, ITV has been coming to the regulator to ask for its expensive public service duties to be reduced. First, regional companies consolidated into a single business; then regions were merged; and now the news budget for ITN is down to £35 million from £55m in the glory days. Budgets for children's output have been halved and cheaper soaps have displaced more choice in prime time.
>
> (Hodgson, 2008: 47)

So market failure remained a feature of the digital era. Public service television broadcasters became, if anything, more central to the provision of a wide range of quality programming. Children's programming provided a classic example. While the output had expanded massively, the result internationally was a commercial market dominated by cartoons, disproportionately American in origin, and a further problem was food advertising contributing to childhood obesity (Livingstone, 2008). Public service television was needed to produce quality content. The BBC's channel for school-age children, CBBC, was required to broadcast 85 hours of news, 665 hours of drama and 550 hours of factual programming each year (D'Arma and Steemers, 2010: 120).

As partisan news sources multiplied on the Internet, the citizenship role of public service media in providing a trusted source of fair, accurate and serious news became more valued. The needs of citizens were recognised as going wider than individual consumer needs: not only do we all have a personal interest as citizens in being well-informed and able to participate in public policy debates, we also have an interest in our fellow citizens being well-informed and aware of a range of perspectives. Serious investment in factual news-gathering and reporting in the round to encompass different viewpoints constitute a 'public good'. The trustworthiness of public service television should be its distinctive feature:

> Arguments for the relevance and social value of public service media organisations in the digital era need look no further than their status as trusted brands. Fulfilling a purpose no others can, public service

media represent islands of safe, reliable, impartial, 'quality' content in the uncertain, unreliable sea of digital online media. Long a key point of difference for public broadcasters, trustworthiness has assumed new significance in a global media marketplace characterised by conglomeration, corporate and government spin, and non-accountable citizen and social networking media.

(Debrett, 2010: 205)

The other major role of public service broadcasting, traditionally, had been to uphold and celebrate national culture. In the face of globalisation and migration, and in the digital multi-channel world, the importance of this role was also recognised, especially in countries where the market was too small or too weak to sustain many commercial services of their own and where many of the new channels were therefore transnational – as in Canada, Scandinavia and the smaller countries of central and Eastern Europe. Nurturing different national and regional cultures and a range of different languages were public purposes which digital technology made easier.

The period of the digital transition thus became one in which public service television – evolving into public service media – reaffirmed its distinctiveness and sought to show the positive role it could play in the digital communications market.

On the face of it, the French broadcasting reform initiated by President Sarkozy in 2008 was a government-led initiative to increase the distinctiveness of public service television. First, the President announced that advertising would no longer be part of its funding. The motive here was, at least in part, to assist the private sector during a difficult economic period and an increasingly competitive commercial market for advertising but there was also a coherent attempt to reshape France's public service broadcasting.

The former analogue public channels, France 2 and France 3, were grouped together with new digital channels, France 4 and France 5 and the France Ô service for overseas departments and territories into the single corporation of *France Télévisions* (Kuhn, 2010). Commercial advertising was withdrawn initially from the period 8 pm to 6 am and a new tax on Internet providers and mobile phone operators was introduced to plug the funding gap. The schedules were intended to become more serious with, for example, a ban on reality TV shows (Levy, 2012).

However, in a move that shocked and disturbed supporters of public service media's political independence, President Sarkozy decided to reclaim from the broadcasting regulator the state's power to appoint the Director-General of the new organisation. To Raymond Kuhn this seemed like a throwback to the Gaullist era, while David Levy diplomatically described it as a surprising outcome from a reform process which had initially been heralded as 'a project for creating a French BBC' (Levy, 2012: 104).

## New pressures build

The digital switchover process was always going to be a temporary phase and, as analogue switch-off took place in Europe and other advanced economies, the warm climate in which public service media had been basking began to cool. Governments no longer needed to inject additional funding into public service television to assist the digital transition and after 2008 the economic recession triggered by extended borrowing both by banks and by governments brought the policy response of public expenditure cuts.

In the UK a decade or so of reasonably generous funding for the BBC came to an abrupt end in 2010 when the licence fee was frozen for six years. Sweden's SVT had received additional licence fee funding for the digital television transition under an arrangement timed to end with analogue switch-off in 2008 (Iosifidis, 2007). In Japan NHK volunteered a cut in its licence fee in 2011. Funding for *France Télévisions* was reduced in 2012/2013. In Spain (where, as in France, advertising had been withdrawn as a means of partially funding public broadcasting) the subsidy for the national public television service was reduced in 2012 and major cutbacks were made in regional public television (Fernández Alonso and Díaz González, 2013). In Portugal public television entered a period of crisis in 2012 when funding was cut and proposals aired for shutting down or privatising some of its channels (New York Times, 2012).

Even before the completion of analogue switch-off, public service television's development was reversed in New Zealand. A change of power from the Labour to the National party in 2008 brought a sharp change in policy. The new government removed the public service Charter which TVNZ had enjoyed since 2003 and required the broadcaster to operate on a fully commercial basis. The finance associated with the Charter was reallocated to NZ On Air to be a contestable fund for quality programming, available to any broadcaster (Norris, 2013). The government also decided not to renew the public funding for TVNZ's two all-digital channels, TVNZ 6 and TVNZ 7, at the end of their six year term, leaving both services at risk. TVNZ 6's mixed programming service was closed and partially replaced by a fully commercial youth channel called U.

TVNZ 7, a news and factual service, closed in 2012 after the failure of a public campaign to save it and was replaced by a time-shifted version of TVNZ 1 (Norris, 2013).

Notwithstanding the events in New Zealand and the uncertainty in Portugal, public service media were not under threat of being stamped out. Admittedly, technology now made this a theoretical possibility. The ongoing march of subscription-based satellite and cable services, the feasibility of conditional access on digital terrestrial television and its use for pay-TV in a number of countries, and the advent of IPTV made technically possible a system of direct financial payment for broadcasting with the sanction of exclusion for non-payment. It became feasible for television, like the Press, to be financed by a combination of advertising and direct consumer charges. In this sense the digitisation of television certainly had potentially dramatic implications, but what *could* be done was a different matter from what *should* be done (Barwise and Picard, 2012).

When the justification for public service had been successfully reaffirmed the high-point of market ideology had passed. James Murdoch's 2009 MacTaggart Lecture, in which he likened the natural operation of the market to Darwinism and regulated public service broadcasting to creationism (Murdoch, 2009) was received with scepticism and criticised by his sister, Elisabeth, speaking from the same platform in 2012 (Guardian, 2012b). For all the occasionally noisy criticism, the public finance ingredient in the media funding mix in practice tends to be quietly sustained by commercial broadcasters who are not keen to see additional competition for their own sources of funding.

## The new battleground

With public service media here to stay in the digital communications world, the central question became what limits to set on their activities. Public service broadcasting's move into multi-media was particularly contentious. In 2006 the Director-General, Mark Thompson, stated the BBC 'should no longer think of itself as a broadcaster of TV and radio and some new media on the side' but should aim 'to deliver public service content to our audiences in whatever media and on whatever device makes sense for them, whether they are at home or on the move' (BBC, 2006). The benefits to viewers and listeners from this development were clear:

- from online services, an extra layer of detail to complement the broadcasts, often at a more local or personally relevant level

- from On-Demand services, freedom from the tyranny of the schedules, on the one hand, and the potential of access to the Archives, on the other
- and from mobile reception, greater convenience at times.

However, public service broadcasters' moves onto the Internet brought them into direct conflict with Press and publishing industry players who were also extending their operations into electronic media. The Press in particular was engaged in a long-term migration from print, overnight trucks and early morning paper-boys to electronic distribution. Well-funded authoritative websites provided by public service broadcasters which were free at the point of use provided a frustrating obstacle to newspapers seeking to charge for their online material. Some European public service organisations, partially funded by advertising, aroused additional newspaper hostility by competing for Internet advertising. Newspapers and publishers were quick to ask the European Union to examine the issues here from the standpoint of competition policy and state aid. In 2004, for example, three leading commercial media lobbies sent a 'White Paper' to the European Commission alleging market distortion by public service organisations (Nord, 2012).

An approach to handling this issue was developed by the BBC in the context of its pre-2006 Charter Review process, drawing on the economic concept of Public Value articulated by Mark H. Moore at Harvard (Moore, 1995). The BBC argued that its services provided a public value which could be assessed analytically and quantified, with reference to:

- audience reach, which research monitored
- quality, which could be assessed from a range of perspectives
- impact, reflecting audience size, memorability, awards won, and other factors
- value for money, behind which lay measures such as level of investment, cost per hour, cost per viewer hour, public willingness to pay and level of overheads (BBC, 2004: 87).

So, when the BBC wanted to expand into a new field, its proposal was subject to a Public Value Test, including an external assessment of its market implications, so that a decision could be made, weighing positive public value against any negative implications for current or potential private sector competitors.

Germany imposed a set of regulatory limitations on PSB multi-media activities, embodied in an Interstate Treaty between the German *Länder*, covering a new category of PSB 'Telemedia' consisting of the Internet and mobile TV (Woldt, 2010). This recognised PSBs' duty to promote the participation of citizens in the Information Society and support media literacy, but prohibited them from offering online content similar to print media content. TV and radio programmes could only be streamed over the Internet for seven days after their original broadcast (for sports programmes, the limit was 24 hours). Archives of historical interest could be offered online without any time limit but this required prior regulatory approval. All online material not directly related to a programme or which the broadcasters wished to offer for longer than a seven day period was to be subject to three tests: (i) was it part of the PSB remit? (ii) would it contribute to pluralism and diversity? (iii) were the budgets reasonable?

In 2009 the European Commission produced a new Communication on State Aid and public service broadcasting requiring an advance assessment along the lines of the BBC Public Value Test but placing the responsibility on national governments:

> In order to ensure that the public funding of significant new audiovisual services does not distort trade and competition to an extent contrary to the common interest, Member States shall assess, based on the outcome of the open consultation, the overall impact of a new service on the market by comparing the situation in the presence and in the absence of the planned new service. In assessing the impact on the market, relevant aspects include, for example, the existence of similar or substitutable offers, editorial competition, market structure, market position of the public service broadcaster, level of competition and potential impact on private initiatives. This impact needs to be balanced with the value of the services in question for society. In the case of predominantly negative effects on the market, State funding for audiovisual services would appear proportionate only if it is justified by the added value in terms of serving the social, democratic and cultural needs of society, taking also into account the existing overall public service offer.
>
> (EC, 2009)

For some public service media supporters these *ex ante* tests are intrusive (Lowe and Steemers, 2012) but they have become part of the new digital way of life in Scandinavia, Belgium and the Netherlands, as well as the UK and Germany. In principle, it is better to have a system and process in place to determine the limits of public service expansion than to have open-ended battles with powerful commercial lobbies with no rules.

## Funding

The other area of pressure was funding – not just the perennial issue of its level, but also its basis and the number of organisations across which the revenue should be spread.

The idea of a licence fee paid by every household with a TV receiver did not survive into the digital world in all countries with public services. In Australia it was abolished in 1974 and replaced by grants from government general revenue. The Netherlands abolished its licence fee in 2000. However, the system has had a long life, especially in Europe, since, as a stand-alone tax at arm's length from the mainstream taxation and public expenditure system, it can protect public broadcasting from direct rivalry for funding with other public priorities such as health and defence.

Convergence posed a new challenge. The ability to receive television and radio services on a computer or a mobile telephone clearly raises a question about the exact type of equipment whose ownership and use is linked is linked to liability to pay. The question is not altogether new. In the UK the licence fee was originally attached to radio receivers and then evolved first to cover both TV and radio receivers and later to apply to TV receivers only. So the equipment link can be altered without undermining the underlying concept. The administrative mechanism is far less important than the principle of a tax which is quite distinct from the concept of a consumer subscription and which is justified by its public benefits.

Indeed, the basis had already shifted from the ownership and use of a particular piece of equipment to the reception of certain types of service regardless of their means of distribution or reception. The 2007 European Union Audio-Visual Media Services (AVMS) Directive, as we saw in connection with regulatory policy, aims to span both broadcasting and the Internet on a technology-neutral basis. It draws a distinction between 'television broadcasts' which are delivered (by whatever means) in a linear transmission schedule, simultaneously to all homes, and 'on-demand' services which are selected on a non-linear basis by the viewer. Licence fee administration in the UK currently rests on this same distinction. Watching TV programmes on Catch-Up TV, even on a TV receiver, does not carry an obligation to pay the licence fee – but watching live television, or recording from live transmission for viewing later, does, even if the receiver is a computer or a mobile device.

A number of others countries which have historically had licence fee systems have started to review them. Denmark has decided to change the basis of the licence fee from the ownership of a TV set to the ownership of any receiving equipment. France has topped up its licence fee revenue with its tax on Internet providers and mobile phone operators. Germany is switching to a charge falling on all households, regardless of the equipment they own, which, of course, simplifies collection and enforcement.

In the UK commercial broadcasters have in the past bid for a slice of the licence fee revenue. In 2003 Charles Allen, Chairman of Granada TV at the time, called on the government to give 10% of the licence fee to ITV while from 2004 onwards Channel 4 argued for some direct public funding to augment its advertising funding. Channel 4's case was ultimately rejected but a debate about using a slice of the licence fee for public service purposes beyond funding the BBC had been ignited. Lord Burns, Chairman of the Independent Panel set up by the government to advise on the BBC's bid for Charter Renewal in 2006, thought that in future there could be an element of competition for licence fee funds in the interest of public service plurality (Burns, 2005). While the Labour government declined this advice, it kept alive the idea of 'top-slicing' the licence fee by using licence fee revenue to fund the digital switchover Help-Scheme.

Then, in freezing the licence fee for six years in 2010, the new Conservative–Liberal Democrat Coalition government extended this precedent. In addition to loading the licence fee with the cost of funding the BBC World Service (hitherto borne by the government), it also required the BBC to spend money on non-BBC public services. Under the settlement the BBC was to become the primary funder of the Welsh language channel S4C, was obliged to make a £150 million annual investment in broadband for four years, and, without any new funding, would contribute to the Secretary of State's priority of developing non-BBC local television.

If the funding available to support public service media is distributed in too many different directions, the outcome could be the Public Service Broadcasting Council advocated back in the 1980s by the Peacock Committee or a body along the lines of New Zealand On Air, where public funding is contestable and rival would-be providers compete. Such an approach has its advocates. For the UK David Elstein advocated a Public Broadcasting Authority in direct receipt of public funding for which the BBC would have to compete 'on equal terms with all other potential producers and broadcasters of public service content' (Elstein, 2008: 87).

However, a grant-making body of this nature manages a range of contracts without having a relationship with its audience of the kind a public service institution develops. Trisha Dunleavy's study of New Zealand On Air noted that its funding had never been sufficient to pay for the range of activities in which it was involved, so that it supported, rather than fully funded, public service projects. She thought that the ideal was for countries to have non-commercial public networks as the centrepiece of their national TV systems but 'not all countries can afford them' (Dunleavy, 2010: 308). Jeremy Mayhew and Luke Bradley-Jones examined the New Zealand model to see whether it had any lessons for other countries. They noted the transparency of the contractual relationships as a strength but commented that the New Zealand funding system had failed to provide sustained high quality, high impact public service content. On the question of whether such a system of contestability should replace the existing institutions in the UK, they came down in favour of the 'experience, skill sets and ethos' which the institutions had built up over an extended period of time (Mayhew and Bradley-Jones, 2005: 169).

Ireland has chosen a mixed economy in which its public service broadcaster, RTE, is financed partly by a licence fee and partly by advertising, while a separate Sound and Vision Fund, also financed by the licence fee, can be tapped by any broadcaster bidding to produce Irish content for Irish audiences.

## Emerging outcome?

Public service broadcasting and public service media have established their place in the digital communications world but their size, scope and sources of funding remain varied and fluid. Gregory Lowe and Jeanette Steemers are apprehensive about their future. Public service broadcasting in the United States, they observe, only started in the 1960s and has always been under attack from the political right; in central and Eastern Europe it is plagued by 'political meddling' and the ghosts of its state broadcasting past; in parts of southern Europe its historic roots go back to military dictatorship; and 'even in its heartland' of north-west Europe it is 'in trouble' (Lowe and Steemers, 2012: 9).

National differences make generalised predictions difficult and national patterns diverge even within Europe. Under the 1997 Protocol of the Amsterdam Treaty, the European Union left its Member States free to determine both the method of funding and the remits of their public service bodies (Iosifidis, 2007) and David Levy's study of policy-making in the UK and France confirmed that, while EU state aid policy was an influence, national governments shaped their public service institutions in different ways from one another (Levy, 2012).

The UK's analogue legacy of public service television, overseen by Ofcom, dilutes the concept by offering ITV and Channel Five 'due prominence' on Electronic Programme Guides in return for diminishing content commitments. Channel 4 has become reconciled to delivering its public purposes without a public subsidy. The BBC's next Charter Review takes place in the run-up to 2016. Key issues will be the licence fee system and the level of funding – with the latter closely linked to the scale and scope of the BBC's remit.

Partly, the debate here will reflect commercial pressures: reducing the size of the BBC and the level of its funding would probably enable the pay-TV companies to extract more money from their subscribers (Barwise and Picard, 2012). However, reviewing media plurality in the wake of News Corporation's bid to take control of BSkyB, Ofcom proposed that the BBC's position would need to be considered in assessing plurality (Ofcom, 2012c). Another Charter Review issue will be whether the BBC should continue to have its own regulator, the BBC Trust, or be brought fully under Ofcom's authority.

The role of public service media in the digital communications industry will not be determined by technology, or the interaction of technology with economics, but by political choice. Their constitutional basis will be re-examined and decided afresh by different countries at different times. Lowe and Steemers believe that public service media need to regain the initiative to secure their future and, within their edited volume, Robert Picard urges public broadcasters to make their case not only to politicians, but to a much wider set of stakeholders, including competitors and consumers (Picard, 2012). While national governments may be in the driving seat, the future of public service media ultimately depends on the views of the public in their role as citizens.

# 10
## The Democratic Dividend

### Summary of the chapter's argument

Digital television switchover was not adopted around the world with the primary intention of strengthening the media's democratic role. Indeed, in some countries outside the orbit of western democracy, a key aim was to maintain the state's political control through the digital transition. However, democratic aspirations are almost universal today and the question of whether digitisation of the media can deliver citizen benefits as an outcome is a pertinent one.

The conversion of television transmission from analogue to digital does not *cause* changes in the media's contribution to democracy: technology is a tool, not a determinant. However, digital television switchover coupled with convergence does create opportunities for strengthening the media's democratic role and, conversely, may create risks.

Case studies and comparative analysis show mixed experiences. Whether the opportunities are taken, or the risks materialise, is determined, country by country, by the decisions of governments, regulators, broadcasters and citizens. It is essentially a matter of political choice.

For this reason a broad understanding of the digital switchover process by civil society is highly desirable. Citizens have an interest in a design for digital switchover in which (within the limits of feasibility)

- the supply and range of news services can be increased
- services from other countries can provide new political perspectives
- regional and local television can be strengthened, including through the provision of services in additional languages if appropriate
- politicians remain or become fully distanced from content regulation

- television can be made more accessible to some groups of disabled people
- complementary television and Internet services can strengthen civic involvement
- the digital dividend is used to reduce the broadband 'digital divide'.

A 'democratic dividend' from digital television switchover will not 'just arrive' as an automatic by-product of the process. It needs to be sought. Most of the benefits available involve public policy in one form or another. Civil society needs to look at digital switchover not as an a-political technology change, nor as an inevitable cause of greater partisanship and prejudice, but as the source of opportunities for citizens which can be secured within the public arena.

## Digital television and democracy

The origins of digital television switchover were in industrial policy, spectrum management, pay-TV, broadcasters' multi-channel ambitions, and the growth of mobile wireless telecommunications. The technology was invented to benefit consumers but not specifically to strengthen the media's democratic role. However, in assessing the emerging *outcomes* from the process, we do need to ask whether, in addition to the consumer attractions, the transition can deliver benefits for the citizen.

### Consumer outcomes

We have seen the outcomes in terms of the new services and features offered to consumers – new channels, widescreen and HDTV, interactive features, Catch-Up and On-Demand TV, access to online videos and 'over the top' services, mobile and tablet reception, and perhaps in the future 3D. The range of available services continues to grow.

In several countries the total amount of TV viewing has shown an increase in response to the wider digital choice, but the level is likely to remain relatively stable, with the more significant change lying in how that total amount of viewing is spread. Simultaneous mass viewing of major events continues, often on an international basis. Outside of these peak viewing occasions, however, the audience is disaggregating.

Some viewers – very probably most viewers in some moods – will continue to view with enjoyment what schedulers offer them at the time it is offered. New original production in television will still provide a focus for interest and attention, just as new film releases and new book publications do. Alongside this, however, especially in the busiest parts of the day, will be a lot of media snacking – on the office computer, on the car radio, on a mobile phone or tablet, or on a big screen at an airport or railway station. News consumption will often be 'on the go', not just a set appointment with a morning newspaper or an evening bulletin.

Another section of the audience – probably most of us at some time – will become active self-schedulers, making use of the full range of recording devices and On-Demand services available, using an on-screen search engine to find individual programmes whether from a major broadcaster or from YouTube. The source of our interest could be respected reviewers, an Electronic Programme Agent which has built up computerised knowledge of our tastes and habits, or friends – in person or via social media. Enthusiasts will find their own highly specialised minority channels, but interest in certain programmes or series will 'go viral'.

Another group will be the active Internet users, ranging from those who simply want to inform or entertain themselves to those who generate material in the hope of reaching an audience. As now, the agile young will multi-task, conversing electronically on one device, while viewing passively on another.

Essentially, from the *consumer* standpoint, the outcomes are greater choice, greater convenience and increased opportunities for input and interaction.

### Citizen outcomes

Any analysis of outcomes for the *citizen* is dependent on national and cultural perspectives. In Western Europe and North America we tend to see a pattern whereby societies evolve through agrarian, industrial and then post-industrial stages and, in doing so, move from tribal, religious and relationship-based sources of authority to nation-states based on the rule of law and political accountability (Fukuyama, 2011). Integrated into this vision of progress is the establishment of a legal framework supporting freedom of speech and the development of a media system which underpins accountable political institutions and serves the wider civil society. We may now scoff at Francis Fukuyama's earlier thesis that with the collapse of Communism and the disintegration of the Soviet Union we could see the 'End of History' (Fukuyama, 1992) but we perhaps hold to Samuel Huntington's picture of the nineteenth and twentieth centuries as characterised by successive waves of democratisation separated by periods of regression (Huntington, 1991). So it seems natural to us to ask whether having more TV channels and increased opportunities for input and interaction is 'good for democracy'.

This assumption of progress towards democracy – and the corollary that media development should support and strengthen democratic institutions and processes – is at odds with the world view of China's Communist Party and of Islamic theocracies and is resented by them. Yet, while non-western regimes have different values and ideologies, research based on the Global Barometer and World Values Surveys indicates worldwide approval for the idea of democratic governance including within countries with no national experience of it. Pippa Norris concludes from this that:

> Although democratic attitudes and values are commonly assumed to be deepest and most widespread in long-standing democratic states in Western Europe and North America, in fact the cross-national picture shows that democratic aspirations are almost universal today, irrespective of the type of regime governing the state.
>
> (Norris, 2011: 101)

The question of digital television switchover's impact upon democracy from a citizen standpoint is therefore an appropriate one to consider on a global basis.

Do more channels and greater opportunities for participation in media lead to increased freedom of expression? Does the digital transformation of the media enhance the citizen's role in shaping political agendas in the 'Public Sphere', a concept fathered by Jürgen Habermas in 1962 in a work only translated into English in 1989 (Habermas, 1989)? Habermas argued that the English coffee shops and French salons of the eighteenth century created a space which was neither governmental, nor commercial, nor private, in which new, critical ideas could be debated and political views developed. The public sphere, he believed, was undermined by the state domination of the economy and the rise of the mass media in the twentieth century, when critical deliberation among citizens could be overridden by prestigious displays and manipulation by those in power. Habermas' historical perspective has been criticised but his Public Sphere concept now features in academic studies of digital communications (Gripsrud, 2010; Coleman and Ross, 2010; Iosifidis, 2011b) and has become a point of reference in an extended debate over whether the digitisation of the media has strengthened public discussion and public decision-making.

As well as a space in which to debate ideas, citizens need information and explanation in order to inform their thinking and deliberations. High quality, wide-ranging and penetrating journalism is required alongside discussion programmes and online forums. The task of the media is to support citizens, the ultimate political authority in democracies, in both respects. Michael Schudson has articulated six distinguishable ways in which the media should perform their democratic function:

- the educational role of informing the public of what its political representatives are doing, what dangers and opportunities for society loom on the horizon, and what fellow citizens are up to, for better or worse;
- the investigative or 'watchdog function', holding government officials to the legal and moral standards of public service;
- the task of analysis, explaining complex issues and making them comprehensible to the public as a whole;
- encouraging social empathy, stimulating help, for example, in the aftermath of natural disasters;
- offering a public forum for dialogue and debate;
- an advocacy role, campaigning on issues of social concern (Schudson, 2010).

On the face of it, a wider channel choice with additional news services and the increased opportunities for interaction provided by the interface of digital television with the Internet might appear potentially beneficial from a citizen perspective. More news should be 'good news' from a democratic standpoint. Looking at how the World Values Survey illuminates the relationship between the media and democracy, Pippa Norris found that the more often people tuned into broadcast news, the more strongly they expressed aspirations for democracy and that regular use of television and radio news tended to strengthen democratic satisfaction (Norris, 2011: 173).

However, even before full digitisation became a factor, Markus Prior argued that the increased choice offered by cable television was adversely affecting democracy (Prior, 2007). He noted that before the advent of cable most Americans were exposed to the news and politics because, at times when the networks screened their news shows, they were virtually forced to watch them since there was no other choice. However, presented with an abundance of channels on cable TV, they could go elsewhere, and did. This left a much smaller committed group of political viewers who chose to watch the news. In this more segmented market (with no Fairness Doctrine) these viewers were offered partisan cable news programmes which accorded with their own views. Not only did this reduce the breadth of the American public's political understanding, it was also leading, Prior argued, to more polarised elections, since the non-political viewers tended to abstain while the partisan political viewers were more likely to vote. The Internet intensified this trend:

> Cable television and the Internet set in motion a re-sorting of the electorate that polarized elections without necessarily making anyone more partisan.
>
> (Prior, 2007: 245)

The United States' ending of the Fairness Doctrine, the development of Fox News and other services with a partisan agenda, and fears about the possible implications of removing the 'due impartiality' requirement in the UK have fed the idea that the more media services we have to choose from, the more likely we are to be trapped by our own prejudices. However, as John Lloyd has noted (Lloyd, 2010), the Oxford Internet Institute's finding of the extent to which the readers of online news chose different sources from their preferred offline newspaper provides some counter-evidence here (Dutton, 2007).

Peter Golding examined the 'expectation that the growth of digital media would enrich and enhance democracy, by generating wider choice and accessibility of political information and by providing the means for a more informed and engaged citizenry' in western countries, and made a number of reservations about whether this ideal was in practice being realised (Golding, 2010). He noted a softer approach to current affairs and a decline in news audiences and newspaper readership, not fully offset by Internet usage; audience fragmentation; the 'commodification' of news and entertainment; the over-simplification of journalists' explanations; and the persistence of a 'digital divide'. Digital broadcasting, and the new media more generally, he concluded, could be liberating and enriching but could also prove narrow and inhibit participation and engagement: 'Neither path is inevitable, and technology is neither the cause nor the reason for either' (Golding, 2010: 221).

The question of whether digital television switchover is 'good for democracy' has no self-evident or general answer.

## Comparative case studies

In 2010 the Soros-financed Open Society Foundations (OSF) embarked on an ambitious Mapping Digital Media project, to examine, initially across some 60 countries, how the core democratic service that any media system should provide – news about political, economic and social affairs – was affected by the switch from analogue to digital broadcasting, the growth of new media platforms and the convergence of broadcasting and telecommunications.

The advisory Editorial Commission (of which I was a member) cautioned against any attempt to prove cause and effect here. It would be a fallacy to state that the conversion of television transmission from analogue to digital *caused* changes in the media's contribution to democracy. Technology is a tool, not a determinant. It was possible, however, to identify the opportunities which changes in technology create for strengthening the media's democratic role and to ask, country by country, whether those opportunities have been or are being taken. Similarly, it was possible to point to risks or threats which could arise during or following the changes and establish, again case-by-case, whether any of these had materialised.

For example, an obvious opportunity is that digital television's extra channel capacity could be used to broaden the range of service providers, creating greater pluralism and introducing extra news channels. Another is the greater scope for audience participation offered by online feedback to programmes. Conversely, one major risk is that either the government or a small group of analogue terrestrial incumbents design switchover so as to limit or exclude the opportunities for new entrants in order to transfer their dominance of the analogue market into the digital one. Another risk is that market forces, in a highly competitive market without influential public service broadcasting or regulatory constraint, produce a 'race to the bottom' in which non-tabloid and non-partisan news programmes are eliminated.

The OSF project had a wider scope than the digitisation of television and its expansion onto the Internet and into mobile reception. It encompassed the new media more broadly, including websites and other Internet activity which had no direct connection with television. Moreover, many of the countries it surveyed had yet to complete digital switchover. While the surveys in total have not presented a tidy coherent answer on the issue of digital television's relationship to democratic values, its individual reports (available at www.mediapolicy.org/mdm) are illuminating. For example, the UK report writers' assessment includes the judgment that 'near universal digital media access has yielded broad benefits for citizenship and democracy', but also expresses concern about financial crises, media concentration and limitations on the reach of quality programmes beyond an engaged and relatively elite audience (OSF, 2011a: 9). The United States report points up the migration of consumers to partisan cable news networks, the segmentation of news audiences, financial pressures and a scaling back of media ownership regulation, noting that

> Regulatory activities directed at preserving and promoting competition, free and independent news production, diversity, and pluralism in the digital space have yet to emerge in any meaningful sense.
>
> (OSF, 2011b: 8)

The OSF report on Russia concludes that 'digitization, understood as both the digital switchover and the spread of online media, has not weakened the dominant role of the State in the media market' (OSF, 2011c: 75), while the reports on Italy and Mexico both express concerns about the continuing dominance of television duopolies (OSF, 2011d and e).

The diversity of national experiences captured in these reports is no surprise. Market conditions – and, of course, political and constitutional characteristics and history – differ hugely and it is unrealistic to expect all countries to be able to exploit the same opportunities as one another. Media policy tends to be conditioned by historical context and the legacy of past policy, as recent scholarship examining the importance of institutional history has shown.

A comparative study by Luis A. Albornoz and María Trinidad García Leiva focussed specifically on digital terrestrial television and examined nine national case studies (one of which I contributed). While it was published in Spanish (for details, see Acknowledgements), the authors have summarised their findings in a Journal article (Albornoz and García Leiva, 2012). They concluded that the digital terrestrial landscape was shaped significantly by the analogue past, state intervention, industrial policy, economic gain and 'diverse power struggles'.

> Consequently, issues of social promotion, inclusion, cultural diversity or political pluralism have been mostly left behind. This is why, when assessing the implementation of DTT [digital terrestrial television] at the international level, it can be concluded that the working models and, consequently, the emergent patterns and tendencies, do not entail deep, real changes in regard to the democratization of the audiovisual field. The implemented policies have not taken into account the citizen as a fundamental backbone of these changes.
>
> (Albornoz and García Leiva, 2012: 317)

In an earlier study comparing the digital transition in the United States and the United Kingdom entitled *New Television, Old Politics,* Hernan Galperin highlighted the role of national governments and pre-existing patterns of broadcasting in shaping digital television. He challenged both the optimist and the pessimist assumptions about new media technology undermining the state's capacity to shape modern communications – optimists believing that power was passing into the hands of users and new entrants and pessimists seeing deregulation as leading to control by big multi-national corporations. His observation was that governments were not in retreat but were simply using new tools to influence the media sector, with different results in different countries. Technology and globalisation were not dictating the outcomes. Galperin concluded:

> Different national media regimes have therefore proved compatible with digital communications on a global scale and the strengthening of political and economic links between nations. This should be good news for those engaged in efforts to democratize media access or protect arrangements aimed at securing the supply of public goods that media markets may undersupply (e.g. minority-oriented programming, political speech), for the future of television seems less wedded to the evolution of technology or global market forces than to politics, as usual.
>
> (Galperin, 2004: 287)

In the light of this review of the evidence – and the literature – we can conclude that the connection between digital television switchover and democracy is a very simple one: the technology change offers opportunities for strengthening democracy but whether or not those opportunities are taken is determined, country by country, by the decisions of governments, regulators, broadcasters and citizens. As Petros Iosifidis put it in a paper for the Open Society Foundations project:

> New communications technology is not inherently pro-democratic: it can be just as effective at sustaining propaganda and authoritarian regimes. New forms of citizenship and public life are simultaneously enabled by technology and restricted by market power and surveillance. What is certain is that media are not the public sphere *per se*; they are a vehicle through which such a space can be created.
>
> (Iosifidis, 2012: 11)

## The potential 'democratic dividend'

Thus the digital switchover process can be designed with the aim of securing democratic benefits, but this is in no way guaranteed. The process can be captured and formulated behind closed doors by vested interests. 'Technical' reasons can be advanced for excluding new entrants to the television market, suppressing opportunities which their citizens perhaps never knew were there. At the outset countries which opted for HDTV faced a genuine problem in expanding the number of broadcasters during the simulcasting stage because of the amount of spectrum an HD channel required. With the development of a second generation of transmission technology, such as DVB-T2, and the advent of the newer compression standard MPEG-4 replacing MPEG-2, such technical arguments have become much weaker. The issues can be complex, however, since, when newer technology first arrives in the market, it can increase the cost of receivers. Lucia Barmošová has described the enormous pressure that the incumbent analogue broadcasters in Slovakia applied to the regulator in Slovakia in 2008, leading it to reverse its choice of MPEG-4 for the country's digital terrestrial television (Barmošová, 2010).

In the case of Bulgaria the European Commission intervened, judging that the process for awarding digital terrestrial television spectrum was disproportionately restrictive and excluded potential candidates. Dissatisfied with Bulgaria's response, in 2013 it referred the issue to the European Court of Justice (EC, 2013).

While civil society needs to be alert to restrictions on new market entrants, idealists do need to understand market constraints. It is simply not possible for digital television switchover to usher in a glorious new age of democratic pluralism in every country, regardless of its market characteristics. As we saw in Chapter 4, small countries such as Portugal, Ireland and Slovenia, facing an adverse economic climate, found that their terrestrial households were simply not numerous enough to support the kind of additional services their governments and regulators would ideally like to have seen.

In order to be able to secure as good a 'democratic dividend' as is feasible, civil society needs to be ready to ask the right questions at the right time. While there can be no standard list of answers, a useful 'checklist' of questions might read:

- can the supply and range of news services be increased?
- can services from other countries provide new political perspectives?

- can regional and local television be strengthened, including through the provision of services in additional languages if appropriate?
- will politicians be fully distanced from content regulation?
- can television be made more accessible to the disabled?
- can complementary television and Internet services strengthen civic involvement?
- can the digital dividend be used to reduce the broadband 'digital divide'?

### Increasing the supply and range of news services

News programming is obviously a central area where digital switchover can make a contribution to the strengthening of democracy. As noted above, Pippa Norris has identified a correlation between regular use of television and radio news and democratic satisfaction. She addressed the commonly voiced idea that exposure to negative news and political scandal tends to foster mistrust of government and dissatisfaction with democratic institutions (which she terms the 'video-malaise thesis') and, from her analysis of survey data, concluded that the reverse is true:

> Contrary to the core claim in the video-malaise thesis, users of television and radio broadcast news proved *more* satisfied with democracy, not less.
>
> (Norris, 2011: 186)

In countries where the source of analogue TV news has been restricted, with the media perhaps dominated by a state broadcaster, it is highly desirable to diversify by adding an additional news provider. This is most obviously achieved by licensing one or more new broadcasters with a requirement that news be an integral part of their schedules. More developed markets, with a range of broadcasters, may have scope for the introduction of specialised news services, including 'rolling news' designed to be accessed anytime, day or night, at the viewer's convenience – news on tap. In North America, where 24-hour news was an established analogue format, the number of news channels expanded at both national and local levels. In France in 2005 BFM TV added an all-news channel to those already in the market. In the UK the BBC introduced a 24 hour digital news channel while BSkyB greatly strengthened the Sky News channel it had initially developed on analogue satellite. Spain's *Canal 24 Horas*, originally launched on satellite, became available on digital terrestrial TV in 2005. In Australia the public broadcaster ABC replaced an HD simulcast channel with ABC News 24 in 2010.

Sustaining full-time news channels in a mature market is commercially challenging. The more competing news programmes there are, the smaller the audience for any one of them is likely to be and, if they rely on advertising finance, market saturation can be reached. In the UK a digital ITV news service, launched in 2000, was forced to close in 2005. News channels are more easily provided by public broadcasters with public funds or by pay-TV broadcasters who can incorporate them in a broader subscription package.

Moreover, the 'rolling news' genre has both strengths and weaknesses. News channels provide ready access to the headlines and are, of course, gripping when dramatic events are unfolding but, as Steven Barnett noted critically:

> 24-hour news channels compensate for periods of inaction through a number of dramatic conventions: opinionated commentary, a 'breaking news' ticker at the bottom of the screen, a manufactured confrontation between protagonists holding mildly different views, or the live 'two-way' where the very element of liveness is designed to inject immediacy in a story where, in truth, very little is happening.
>
> (Barnett, 2011: 205)

So news channels are not always in practice the answer to a democrat's prayer.

Nonetheless, an expansion and diversification of news programming, with full regard to both financial viability and quality, is a significant potential citizen benefit of digital television switchover. Debates about the plurality of news provision, and attempts to measure plurality, feature most often when a takeover or merger is in prospect, but the topic is one which civil society should seek to air during the formulation of digital switchover policy, especially during deliberations on the criteria for the selection of multiplex licensees and channel providers. At the very least, there is an opportunity to reduce the risk of one or two powerful voices (government or commercial) having an excessive influence on public opinion and the political agenda. At best, the outcome could be a more wide-ranging and inclusive news agenda, enhancing the educational, watchdog, analytical, social, facilitating and advocacy roles which news journalism can play.

### Drawing in political perspectives from other countries

Another 'citizen interest' opportunity arising from digital television switchover is greatly increased access to the broadcasts of other countries and cultures. The economics of switchover positively encourage this, in that the expansion in the number of channels is usually far greater than any expansion in the resources for funding new production, so carrying foreign TV services is common not only on satellite and cable but on digital terrestrial television too. *Freeview* viewers in the UK are offered Al Jazeera, for example.

Television has always had an international dimension, based on the import and export of programmes, and analogue satellite provided the basis for the launch of CNN as a global news service. However, with conspicuous exceptions like the BBC, a great deal of analogue international television was one-way traffic from the United States to other countries – which worried about the implications of this 'cultural imperialism' for their own languages, cultures and news agendas.

In recent decades, particularly with the proliferation of digital satellite channels and the spread of cable distribution, the pattern has changed. Japan's NHK World Television, Germany's Deutsche Welle (DWTV), Russia Today, China's CCTV and Qatar-based Al Jazeera's are now widely available around the globe. Other countries have expanded their domestic native-language services and made agreements for them to be carried by foreign countries, often for reception by diaspora communities. The international availability of video services via the Internet to broadband users is now opening up even greater access to foreign television material. Programmes from their native land or in their native language can play a support role within immigrant communities.

Meanwhile the United States has become a major importer of Spanish-language programming, mainly from Mexico, to serve its growing Spanish-speaking population. Surveying the full range of global media changes, Jeremy Tunstall replaced his 1977 book *The Media Are American* with a twenty-first century version *The Media Were American* (Tunstall, 2008). In digital television globalisation need not be synonymous with Americanisation. As digital television spreads across the world, it can potentially supply a foundation for an increased understanding of the perspectives of other countries.

### Strengthening regional and local television and providing services in additional languages

While digital switchover policy tends to be formulated primarily at national level, the expansion of channel capacity offers great scope for strengthening regional and local television. Spectrum may be available for this from the outset, when digital terrestrial simulcasting begins, and, if there are constraints here, this is one of the purposes for which released spectrum can be used. Moreover, because digital terrestrial transmission requires lower transmitter power than analogue for the same result, new opportunities for local television can be found in new gaps within the established network of national transmission frequencies – the so-called 'White Spaces'.

Spain and France provide examples of countries which have increased regional and local provision. When Spain re-launched its digital terrestrial television services in 2005, capacity was earmarked for over 20 regional and local digital TV services, including local language broadcasts. Spain's political structure of regional autonomy and the strength of the Catalan and Basque languages perhaps make it a special case, but France, with a contrasting history of centralisation, also set aside two digital terrestrial multiplexes for regional and local TV.

While the UK recognised the importance of Welsh and Gaelic language broadcasting, its digital switchover policy initially made no provision for any expansion of regional and local television – indeed, the trend was in the opposite direction as ITV reduced some of its regional commitments. As Secretary of State for Culture, Media and Sport the Conservative Minister Jeremy Hunt subsequently took a personal initiative to plant the seeds of local television. As switchover proceeded, spectrum became available; the main issue was the economics of the business and it remains to be seen whether the combination of regulatory help and some licence fee funding can produce a flourishing local tier of television. It would not have started without the political impetus.

### Keeping politics out of content regulation

Even in countries where public broadcasters are independent of the government, political interventions to try and block the transmission of politically contentious material can occur. In the UK in the analogue era Ministers would occasionally attempt to persuade the politically appointed chairmen of broadcasting's governing authorities not to broadcast a programme known to be in the pipeline. Examples where government intervention was tried but failed were the BBC's *Question of Ulster* programme in 1972 and ITV's *Death on the Rock* in 1988; an example where Prime Ministerial intervention temporarily succeeded was the BBC's *Real Lives* documentary in 1985.

Increasing the distance between government Ministers and programme publishers by establishing the principle that regulatory bodies should not view programmes in advance of transmission has curbed this tendency. Greater plurality in broadcasting and the role of independent production have also reduced the risk of pre-transmission government intervention. In twenty-first century outbreaks of hostility between governments and broadcasters over particular programmes, such as the BBC radio broadcast on the Iraq dossier in 2004, conflict tends to be *after* transmission.

The development of an all-digital communications pattern should further reduce the risk of political pressure over contentious programmes. Pre-transmission regulation of a greatly expanded number of TV channels is impractical and an independent producer who cannot secure a broadcast slot for a controversial programme can always distribute it over the Internet.

The all-digital communications environment *could* lead to the removal of politicians from any oversight of television content. Conceptually content regulation of digital communications can be done by

a) no one (just left to the law)
b) an independent body, separate from both media organisations and the state
c) a regulatory body appointed by the state
d) the government.

As discussed in Chapter 8, Americans may have a cultural preference for option (a) but, for other societies which do not, digital convergence provides an opportunity to adopt option (b) on a cross-media basis, uncoupling television content regulation from the state's licensing of spectrum.

### Making television more accessible to the disabled

Television plays an important part in shaping communities and a sense of belonging, as well as supporting democratic processes and institutions, and digital switchover provides a major opportunity to improve access to the medium for those who may otherwise be excluded from it through disability.

Digital television can offer two forms of help to the deaf and hard-of-hearing – subtitling and sign language. For the partially sighted it can offer audio-description – a verbal description of what is happening on the TV screen carried in between the dialogue. These services need to be implemented both at the transmission and the reception end of the broadcasting chain. While broadcasters may choose to what extent they provide them – the BBC, for example, subtitles all its TV programmes, provides audio-description for around 10% and signing for over 5% – this is an area where regulators can appropriately set requirements and targets. These are issues to be aired during the process of digital switchover policy formulation.

### Complementary television and Internet services

The idea of referring television viewers to the broadcaster's website for additional information and explanation is a familiar one – and its use is growing. It facilitates a more detailed exposition of subjects; it allows the viewer to find detail of more local or personal relevance; and, as news topics develop, it provides a point of reference for those who missed the starting-point or want to be reminded of the background. Such a complementary relationship between television and online services can strengthen the information and education role digital television broadcasters play in supporting democracy.

In practice, the potential of this relationship has been restricted by the fact that the dual modes of distribution (television by broadcasting, Internet via broadband) have hitherto required two separate forms of reception. Viewers in the sitting-room watching television news, when told that they can find out more about the government's proposed tax reforms by going to the broadcaster's website, do not get out of their chairs and go into another room to turn on the computer unless very strongly motivated. However, two aspects of convergence could change this. One is the Connected TV set, plugged into both broadcasting and broadband feeds, where the viewer can flick from one source to another without changing rooms or receivers. If the drawback with this is that the following item on the broadcast programme might be missed, the other option is to access the website on the mobile phone while continuing to watch TV. As technology convergence proceeds, and dual-screen viewing grows, editorial opportunities arise here.

The relationship between the Internet and democracy is a much wider subject, outside the scope of this book, but the interface between broadcasting and the Internet can certainly be exploited to enhance the contribution to democracy which digital television can make. The best known example was the western media's reliance on social media and user-generated video material from the Middle East, from the Iranian elections of 2009 through the Arab risings of 2010–2012, at times or in places where their own correspondents could not operate freely. The risk of 'media capture' by particular dissident groups needs to recognised and avoided but a well-managed relationship between the mainstream media, on the one hand, and citizens anywhere with cameras in their phones and access to the Internet, on the other, can shine a light of publicity within areas of the world where dictatorship or oppression has been shielded in obscurity.

It is a relationship relevant to domestic as well as international news. Alan Rusbridger, Editor of the *Guardian* newspaper, has outlined a vision of collaborative journalism in which the established media can enlist the support of the digitally active public in ferreting out information. As an example, he cites the work of *Guardian* journalist Paul Lewis who used *Twitter* to track down video evidence of a police constable assaulting a pedestrian who subsequently died at the G20 Summit in London in 2009, securing evidence from a witness who might not otherwise have been found (Rusbridger, 2009).

More widely, it is open to broadcasters to develop their relationship with social media and other forms of citizen self-expression to facilitate greater public participation in policy debates and public consultations. One-way analogue broadcasting often saw its citizen role as seeking to provide the public with the information and education professionals judged to be needed. The evolution of digital television into digital multi-media, which can be multi-directional in character, makes it possible to go much further, at both national and local levels, in promoting civic involvement and participation.

### Reducing the broadband 'digital divide'

The opportunities to strengthen democracy discussed above essentially relate to the uses which can be made of spectrum earmarked for television. Finally, it is also worth considering whether any contribution to democracy can be made by the spectrum released by analogue switch-off for other potential uses.

As Pippa Norris first stated (Norris, 2001), there are different kinds of 'digital divide', between countries and within them, between those who can afford certain equipment and those who cannot, between those who have certain skills and those without them. However, in advanced societies where the penetration of personal computers is high, a particular issue is the divide between those with access to high-speed broadband and those, often in rural areas, who are still waiting for it. Broadband is increasingly seen now as an essential service for economic, social and political participation in a modern state. While only a few countries have committed to making it universal in practical terms, most advanced economies now have this as an aspiration. The extension of fixed line broadband access is normally the primary answer to this need but wireless access networks can also have a role, especially in remote rural areas. Spectrum released by digital switchover for telecommunications use can be relevant here.

In the United States the role which released broadcasting spectrum could play in enabling wireless broadband to be provided to remote areas was one of the arguments pressed by high-tech companies for proceeding with analogue terrestrial television switch-off. In 2005, when Senate Committee hearings were being conducted on the case for naming a hard date for switch-off, Aloha Partners pointed out that in rural states the wireless broadband beneficiaries of digital switchover could outnumber the households still dependent on analogue terrestrial:

> For example, Montana has an estimated 86 percent of its homes covered by satellite and cable. That leaves about 50,000 of the households that are receiving TV Over-The-Air and potentially in need of assistance to complete the transition. On the other hand, more than 175,000 households are estimated to be unable to receive broadband because they live in low density areas. In other words, the number of households in Montana that are being deprived of broadband is over three times as large as the number of households that may be affected by the DTV transition. Montana is not an isolated case. A number of states represented on this committee face the same situation: Arkansas, Louisiana, Maine, Mississippi, Nebraska, North Dakota, South Carolina, Virginia, and West Virginia.
>
> (United States Senate Committee on Commerce,
> Science and Transportation, 2005).

In the UK in 2012 the House of Lords Committee Select Committee on Communications, investigating how best to provide broadband to everyone, looked to the part which wireless broadband could play in rural areas where installing fibre would be prohibitively expensive:

> Wireless technologies... seem to us to have a complementary role, standing in for fibre where there is none, and supplementing it, where there is.
>
> (House of Lords, 2012: 13)

When Germany designed its auction of spectrum for 4G, the quickest possible expansion of broadband supply to rural areas was made an explicit objective of the process.

## Securing the 'democratic dividend'

From the possibilities outlined above, it will be apparent that a 'democratic dividend' from digital television switchover will not 'just arrive' as an automatic by-product of the process. It needs to be sought. While complementary online services and synergy with social media, for example, can be achieved by individual broadcasters, others are a matter of broader public policy. Government and regulators set the criteria for selecting the services to be carried on digital terrestrial multiplexes and authorise the provision of new services, such as new 24 hour news by public broadcasters, for example. It was government broadcasting policy which stimulated, and designed support for, the development of local television in the UK. Regulators are involved in specifying minimum levels for access services for the disabled. Governments would need to be involved in any decision to withdraw state licensing bodies from content regulation – and, of course, governments and regulators are central to decisions about the re-use of released broadcasting spectrum for wireless broadband.

Most of the elements of the 'democratic dividend' discussed above have been achieved in Western Europe, as the examples from the UK, France and Germany illustrate, but primarily as a result of public policy of one form or another. There is an agenda here for civil society: citizen benefits from digital switchover need to be sought and secured in the public arena.

# In Conclusion

## Does it add up to a revolution?

We have charted the progress of digital television switchover from its origins through to convergence and the advent of the Connected TV, and seen how it has spread from North America and Europe across the globe, even to developing countries. The process began in the 1990s, around 30 countries had completed analogue terrestrial switch-off by the end of 2012, many more will have done so by 2015 but the full global transition will have a long tail. Does it add up to a revolution?

Historians use the term rather sparingly – for example, to describe the political upheavals of the French Revolution and the Russian Revolution and the economic and social transformations we know as the Agricultural Revolution and the Industrial Revolution. In relation to the contemporary world, the term is often used more casually to characterise social, technical and economic change: thus we might talk of the revolution in the airline industry – and in business and tourism – associated with the advent of the jet engine. The context can vary considerably, therefore, but 'revolution' does imply a transformation in which an old order is replaced by a new one at a relatively swift, rather than gradual, speed.

Does the transformation of television from analogue to digital technology replace an old order with a new? The answer is 'yes' within a much wider change, sometimes termed the electronic Information Revolution, which has had, and continues to have, an all-pervading influence on our economic, social and political systems. Within the field of television digital switchover is bringing about dramatic change when seen in conjunction with the development of new platforms and the interface with the Internet.

The counter-argument is that, while digital switchover has brought us a much greater choice of channels and we therefore watch a little more television, our viewing habits have not yet changed that much. From the menu of 50–500 channels many of us still choose the same four or five regular favourites. However, there is a bigger picture.

In the analogue world both broadcasters and audiences constituted coherent groups. In many countries the broadcasters were institutions – state broadcasters and public broadcasters founded and funded by the state – together with a select number of commercial broadcasters overseen by a regulator who watched over the balance of their schedules and the impartiality of their news and current affairs. The small number of channels meant a small choice of programmes available at any one time. Most of us viewed the same programmes as one another in groups sufficiently large for commercial broadcasters to sell to advertisers and in peak-time audiences could be very big indeed. Aside from whatever compulsory tax financed the state or public channels, viewing was free.

Governments tended to attribute great power and influence to individual programmes and, even in the UK with its tradition of editorial independence, would occasionally try and lean on the regulatory institutions they had appointed to prevent the showing of a politically controversial programme.

At first the transformation was gradual. To begin with, those coherent groupings were loosened. The broadcasting institutions were joined by new broadcasters and obliged to carry the work of independent producers. With the advent of satellite and cable, a proportion of households were taken into a multi-channel world: subscription supplied a new source of finance and pay-TV broadcasters formed new agreements with movie houses and sporting bodies to remove 'premium' programmes from free-to-view television. Audiences spread out over more channels and made increasing use of recording technology.

Then the digital TV revolution brought a sharp upward gear-change to these trends. Whole nations were shifted into multi-channel television by government decision. The number of channels proliferated, the number of broadcasters and content producers expanded, the power of subscription finance started to eclipse the power of advertising finance, the recording technology became more sophisticated and user-friendly, and the audiences dispersed more widely, though coming together for major events.

Television became ubiquitous. In the fields of news and sport, more started happening faster, in real time around the clock. Meanwhile, drama and comedy programmes acquired a much longer life, independent of TV schedulers. Television could be viewed on the Internet, which provided On-Demand Catch-Up TV, liberating viewers from the constraint of time. Mobile technology freed viewers from the constraint of a fixed reception place. Connected TV brought the Internet to the main TV screen alongside broadcast programmes and, with broadband now an additional platform, the technology is evolving towards a hybrid broadcast—broadband TV.

The increased access to content is not just a matter of more TV channels and easier access to the archives. The tenfold increase in terrestrial channels and the supermarket of 500 channels available on satellite and cable constituted the first wave of change but, with convergence and the arrival of the Connected TV set, the next phase is access on the same TV device to the Internet and its cornucopia of video content. Entry barriers to the business of producing and distributing video material have been taken down.

Digitisation has brought a step-change in interactivity between the public and the mainstream broadcasters, with the feedback mechanisms of e-mail, texting and the use of TV remote control buttons – and by the interface with social media. The proactive side of this interactivity is User-Generated Content, material supplied to the broadcaster direct from members of the public. Every member of the public with a camera-equipped mobile phone is a potential television contributor and, in countries where professional journalist access is restricted, this has become politically significant.

Digital television has a global dimension. Historically, television was largely confined within national frontiers, albeit with some cross-border reception and with some international broadcasting. However, the explosion of satellite broadcasting and the delivery of online video services via the Internet have created a globalised industry.

We are seeing a long-term trend away from terrestrial television. In some nations – both heavily cabled countries of northern Europe and countries in the Middle East where satellite predominates – its role is being marginalised. Even in countries where it continues to play a major part, it may no longer be expected to achieve near-universal coverage: instead of multiplying the number of small transmitters to reach into every last corner, countries find it more economic and sensible to fill out national coverage using satellite. In the long run broadband may become the preferred way of distributing much of what we now call 'television'.

The ability to use terrestrial spectrum for many more television channels while at the same time releasing large chunks of it for use by telecommunications, facilitating wireless and mobile broadband services, represents a dramatic technical change. Broadcast television technology now has to fight for the spectrum resources it uses and its leaders are looking beyond the 'standards wars' of the switchover process towards a more collaborative global approach.

Convergence, involving the Press now as well as broadcasting and telecommunications, is undermining the analogue foundations of broadcasting regulation and the concept of separate regulatory silos for different media depending on their means of distribution. While many countries will still want regulation by an independent body both to enhance quality and to prevent harm, governments will find it harder to prevent the broadcasting of specific programmes. The state's role in content regulation, other than for public services, could be further reduced if the licensing of spectrum ceases to be a content management tool.

The world of digital television is therefore not simply the world of analogue television with more channels, more robust signal quality, the option of high-definition and new widescreen TV sets. The transformation taking place is broader and more complex, creating new sets of relationships between communicators, audiences, regulators and governments.

It is said that revolutions often take longer but go further than those in the midst of them expect. Although analogue television transmission systems are rapidly being closed down, we have yet to see the full outcomes of the converged pattern of all-digital communications.

## Managing outcomes

It has been a theme of this book that digital television switchover can be proactively managed. It is not a process whose outcome is technologically determined, nor one that need leave television driven by untrammelled market forces in directions we find damaging to our cultures and democracies. Governments and regulators can shape it. So can civil society.

Rapid change sometimes presents clearer decision points than evolutionary development. Digital television switchover is not a process of gradual technological change, it is at heart a political project involving a series of events which need to be deliberately planned. Some of the design work is highly technical or legal and thus specialised – and many of the decisions are commercial. However, from the point of view of citizens wishing to influence it, certain key points at which the voices of civil society should be heard are:

- at the start of digital terrestrial television when the criteria for the selection of new services are being drafted;
- as analogue terrestrial switch-off approaches and further new television services become feasible;
- when the auctioning or reallocation of released spectrum is being planned;
- when the regulatory system is redesigned to cope with convergence;
- when the roles of public service broadcasting and public service media organisations are reconsidered in the new all-digital environment.

We have identified some of the main risks for citizens of regarding the digital television revolution as 'too difficult', 'too technical' or 'the product of impersonal technical and commercial forces outside of our control'. Without civil society's understanding of the process and involvement, governments in authoritarian societies will replace political control of analogue broadcasting with political control of the digital media. Market-dominated countries may see analogue media barons using their political muscle to turn themselves into digital media barons. Liberal regimes may fail to see how to prevent a fragmented and unregulated market from destroying high-quality television journalism and replacing it with opinionated commentaries with a politically partisan agenda.

None of these scenarios is inevitable. Many countries have a media history that makes them prone to one or other of these risks, but this can be combated by a well-informed proactive civil society with an understanding of how the digital transition works.

# References

Advanced Television, 2012a, 'Nielsen: internet-only TV homes surge 23%', 10 February, http://advanced-television.com/index.php/2012/02/10/nielsen-internet-only-tv-homes-surge-23/, accessed 17 April 2012.

Advanced Television, 2012b, 'Australia: traditional TV viewing on the rise', 20 February, http://advanced-television.com/index.php/2012/02/20/australia-traditional-tv-viewing-on-the-rise, accessed 10 March 2012.

Albornoz, L. and García Leiva, M.T., 2012, 'The political economy of DTT: an international overview' in *The International Journal of Digital Television*, 3:3, 301–319.

Alvarez-Monzoncillo, J., 2011, *Watching the Internet: The Future of TV?* Formalpress/Media XXI, www.mediaxxi.com

Armstrong, C. and Collins, R., 2011, 'Digital turmoil for South African TV' in *The International Journal of Digital Television*, 2:1, 7–29.

Arrese, A. and Herrero, M., 2005, 'Spain: A Market in Turmoil' in: Brown, A. and Picard, R., (eds), *Digital Terrestrial Television in Europe*, Mahwah, New Jersey, Lawrence Erlbaum Associates.

Australian Government, 2012a, *Digital Tracker: Summary Report for Quarter 1, January to March 2012*, Department of Broadband, Communications and the Digital Economy.

Australian Government, 2012b, *Convergence Review: Final Report*, Canberra, Department of Broadband, Communications and the Digital Economy.

Barmošová, L., 2010, 'Digitalization of TV broadcasting in Slovakia' in *The International Journal of Digital Television*, 1:3, 361–366.

Barnett, S., 2011, *The Rise and Fall of Television Journalism*, London, Bloomsbury Academic.

Barwise, P., 2011, 'Waiting for "Vodot": why "video on demand" won't happen' in *Market Leader*, Quarter 2.

Barwise, P. and Picard, R., 2012, *The Economics of Television in a Digital World*, Oxford, Reuters Institute for the Study of Journalism.

BBC, 1992, *Extending Choice: The BBC's Role in the New Broadcasting Age*, London.

BBC, 2004, *Building Public Value*, London.

BBC, 2006, 'Creative future', press release, 25 April.

Bell, M.L., 2007, *Inventing Digital Television*, Sudbury, The London Press.

Bell, M.L., 2010, 'The UK's Freeview HD dilemma and the DVB-T2 solution' in *International Journal of Digital Television*, 1:3, 273–287.

Bhat, R., 2012, 'Television in India: the starting point for digital switchover' in *The International Journal of Digital Television*, 3:1, 73–83.

Birt, J., 2002, *The Harder Path*, London, Time Warner Books.

BIS (Department for Business Innovation and Skills) and DCMS (Department for Culture, Media and Sport), 2009, *Digital Britain*, London.

BIS and DCMS, 2010, *Britain's Superfast Broadband Future*, London.

Bonin, G., 2010, 'Canada's transition to digital television: from policy to reality' in *The International Journal of Digital Television*, 1:2, 135–154.

Bottomley, V., 1995, Letter to *The Times*, 11 August.

Briggs, A, 1965, *The History of Broadcasting in the United Kingdom, Volume II, The Golden Age of Wireless*, Oxford, Oxford University Press.

Brinkley, J., 1997, *Defining Vision: The Battle for the Future of Television*, New York, Harcourt Brace & Company.

Broadband TV News, 2011a, 'Russia goes for DVB-T2', 29 September http://www.broadbandtvnews.com/2011/09/29/russia-goes-for-dvb-t2/, accessed 10 January, 2012.

Broadband TV News, 2011b, 'France withdraws "bonus channels"', 30 November http://www.broadbandtvnews.com/2011/11/30/france-withdraws-%e2%80%98bonus-channels%e2%80%99/, accessed 5 January 2012.

Broadcast magazine, 2003, 'ITV Digital "never stood a chance"', 20 June.

Brown, A., 2005a, 'Sweden: The Digital Threat to Cultural Sovereignty' in: Brown, A. and Picard, R., (eds.), *Digital Terrestrial Television in Europe*, Mahwah, New Jersey, Lawrence Erlbaum Associates.

Brown, A., 2005b, 'Finland: Uncertain Digital Future in a Small Market' in: Brown, A. and Picard, R. (eds.), *Digital Terrestrial Television in Europe*, Mahwah, New Jersey, Lawrence Erlbaum Associates.

Burns, T. (Lord), 2005, Letter to the Secretary of State for Culture, Media and Sport, accompanying report of an Independent Panel on the BBC's Charter renewal, 27 January.

CITU (Central Information Technology Unit), 2000, *Modernising Government – Framework for Information Age Government, Digital TV*, Cabinet Office.

Chin, Yik-Chan, 2007, 'From the Local to the Global: China's Television Policy in Transition' in: Kops, Manfred and Ollig, Stefan (eds.), *Internationalization of the Chinese TV Sector*, Berlin, LIT.

China Daily, 2010, '*National* cable TV network soon', 25 August, http://chinadaily.com.cn/china/2010-08/25/content_11198025.htm

Chippindale, P. and Franks, S., 1991, *Dished! The Rise and Fall of British Satellite Broadcasting*, London, Simon and Shuster.

Coleman, S. and Ross, K., 2010, *The Media and the Public: "Them" and "Us" in Media Discourse*, Chichester, Wiley-Blackwell.

Consumers' Association, 2001, *Turn On, Tune In, Switched Off – Consumer Attitudes to Digital TV*, London.

Darlington, R. and Tambini, D., 2011, 'Regulating content as communications converge' in *The International Journal of Digital Television*, 2:3, 285–296.

D'Arma, A. and Steemers, J., 2010, 'Public Service Media and Children: Serving the Digital Citizens of the Future' in: Iosifidis, P. (ed.), *Reinventing Public Service Communication: European Broadcasters and Beyond*, Basingstoke, Palgrave Macmillan.

Debrett, M., 2009, 'Riding the wave: public service television in the multi-platform era' in *Media, Culture and Society*, 31:5, 807–827.

Debrett, M., 2010, *Reinventing Public Service Television for the Digital Future*, Bristol, Intellect.

Del Monte, A., 2006, 'The development of digital broadcasting in Italy' in: Cave, M. and Nakamura, K. (eds.), *Digital Broadcasting: Policy and Practice in the Americas, Europe and Japan*, Cheltenham, Edward Elgar.

Denicoli, S. and Sousa, H., 2012, 'The implementation of DTT in Portugal: a case of public-private interplay' in *The International Journal of Digital Television*, 3:1, 39–52.

DCMS (Department for Culture, Media and Sport) and DTI (Department of Trade and Industry), 2003, *Cost Benefit Analysis of Digital Switchover*, London.

DCMS, 2005, *Review of the BBC's Royal Charter: A Strong BBC, Independent of Government*, London, Green Paper.

DCMS and DTI, 2005, *Report of the Digital TV Project*, completed November 2004, London.

DCMS, 2006, *Broadcasting: Copy of Royal Charter for the Continuance of the British Broadcasting Corporation*, Cm 6925, presented to Parliament, October.

DCMS, 2011a, *Local Media Action Plan*, London.

DCMS, 2011b, Digital Radio Action Plan, Version 5, London.

Department of National Heritage (DNH, subsequently the Department for Culture, Media and Sport), 1995a, *Digital Terrestrial Broadcasting: The Government's Proposals*, London, HMSO, Cmnd. 2946.

DNH (Department of National Heritage), 1995b, press release 15 December.

Department of Trade and Industry (DTI, subsequently BIS, Department for Business, Innovation and Skills), 2001, Enterprise, *Skills and Innovation*, London, White Paper.

De Renesse, R., 2011, *Mobile TV: Challenges and Opportunities Beyond 2011*, a 'Mapping Digital Media' paper, Open Society Foundations, available at www.mediapolicy.org

DigiTAG, 2010, *Web Letter*, January, http://www.digitag.org/WebLetters/2010/External-Jan2010.html

DigiTAG, 2011a, *Web Letter*, October, http://www.digitag.org/WebLetters/2011/External-Oct2011.html

DigiTAG, 2011b, *Web Letter*, January, http://www.digitag.org/WebLetters/2011/External-Jan2011.html

DigiTAG, 2012a, *Web Letter*, August, http://www.digitag.org/WebLetters/2012/External-Aug2012.html

DigiTAG, 2012b, *Web Letter*, February, http://www.digitag.org/WebLetters/2012/External-Feb2012.html

DigiTAG, 2012c, *Web Letter*, March, http://www.digitag.org/WebLetters/2012/External-Mar2012.html

Dunleavy, T., 2010, 'New Zealand on Air, Public Service Television and TV Drama' in: Iosifidis, P. (ed.) *Reinventing Public Service Communication – European Broadcasters and Beyond*, Basingstoke, Palgrave Macmillan.

Dutton, W., 2007, *Through the Network (of Networks) – the Fifth Estate*, Inaugural Lecture, University of Oxford, 15 October, available at ssrn.com/abstract=1134502

Dutton, W., di Gennaro, C. and Millwood Hargrave, A., 2005, *The Internet in Britain: The Oxford Internet Survey*, Oxford, Oxford Internet Institute.

Dyke, G., 2004, *Inside Story*, London, Harper Collins.

Elstein, D., 2008, 'How to Fund Public Service Content in the Digital Age' in: Gardam, T. and Levy, D. (eds.), *The Price of Plurality*, Oxford, Reuters Institute for the Study of Journalism.

European Commission (EC), 1994, *Europe and the Global Information Society: Recommendations to the European Council*, report from the High Level Group on the Information Society, Brussels, European Commission.

EC, 2003, *Communication on the Transition from Analogue to Digital Broadcasting (From Digital Switch-Over to Analogue Switch-Off)*, COM (2003) 541 final, Brussels, European Commission.

EC, 2005a, *Communication on Accelerating the Transition from Analogue to Digital Broadcasting*, COM (2005) 204 final, Brussels, European Commission.

EC, 2005b, press release, *State Aid: Commission Rules Subsidy for Digital Terrestrial TV (DVB-T) in Berlin-Brandenburg Illegal; Explains how Digital TV can be Supported*, 9 November, Brussels, European Commission.

EC, 2009, *Communication from the Commission on the Application of State Aid rules to Public Service Broadcasting*, Brussels, European Commission.

EC, 2013, press release, *Antitrust: Commission takes Bulgaria to Court over assignment of Digital Terrestrial Broadcasting Authorisations*, 24 January, Brussels, European Commission.

Fanucci, F. and Brevini, B., 2013, 'Digital television in Italy: from analogue to digital duopoly?' in *The International Journal of Digital Television*, 4:1, 7–19.

Federal Communications Commission (FCC), 1997, *Fifth Report and Order*, April, Washington DC, FCC.

FCC, 2002, *Second Report and Order*, August, Washington DC, FCC.

FCC, 2010, *National Broadband Plan*, www.broadband.gov, accessed 16 April 2012.

Fernández Alonso, I. and Díaz González, M-J., 2010, 'Digital terrestrial television roll-out policies in Spain and the changing television scene in the context of analogue switch-off' in *The International Journal of Digital Television*, 1:3, 289–307.

Fernández Alonso, I. and Díaz González, M-J., 2013, 'Pluralism in Crisis: Transformations of the Spanish DTT Market in the context of the Recession' in *The International Journal of Digital Television*, 4:1, 81–86.

Fielden, L., 2011, *Regulating for Trust in Journalism – Standards Regulation in the Age of Blended Media*, Oxford, Reuters Institute for the Study of Journalism in association with City University.

Fielden, L., 2012, *Regulating the Press – A Comparative Study of International Press Councils*, Oxford, Reuters Institute for the Study of Journalism.

FOBTV (Future of Broadcast Television), 2012, *Memorandum of Understanding*, available at www.fobtv.org

Fukuyama, F., 1992, *The End of History and the Last Man*, London, Hamish Hamilton.

Fukuyama, F., 2011, *The Origins of Political Order*, London, Profile Books.

GAO (General Accounting Office, United States), 2005, *Digital Broadcast Television Transition: Estimated Cost of Supporting Set-Top Boxes to Help Advance the DTV Transition*, GAO 05-258T, Washington D.C.

Galperin, H., 2004, *New Television, Old Politics: The Transition to Digital Television in the United States and Britain*, Cambridge and New York, Cambridge University Press.

García Leiva, M.T, 2010, 'The introduction of DTT in Latin America: politics and policies' in *The International Journal of Digital Television*, 1:3, 327–343.

García Leiva, M.T. and Starks M., 2009, 'Digital switchover across the globe' in *Media Culture and Society*, 31:5, 787–806.

Gardini, F. and Galperin, H., 2005, 'Italy: Slow Penetration, High Potential?' in: Brown, A. and Picard, R., (eds.), *Digital Terrestrial Television in Europe*, Mahwah, New Jersey, Lawrence Erlbaum Associates.

Given, J., 2010, 'TV competition livens up down under' in *The International Journal of Digital Television*, 1:2, 231–234.

Given, J., 2012, 'Australia's convergence review' in *The International Journal of Digital Television*, 3:3, 293–300.

Given, J. and Norris, P., 2010, 'Would the real Freeview please stand up?' in *The International Journal of Digital Television*, 1:1, 51–68.

Goggin, G., 2012, 'The eccentric career of mobile television' in *The International Journal of Digital Television*, 3:2, 119–140.

Golding, P., 2010, 'The Cost of Citizenship in the Digital Age' in: Gripsrud, J. (ed.), *Relocating Television: Television in the Digital Context*, Abingdon, Routledge.

Gómez Garcia, R. and Sosa Plata, G., 2013, 'Digital terrestrial television policies in Mexico' in *The International Journal of Digital Television*, 4:1, 33–48.

Goodwin, P., 2005, 'United Kingdom: Never Mind the Policy, Feel the Growth' in: Brown, A. and Picard, R. (eds.) *Digital Television in Europe*, Mahwah, New Jersey, Lawrence Erlbaum Associates.

Grimme, K., 2002, *Digital Television: Standardization and Strategies*, Boston and London, Artech House.

Gripsrud, J., 2010, (ed.) *Relocating Television: Television in the Digital Context*, Abingdon, Routledge.

GSMA and A.T. Kearney, 2011, *African Mobile Observatory 2011*, London, GSMA.

Guardian, 2012a, 'Iran's press TV loses UK licence', 20 January.

Guardian, 2012b, 'Elisabeth Murdoch rounds on her brother in MacTaggart Lecture', 23 August.

Habermas, J., 1989, *The Structural Transformation of the Public Sphere*, Thomas Burger and Frederick Lawrence (trans.), Cambridge Massachusetts, MIT Press.

Hart, J.A., 2004, *Technology, Television and Competition: The Politics of Digital TV*, Cambridge and New York, Cambridge University Press.

Hart, J. A., 2010, 'The transition to digital television in the United States: the endgame', in *The International Journal of Digital Television*, 1:1, 7–29.

Helm, D., 2005, 'Consumers, Citizens and Members: Public Service Broadcasting and the BBC' in: BBC commission, *Can the Market Deliver?* Eastleigh, John Libbey Publishing.

Hodgson, P., 2008, 'Public Purpose versus Pluralism?' in: Gardam, T. and Levy, D. (eds.), *The Price of Plurality*, Oxford, Reuters Institute for the Study of Journalism.

Home Office, 1986, *Report of the Committee on Financing the BBC*, Cmnd. 9284, London, HMSO.

House of Commons, 2002, Statement by the Secretary of State at the Department of Culture Media and Sport, Tessa Jowell, 26 April.

House of Lords, 2010, *Digital Switchover of Television and Radio in the United Kingdom*, Report of the Select Committee on Communications, HL Paper 100, London.

House of Lords, 2012, *Broadband for All – An Alternative Vision*, Report of the Select Committee on Communications, HL Paper 41, London.

Hu, Z. and Hong, L., 2011, 'The issues and challenges facing three-network convergence in the Chinese media landscape' in *The International Journal of Digital Television*, 2:2, 215–221.

Hundt, R.E., 2000, *You Say You Want a Revolution: A Story of Information Age Politics*, New Haven, Yale University Press.

Huntington, S., 1991, *The Third Wave: Democratization in the Late Twentieth Century*, Norman, University of Oklahoma Press.

Iosifidis, P., 2007, *Public Television in the Digital Era*, Basingstoke, Palgrave Macmillan.

Iosifidis, P., 2011a, 'Growing pains? The transition to digital television in Europe' in *European Journal of Communication*, 26:1, 3–17.

Iosifidis, P., 2011b, *Global Media and Communication Policy*, Basingstoke, Palgrave Macmillan.

Iosifidis, P., 2012, *Digital Television, the Public Interest and European Regulation*, Reference paper for the Mapping Digital Media Project, Open Society Foundations, www.soros.org

J'son and Partners, 2011, 'Television and On-Demand Audiovisual Services in the Russian Federation', *Report for the European Audiovisual Observatory*, October, Strasbourg, Council of Europe.

Jung, I., 2010, 'Digital switchover of terrestrial broadcasting in Korea: legal background and major policy issues' in *The International Journal of Digital Television*, 1:3, 351–359.

Katz, E., 2009, 'The end of television' in *The Annals of the American Academy of Political and Social Science*, 625, September, 6–18.

Kleinsteuber, H., 2011, 'Digital television in Germany' in *The International Journal of Digital Television*, 2:1, 87–93.

Ko, H-T., Chang, C. and Chu, N-S, 2011, 'The positioning and current situation of Taiwan's digital TV' in *The International Journal of Digital Television*, 2:1, 95–107.

KPMG, 2012, *Media and Entertainment Barometer: Breakthrough for Online Streaming*, London.

Kuhn, R., 2010, 'France: Presidential Assault on the Public Service' in: Iosifidis, P. (ed.), *Reinventing Public Service Communication – European Broadcasters and Beyond*, Basingstoke, Palgrave Macmillan.

Kuhn, R., 2011, 'The French connection: digital television in France' in *The International Journal of Digital Television*, 2.3, 269–283.

Kumabe, N., 2012a, 'DTT switchover accomplished in most areas of Japan' in *The International Journal of Digital Television*, 3:1, 85–87.

Kumabe, N., 2012b, 'Challenges of television after digital switchover in Japan' in *The International Journal of Digital Television*, 3:3, 349–355.

Laurence, H., 2011, 'Digital television and technology diffusion' in *The International Journal of Digital Television*, 2:3, 359–366.

Lax, S., 2011, 'Digital radio switchover: the UK experience' in *The International Journal of Digital Television*, 2:2, 145–160.

Leveson, Lord Justice, 2012, *An Inquiry into the Culture, Practices and Ethics of the Press*, London, The Stationery Office.

Levy, D., 1999, *Europe's Digital Revolution, Broadcasting Regulation: The EU and the Nation State*, London and New York, Routledge.

Levy, D., 2012, 'PSB Policymaking in Comparative Perspective: The BBC and France Télévisions' in: Lowe, G. F. and Steemers, J. (eds.), *Regaining the Initiative for Public Service Media*, Gothenburg, Nordicom.

Levy, D. and Nielsen, R., 2010, *The Changing Business of Journalism and its Implications for Democracy*, Oxford, Reuters Institute for the Study of Journalism.

Livingstone, S., 2008, 'On the Future of Children's Television – A Matter of Crisis?' in: Gardam, T. and Levy, D. (eds.), *The Price of Plurality*, Oxford, Reuters Institute for the Study of Journalism.

Lloyd, J., 2010, 'The Press We Destroy' in: Levy, D. and Nielsen, R. (eds.), *The Changing Business of Journalism and its Implications for Democracy*, Oxford, Reuters Institute for the Study of Journalism.

Lotz, A.D., 2009a, 'What is US television now?' in *The Annals of the American Academy of Political and Social Science*, 625, September, 49–59.

Lotz, A.D. (ed.) 2009b, *Beyond Prime Time: Television Programming in the Post-Network Era*, New York, Routledge.

Lowe, G. F. and Steemers, J. (eds.), 2012, *Regaining the Initiative for Public Service Media*, Gothenburg, Nordicom.

Lunt, P. and Livingstone, S., 2012, *Media Regulation – Governance and the Interests of Citizens and Consumers*, London, Sage.

Mac Síthigh, D., 2011, 'Co-regulation, video-on-demand and the legal status of audio-visual media' in *The International Journal of Digital Television*, 2:1, 49–66.

Mayhew, J. and Bradley-Jones, L., 2005, 'Contestable Funding: Lessons from New Zealand' in: BBC commission, *Can the Market Deliver?* Eastleigh, John Libbey Publishing.

Moore, M., 1995, *Creating Public Value*, Cambridge MA and London, Harvard University Press.

Murdoch, J., 2009, 'The Absence of Trust', MacTaggart Lecture, Edinburgh International Television Festival, 28 August.

Murphy, K., 2010, 'Digital television policy and regulatory neutrality in small western states: Ireland, Greece, Finland, Austria and New Zealand' in *The International Journal of Digital Television*, 1:2, 151–171.

Negroponte, N., 1995, *Being Digital*, London, Hodder & Stoughton.

*New York Times*, 2012, 'Portuguese Chafe as Government Examines Privatizing Broadcaster', 9 September.

Nord, L., 2012, 'Losing the Battle, Winning the War' in: Lowe, G. F. and Steemers, J. (eds.), *Regaining the Initiative for Public Service Media*, Gothenburg, Nordicom.

Norris, Paul, 2010, 'The progress to digital television in New Zealand: an update' in *The International Journal of Digital Television*, 1:3, 345–349.

Norris, Paul, 2013, 'The progress to digital in New Zealand' in *The International Journal of Digital Television*, 4:1, 21–32.

Norris, Pippa, 2001, *The Digital Divide*, Cambridge and New York, Cambridge University Press.

Norris, Pippa, 2011, *Democratic Deficit*, New York, Cambridge University Press.

Ofcom, 2004a, *Digital Replacement Licences to be Offered to Channels 3, 4 and 5 and Public Teletext*, Consultation.

Ofcom, 2004b, *Ofcom Review of Public Service Television Broadcasting: Phase 2 – Meeting the Digital Challenge*, Consultation.

Ofcom, 2005, 'Conclusion of the review of Channel 3 and Channel 5 financial terms', 29 June.

Ofcom, 2006, *Digital Dividend Review*, Consultation.

Ofcom, 2007, Annual Lecture by Ed Richards, *Citizens and Consumers in a Converged World*, 16 October.

Ofcom, 2010, *International Communications Market Report*, 2 December.

Ofcom, 2011, *International Communications Market Report*, 14 December.

Ofcom, 2012a, *Communications Market Report: UK*, 18 July.

Ofcom, 2012b, *Securing Long Term Benefits from Scarce Spectrum Resources: A Strategy for UHF Bands IV and V*, 29 March.

Ofcom, 2012c, *Measuring Media Plurality*, 19 June.

O'Neill, B. and Shaw, H., 2010, 'Radio Broadcasting in Europe: The Search for a Common Digital Future' in: O'Neill B., Ala-Fossi M., Jauert P., Lax S., Nyre L. and Shaw H. (eds.), *Digital Radio in Europe: Technologies, Industries and Cultures*, Bristol, Intellect.

Open Society Foundations, 2010, *Mapping Digital Media: Thailand*, report 23 December, http://www.mediapolicy.org/mdm

Open Society Foundations, 2011a, *Mapping Digital Media: United Kingdom*, report 9 December, http://www.mediapolicy.org/mdm

Open Society Foundations, 2011b, *Mapping Digital Media: United States*, report 24 August, http://www.mediapolicy.org/mdm

Open Society Foundations, 2011c, *Mapping Digital Media: Russia*, report 10 August, http://www.mediapolicy.org/mdm

Open Society Foundations, 2011d, *Mapping Digital Media: Italy*, report 10 August, http://www.mediapolicy.org/mdm

Open Society Foundations, 2011e, *Mapping Digital Media: Mexico*, report 4 February, http://www.mediapolicy.org/mdm

Picard, R., 2012, 'The Changing Nature of Political Case-Making for Public Service Broadcasters' in: Lowe, G. F. and Steemers, J. (eds.), *Regaining the Initiative for Public Service Media*, Gothenburg, Nordicom.

Prior, M., 2007, *Post-Broadcast Democracy: How Media Choice Increases Inequalities in Political Involvement and Polarizes Elections*, New York, Cambridge University Press.

Purvis, S., 2010, 'Calling Time on Analogue Regulation – an agenda for the next Communications Act', Royal Television Society Fleming Memorial Lecture, 11 November.

Reith, J., 1924, *Broadcast Over Britain*, London, Hodder and Stoughton.

Richter, A., 2010, 'The Russian approach to the line-up of digital TV channels', in *The International Journal of Digital Television*, 1:2, 235–238.

Richter, A., 2012, 'The trends in digital switchover of Russia and other CIS countries' in *The International Journal of Digital Television*, 3:3, 279–291.

Rogers, E. M., 2003, *Diffusion of Innovations*, 5th Edition, New York, Free Press.

Rozgonyi, K. and Lengyel, M., 2010, 'Digital Switchover in Hungary' in *The International Journal of Digital Television*, 1:2, 173–191.

Rusbridger, A., 2009, 'I've seen the future and its mutual' in *British Journalism Review*, 20:3, 19–26.

Schudson, M., 2010, 'News in Crisis in the United States: Panic – and Beyond' in: Levy, D. and Nielsen, R. (eds.), *The Changing Business of Journalism and its Implications for Democracy*, Oxford, Reuters Institute for the Study of Journalism.

Seel, P., 2011, 'Report from NAB 2011' in *The International Journal of Digital Television*, 2:3, 371–377.

Shott, Nicholas, 2010, *Commercially Viable Local Television in the UK, a Review for the Secretary of State for Culture, Olympics, Media and Sport*, London, DCMS.

Smith, A., 1973, *The Shadow in the Cave – The Broadcaster, the Audience and the State*, London, Allen & Unwin.

Smith, Chris, 1999, 'Secretary of State at the Department of Culture, Media and Sport', speech to the Royal Television Society in Cambridge, 17 September.

Starks, M., 2007, *Switching to Digital Television: UK Public Policy and the Market*, Bristol, Intellect Books.

Starks, M., 2010, 'Digital television switchover: China goes it own way' in *Westminster Papers*, 7:1, 27–42.

Starks, M., 2011, 'Can the BBC live to be 100? Public service broadcasting after digital switchover' in *International Journal of Digital Television*, 2:2, 181–200.

Stirling, A., 2012, 'Africa is pushing ahead in the race for 700 MHz' in *The International Journal of Digital Television*, 3:3, 339–348.

Stoller, T., 2010, *Sounds of Your Life: The history of Independent Radio in the UK*, New Barnet, John Libbey.

Strukov, V., 2011, 'Digital switchover or digital grip: transition to digital television in the Russian Federation' in *The International Journal of Digital Television*, 2:1, 67–85.

Suárez Candel, R., 2008, 'DTV in Spain' in: Van den Broeck, W. and Pierson, J., (eds.), *Digital Television in Europe*, Brussels, VUBpress.

Suárez Candel, R., 2011, 'Public policy best practice in the field of digital terrestrial television: lessons from Sweden and Spain' in *International Journal of Digital Television*, 2:3, 297–321.

Suter, T., 2013, 'The future of television regulation' in *The International Journal of Digital Television*, 4:1, 67–80.

Tay, J. and Turner, G., 2010, 'Not the apocalypse: television futures in the digital age' in *The International Journal of Digital Television*, 1:1, 31–50.

*Times*, 2011a, 'Click after the break – web adverts overtake television', 5 October.

*Times*, 2011b, 'Minister summons mobile chiefs to kick-start race for super-fast services', 8 October.

*Times*, 2012a, 'Rivals try to outsmart Apple with a TV that does it all', 12 January.

*Times*, 2012b, 'Sky's the limit for Netflix's next ambition', 2 April.

Tracey, M., 1998, *The Decline and Fall of Public Service Broadcasting*, Oxford, Oxford University Press.

Tunstall, J., 2008, *The Media Were American*, Oxford, Oxford University Press.

Urbán, Á., 2008, 'DTV in Hungary' in: Van den Broeck, W. and Pierson, J. (eds.), *Digital Television in Europe*, Brussels: VUB Press.

U.S. Senate Committee on Commerce, Science and Transportation, 2005, Testimony of Charles C. Townsend, President Aloha Partners, 12 July.

Wheeler, M., 2012, 'European Union State Aid, public subsidies and analogue switch-off/digital switchover' in *The International Journal of Digital Television*, 3:1, 7–22.

Winston, B., 1998, *Media Technology and Society: A History from the Telegraph to the Internet*, London and New York, Routledge.

Woldt, R., 2010, 'Public Service Broadcasting in Germany: Stumbling Blocks on the Digital Highway' in Iosifidis, P. (ed.), *Reinventing Public Service Communication: European Broadcasters and Beyond*, Basingstoke, Palgrave Macmillan.

Wood, D., 2011, 'Technical Standards' in *The International Journal of Digital Television*, 2:1, 109–115.

# Index